After the Plane Landed

Eugenia Jenny Williams

Also by Eugenia Jenny Williams

Yenni: A Life Between Worlds

Yenni: In the Rhythm of Everyday

The Chessboard of Destiny

The Stone Fiddler

After the Plane Landed

EUGENIA JENNY WILLIAMS

First Published 2009 by Transit Lounge Publishing as 'Jenny's Coffee House'
This 2nd edition 2018 by
DoctorZed Publishing
10 Vista Ave
Skye, South Australia 5072
www.doctorzed.com
info@doctorzed.com

Cover image adapted from photograph © Dr. Koman Tam
Email: komantamphotography@icloud.com
Website: http://www.flickr.com/photos/komantamphotography
Back cover image: Matthew Elliott www.chaosboi.com
Design adapted by Scott Zarcinas

DoctorZed Publishing is a proud member of the A.P.A. (Australian Publishers' Association) and A.D.P.G. (Australian Digital Publishing Group)

Cataloguing-in-Publication information can be found at the National Library of Australia

ISBN: 978-0-6483871-8-3 (hc)
ISBN: 978-0-6483871-9-0 (sc)
ISBN: 978-0-6483871-7-6 (ebk)

Printed in Australia, UK and USA

DoctorZed rev. date 14/08/2018

To three children: Istvan, Zsuzsi and
Roman who arrived on the TAA aeroplane
on the 31st of May 1969 at Hobart airport
as assisted migrants and became proud
and upright Australians.

Contents

Prologue

It was an unforgettable, heart-piercing moment to leave my grandparents, Omama and Opapa, behind. They were both in their seventies. I still feel the touch of Omama's warm, tear-drenched cheek on mine. I still feel her last kiss. My heart still aches.

I am Yenni and it was I who thought it all out. No future for us or our children in this country after the occupation by the USSR in August 1968. No prospect of keeping our jobs, no university studies for the children, no security. Only tanks with Russian soldiers sitting in turrets with their Katyuskas at the ready.

There were seven of us, four adults and three children – my husband Yano, my mother, who we called Mami, my sister Chopi, six years my junior, her one-year-old son Roman, myself and our two children, Ishtvan and Zsuzsi, then aged twelve and nine. Together we illegally escaped in February 1969 from the country behind the Iron Curtain then called Czechoslovakia.

Before our departure we read the pamphlets about the Australian way of life, which were sent over from the Australian Embassy in Vienna by a friend who had already escaped. We compared the minimum wages, the housing, the schooling, the prices, the freedom. We were well informed; even worked out that after our weekly shopping of groceries, and adding some small luxuries, we would still have $5 saved from our minimum wages. Five whole dollars. *What a country,* I thought. And then there was Yannibachi, Omama's brother, who lived in Hobart, Tasmania, with his wife Hedineni and their daughter Nana. In their letter to us they promised to give us moral support.

But did I know what it meant to drag the whole family out of their comfort zone into emigration? Did I consider the moral and financial consequence for Mami in leaving her job as legal adviser to a large wholesale firm, for Chopi to leave her teaching position and for me to give up my position of secretary to the Invalid Committee? And Yano, who had 150 people working under him?

All right, all right, I argued, it was a big world out there with all its insecurities, unknown problems and languages, but the hardest part surely had to be to get over the border. Once we were safe in a free country things would be good. A little hardship for a short while, that's all. We are all healthy, well-meaning, hard-working people.

That belief and my ability to voice my opinion with self-confidence and assuredness helped. They all listened and believed in the picture I painted about our bright future.

One cold winter morning, with the snow weighing down the bare branches of trees and the streets looking like an enchanted fairytale, we turned the key of our flat on the second floor, closing the door on our world, the furniture, the doonas and bedsheets, coats and parkas, the porcelain, books and paintings. We carried the three suitcases, which from then on represented all our belongings, to the railway station to catch the train to Vienna, supposedly only for a few days over the school holidays. But I knew better.

A group of four uniformed men enter the carriage compartment. 'So, where are we going with the children?' they ask.

'Just visiting an aunt in Vienna.'

'Uh-um,' they say. Two of them step back, keeping the door open, and the other two kneel on the floor looking under the seats with torches. Through the window we see men in uniforms with guns hanging off their shoulders and sniffer dogs at their heels walking on the platform. More soldiers get on the train. Another thirty minutes. When the train finally starts up my hands slide into the pockets of my skirt, searching for my handkerchief, and I wipe the pearls of sweat above my lip.

We left behind all we knew – not just our belongings – we left the streets we knew how to walk on, the shops we knew how to shop in, the language we knew how to communicate with, the system that we had learned to find our way in. We left behind our culture, our identity. And friends, good friends like Svetya and others.

Our future became a clear slate with no mark on it. Nothing of what we knew was of any use to us. And like a newborn we had to learn to exist.

CHAPTER ONE

Looking for the Familiar, Finding Beauty

Under the aeroplane the large sheet of water is fretted, edged into small bays, and is reflecting the setting sun in long orange strips. We are losing altitude. The waves, smooth and heavy like oil, come close to the wing of the plane and the small window I am looking out of, but I am too tired to worry. The plane levels its wings and slides onto the tarmac, leaving the water behind. Hobart, Tasmania, on the other side of my old world. No more getting on and off planes and sitting in airports. After thirty hours we have arrived.

In front of a low oblong building is a group of people, some waving frantically. When the plane taxies closer I recognise Yanibachi and his wife Hedineni as I remember them from the photos on the wall of Omama's bedroom. The rest of the people I don't know.

For a second I am worried about my appearance, then begin fussing about the children, straightening their coats and shirts as we progress through the narrow passage and onto the stairs. Descending in single file, Zsuzsi wriggles herself to the front and runs across the concrete expanse towards Yanibachi. Yano follows with Roman on his arm, Isthtvan next to him, then Mami and Chopi. I am the last one to touch the Tasmanian ground. The group of people seemingly jump out of their background and become larger as we walk closer to them. It seems such a long walk to the building.

Hugs to Yanibachi and Hedineni, introductions to a Hungarian husband and wife, Elizabeth and Stephen, and another couple, English-speaking people whose names I can't memorise because of their unfamiliar sounds. It is comforting to be recognised and welcomed in this faraway land. I would like to be warm and thankful but can't make myself step over the threshold of the automatic responses.

Three cars are lined up outside the airport. The luggage is loaded into the boots. Mami, Chopi and the children are divided between two cars. Yano and I travel in another, a Valiant, I later discover, with Stephen and Elizabeth.

We drive through green open country that funnels into a narrow road surrounded by hills thickly covered with silver-green trees, curly in appearance, like tightly packed heads of broccoli. Along the road in various stages of completion are the clumps of houses, some brick with tin roofs, some with horizontal planks of cladding in pastel colours, but mainly off-white. The houses are surrounded by grass patches that look very green, lush against the dull silver colour of the surrounding bushes.

'Government housing estate – Housing Department houses,' Elizabeth comments. 'You might be able to apply for one of those.'

I can't absorb the information. *What does she mean?* Getting a government flat I know to be a privilege of the working class only in socialist countries. Looking at the houses, they seem so large. *Would the government let us rent a house instead of a flat?*

We have to cross the bridge. We would also have a view of Mount Wellington embracing the city but it doesn't register. I know that it had to be that way, only because the airport is on the other side, across the river, on the Eastern Shore, as Yanibachi explained in one of his letters. Some long streets follow, lined with small houses and strange canopies, roofs extended over the walkways. The car is weaving in and out of the lanes, travelling parallel with other cars, stopping at lights, and then it turns into a wider street.

'This is Elizabeth Street, the main street of Hobart,' Elizabeth says proudly. 'And, this is the Polish Club.' She points to a corner building of dark brick, which to me appears unfinished because the bricks are not clad.

The main street? And the buildings! Small, red-brick homes and houses constructed from wooden planks, verandahs and more canopies above the shop windows, the houses are climbing up the curly hill with the backdrop of a large dark mountain. This must be Mount Wellington. *Very picturesque, very beautiful, but my God, is this the city? Is this the main street?*

Some more turns. The car stops in front of a red-brick house. My eyes are caught by a bush of hydrangeas at the entrance door with flowers as big as a basketball. In my native country it would be kept in a pot inside the house and the flowers would grow to the size of a tennis ball, if lucky.

The cars carrying Mami, Chopi and the children had arrived before us. While trying to fit the key into the door Yanibachi explains that he rented this house for us until we find something more suitable. It wasn't easy to find it, he says. The landlords are suspicious of newly arrived migrant families with children. Yanibachi and Hedineni furnished it with the help of the Hungarian Club. Only basics, you understand, no luxuries.

Basics? Is he kidding? Five rooms and a sunroom? All furnished? Hedineni is telling us that this house has three bedrooms. *Is this how they count the rooms in houses?*

Inside, all the bedrooms are fitted out with beds, bedsheets wrapped outside the blankets, tucked in under the mattresses, looking like they are from an army barracks. On top of them are laid out pyjamas and nighties for each of us.

The kitchen is just the way I know a built-in kitchen should look. Unexpectedly all the cupboards are filled with crockery and pots, and the drawer with cutlery.

I walk in front of the overhead kitchen cupboards in a dreamlike exhaustion, while Elizabeth is opening one cupboard door after another, explaining to the smallest detail the packets of groceries and what they are good for, throwing in the recipe for biscuits made from cornflakes. And I learn that the cornflakes are a breakfast cereal eaten with milk and perhaps fruit and not as I did on the aeroplane coming to Australia, nibbled like potato chips. My tears are flowing uncontrollably, my heart filled with gratitude. With an unfocused and vague mind, I promise myself to thank everyone, absolutely everyone, for their humane thoughtfulness.

The fridge is turned on and packed with butter, milk, cheese, salami and God knows what, even a cask of wine. Who bought all this?

'Yanibachi, Hedineni and the Hungarian community,' explains Elizabeth.

'How are we going to thank you, how are we going to repay you for this, this ...?' I run out of words.

'You always return the favour to the next lot of emigrants,' she says simply, as if it was the most natural thing to do.

Yano and I have our own bedroom. Everyone has plenty of room.

That evening Yanibachi leaves us to settle for a few days. He will come on Sunday evening and will take us to their place for dinner. 'Goodnight.'

As I stretch out in our double bed, the worrisome dream about the fifty brides in white dresses with pearls around their necks, which haunted and threatened me throughout our travel with the imagined crash of the whole planeload of migrants on the flight from Vienna, loses its significance for good.

Knock knock. I crawl out of bed and struggle with the doorknob.

'Turn the knob,' Yanibachi says on the other side of the door.

A-a-a-ah! It slides between my fingers but after a few unsuccessful tries the mechanism takes a grip and the door opens.

'What time is it?' I ask, rubbing my eyes.

'It's Sunday evening,' Yanibachi says, somewhat surprised.

The rest of the family, tucked in their beds, are still asleep. For two whole days. No food, no toilet, only sleep.

❦❦❦

Yanibachi and Hedineni lived in an apartment block only a short distance from us on a wide street with a Roman-sounding name, Augusta Road. They called their flat a *unit*. Nice. I found the furniture old-fashioned and without any style. The non-descriptive brown tones to me were without personality, along with the vinyl seats and couches. I longed for the glass-topped coffee tables and slimline furniture of light wood in Scandinavian style. I missed the living plants, which would give the room life and colour, the ceramic statues, which, sitting on colourful homespun doilies on the shelves of a book-lined wall unit, would give character and tell about the culture of the people living there.

Except for the loungeroom, which was heated by an electric radiator, the rooms were freezing cold, especially their bedroom. They told me to slip my hand under the bedcover.

'A-a-a-ah ...!'

'Electric blanket.'

Never heard of it.

That evening we met our cousin Nana, Yanibachi and Hedineni's daughter, who worked for the Commonwealth Bank. Our new Hungarian friend Stephen told us that she was clever and very beautiful. He was right. Nana was in her late thirties, tall, slim, with soft, vulnerable dark eyes.

After a great dinner we warmly thanked Yanibachi and Hedineni for their loving care, reassured them that we knew our way home, said goodnight and, as soon as we stepped out of the entrance door, got lost. Walking uphill for too long we realised that none of us remembered which street we were supposed to turn into, so Ishtvan walked down all the side streets until he found ours.

Tasmanian winter. So far all the houses we had been invited to were cold. I was cold in our house too and my body needed to soak up heat somehow, somewhere. A couple of open fireplaces, which had not seen fire for years, stared at us black and cold. I wondered what they were good for.

The only heating we had was from two electric radiators, one keeping the kitchen and the adjoining family room temperate. Another small radiator was used to warm the children's bedroom. To us the radiators were also a novelty. I had never heard of electric radiators, not needing them in the centrally heated flats in my country.

Our bedroom was the coldest of the lot and I missed my doona with the lacy cover. The sheets and blankets tucked in at the sides of the mattress restricted me from pulling them up to my chin and pushed me heavily into the bed. In the mornings I would find the sheets at my feet with only the prickly blankets against my body. Anyway, a couple of blankets couldn't keep us warm in a Tasmanian winter, not after experiencing two winters with no summer in between.

Yano and I decided to move our bed into the family room next to the kitchen and planned to buy electric blankets as soon as we could afford them. Seven in number, one to each member of the family.

In the early morning twilight I trot to the toilet, which is outside the glass-panelled kitchen door. The frost has laid a white blanket over the garden and I think of my winter pyjamas, which I sent back to my native country from Vienna with the rest of our winter gear, because everyone in Europe knew that Australia is a hot country. On the way back, as my frozen fingers reach for the doorknob, through the glass pane my eyes lift to the wall above our bed.

Funny, I can't remember that small picture being there the night before. Suddenly the picture moves.

Oh-h-h! It is that, that thing, that spider, which Nana was talking about last night. She said it was very fast and when you finally manage to get it off the ceiling it flops onto the carpet like a leather glove. Oh my God and Yano is asleep while that thing is crawling all over the wall.

I am not going inside, I decide, and in my nylon nightie, teeth chattering, settle to wait it out, until someone wakes up in the house.

After half an hour Mami, in total disbelief, finds me shivering on the other side of the kitchen door. In our desperation and horror we all get into chasing the Huntsman, that poor creature, around the room, until it disappears behind the architrave, to haunt us another day.

For a week we were organising the wardrobes and cupboards and familiarising ourselves with our new home. We looked suspiciously through the packets of groceries lined up in the kitchen cupboard. None of us dared to get out of the house. Nana visited, and Yanibachi with Hedineni. They explained this and that. 'Are you all right?' they kept asking. 'Yes, yes, of course we are all right, thank you very much.'

When they left, between us we tried to recall what they had said. What did they say about adults going to school? What was it about our documents needing to be taken to the Commonwealth Bank, to the Immigration Department for translation? What was it about private medical insurance? Aren't we insured with the government, as back in our country?

The following Monday Hedineni turned up to take Zsuzsi and Ishtvan to the Lenah Valley Primary School. Leaving the house the children clung to Hedineni on both sides, looking back at us. They didn't know a word of English.

'They will be all right,' she said. 'I had a word with the headmaster, the teacher is expecting them this morning.'

My heart sank. My poor kids. This time I couldn't give them any moral support.

Funny thing about children, that very first day Ishtvan came home with a friend. Allan was his name; he lived just up the road.

Ishtvan told me that his name in English was Stephen and Zsuzsi was Susan. We all received new names. Yano became John, Mami Martha, Chopi was Martha too and I changed my name from Yenni to Jenny. At least this way our names were pronounceable.

Hedineni and Yanibachi kept to their promise to stand by us, helping us with our first steps. We were assigned to evening English classes for migrants. At the Hobart Matriculation College Nana walked us through numerous long corridors and deposited us in a classroom full of 'New Australians'. Yano, Chopi and I attended the classes twice a week while Mami minded the children at home.

'I am. You are. We are,' said the teacher pointing with her finger to her, to another person and then to all of us.

'Now, repeat everybody,' she said.

'I am. You are. We are,' we sang in chorus.

The same words over and over, lesson after lesson, for weeks, because at every lesson there would be a couple of new, non-English-speaking pupils walking into the classroom and the whole process started from the beginning.

'I am. You …'

That morning Hedineni knocked on the door and told Chopi and me to get ready. She was going to take us to the Silk and Textiles Company, the very factory that manufactured the 120 metres of silk material that had been sent over to our home town of Košice (pronounced Kosheesa) by Yanibachi in my teenage years, and which kept us all dressed in the latest fashion.

The Silk and Textiles factory traditionally employed a large number of migrants. Yano came with us for something to do. He finished up being employed; Chopi and I didn't.

Yano was assigned to the screen room where his job was to apply designs and colours to new materials and, just like Yanibachi before him, collected his monthly parcel of many metres of silk for a dollar. After Mami sewed up dresses for all of us on her *new* secondhand electric sewing machine, just like Yanibachi had done, we too started sending parcels of materials back to the old country, creating a false assumption about our achieving instant wealth after only a few months living in Australia.

It is right to describe emigration from one country to another as a cultural shock. The shock doesn't relate only to the culture, language, tradition and habits. It relates to everyday matters, to impulses, instincts we had been taught in childhood and grown up with.

I can still see myself struggling to turn doorknobs because I was used to door handles. Battling with an old wooden-framed window I would not have guessed, unless someone explained, that they had to be pushed up. Different from the casement windows in Europe, where to open them they had to be pulled in. Everything was opening and closing in the direction opposite to what I was expecting. Crossing the road, turning my head to check the traffic first to my left and then to my right, I constantly found myself in the way of cars.

Thirty years of my life, my experiences, grooming, ethics and knowledge, were no good. Emotions are wordless; they can be expressed only through an image that provokes emotions. We need terms in which we can identify them. Someone told me: 'Take away the language; take away the identity.' Through my inability to express myself I was deprived of my personality and individuality, the very essence of me, of which I was so very proud.

The ethics were very different too. I had to learn to hold my hand behind my back to resist the urge to shake the hands of strangers. Women don't shake hands in Australia, Stephen had told me. Walking into a shop or office no words of greeting were exchanged, no need to knock on doors, a gesture I was brought up with, to recognise the privacy of the ones behind the door. People walked in and out of places, including homes, without saying a word, as if the ones inside didn't exist, or at least did not matter.

And the shocks, both pleasant and unpleasant, kept coming.

Where were the birds? Yanibachi said there were no birds because there were no trees in the suburbs; where would the birds live then? There were plenty of birds outside the city, all sorts, unusual birds and cockatoos, black, white, even pink, he said. And the people? Where were they? We peered out the windows of our new home in wonder. The suburban streets were empty all day long. Around three o'clock kids coming out of school dressed in lovely uniforms and wide-brimmed hats, like little mushrooms, marched towards their doors and disappeared for the rest of the day.

My first independent bus trip, though, was a triumph!

'City,' I said to the bus driver and received a ticket. *He understood, he understood!* I cheered silently. The bus seemed old-fashioned and I couldn't get over the fact that passengers smoked at the back of it. Leaving the low houses of suburbia behind, approaching the city I could see the wharf and the blue waters of the sea at the end of Elizabeth Street. *A real seaport at the end of the main street!*

I was relieved to find that downtown Hobart looked more what I considered a city to be. Still, most buildings were painted in bright colours and no higher than two storeys with extended roofs above the display windows. It resembled the Wild West, the way I had seen it in American movies.

I was so taken by it that I bought a pretty postcard of Hobart, addressed it to the Collective of the Social Security Department at MsNV Košice and wrote:

A handful of thoughts and memories to you all from the Wild West.

Yenni

Everything around me was strange. I was in a new country, which offered a future but no past. Will I ever be able to reinvent myself as an Australian? I thought of myself as being worthy at least of a glance, but people around me thought differently. No longer was I recognised in streets with a tilt of a head or a handshake, no man in passing ever laid eyes on me, even though I had just adopted the new and to me daring fashion of a miniskirt.

I could not make out the fashion either. *Was it backwards or ahead of Europe?* How come children in the middle of winter were dressed in lacy short-sleeved dresses, like little dolls, pushed in prams facing the wind, while their mothers wore fur coats with summer dresses underneath them? How come little babies were carried, without any support of the *pólya.* These down-filled pillows are wrapped around a baby's body to give support and warmth for the first six weeks. Here their little bare heads are blown by chilly winds down Elizabeth Street, as they dangle on the arms of mothers or fathers, others lying on their stomachs in pushers. Did those people know something new I'd never heard of, or hadn't they been told yet?

I visited Nana in the Commonwealth Bank. Very impressive. It was the first building I could identify with. A modern, grey stone building of several storeys. I was told this had been Hobart's tallest building until they built the AMP just a corner away. A mural on the back wall showed me how Tasmania was settled and told me that this building was opened in 1954.

Inside the bank was an air of authority, warmth and organised professionalism. Nana piled up our documents, typed out an application requesting the translation of them and while doing so consulted her English dictionary several times.

'English is a very complicated language; every employee is supplied with a dictionary,' she smiled.

Really? I thought. *Don't they teach the English grammar and spelling in schools?* If I hadn't known my grammar and spelling back in my old country I wouldn't have had a job in an office.

All done, she gave me a grand tour of the bank. The whispered conversation between hurried personnel dressed in very smart dark-blue uniforms felt just right.

Nana needed to get something in Myer. 'It is a large department store just around the corner. Would you like to come?'

Okay. The department stores in Vienna were big and bright, with lots of merchandise. But Myer? I had never seen anything like this in my entire life. Nana told me to wait for her in the cosmetic department. No room for fantasy; all was laid out to be seen. My feet struck roots as I stood there mesmerised by the light, the scents, beautiful women behind the counters, the sound of English around me and the sheer excess of it all.

After that visit I decided that Tasmania is a very product-oriented society, miles ahead of Europe in consumer culture.

I explored more of the city, looking for the familiar, finding beauty in the new. I dared to get past the tall AMP building and, having to tilt my head back to face the sky, looked up to the top and counted thirteen storeys. *Fancy building thirteen storeys; perhaps I counted wrong.* The small stones in the rendering twinkled mauve in the sun. Following the street to where it met with the sea, I passed a three-storey sandstone building next to the Post Office. Its entrance was supported by two pillars, which stretched up to the second floor. I liked the grandness of it. *Stepping through this entrance would surely give a sense of arrival,* I thought. *Would I understand what was written in English on the plaque?* The date of 1934 was obvious. But it said something more about the Commonwealth Bank, which I couldn't quite make sense of. Had this building housed the bank before the one I had just walked out of? Past the Post Office I peeped around the corner. More grand sandstone buildings and to my right a beautiful park with statues and a fountain. *I will have to come this way next time,* I promised myself. Looking back to where I came from, I felt that I had walked too far to remember how to get back.

Nana instructed me to tell the bus driver one ticket to Augusta Road. That was a long sentence; all I remembered was that I wanted *one ticket.* To make sure the driver understood I stuck my index finger up in the air, handing over the 13 cents. The driver smiled and gave me the ticket. All the people in the bus smiled. *What a friendly lot,* I thought, *lovely people,* and satisfied with my success I smiled back.

Days later Yanibachi explained the no-no in Australia, mentioning the finger stuck up in the air. So many new and unexpected experiences, which needed to be shared, talked and laughed about.

At the same time I longed for the past, desperately wanting to capture the reality of that time when I was sure and familiar with everything. Nostalgia is about discontinuity. The image of my past was frozen in time.

I wrote a ten-page letter to Svetya. Half of it about Myer, the other half about remembering our black-marketing trip to Poland.

Black marketing had become the way of life in our country. For the lack of money and merchandise, and to get what we needed, we looked for the 'other' way. Just as water can't be squeezed into a smaller container because it will overflow, when people are contained in suppressed conditions they also look for loopholes. Free enterprise through the back door was born and, as expected, the government missed out on profit. Czechoslovakia was sandwiched between Germany, Austria, Hungary, the USSR and Poland. Košice was in a better position still, being one hour by bus from the border of the USSR, two hours from the border of Poland and about twenty minutes from Hungary – all good opportunities to exchange our goods for their money. We knew exactly what was in demand, what the going price was and what to buy with the money we made in each country. We knew what to expect at the border crossings, and counted on some border guards being more tolerant than others.

Anyway, the border checks were only a big pretence. We suspected that the 'tours' were organised with the blessing of the authorities, for how else could it have been that almost all the trips to Poland happened in November – the month when everyone was getting ready for the winter – and Poland was known for good-quality cheap parkas and woollen goods. The Hungarian trips were organised during the summer months, when the Hungarian markets were loaded with food and fresh fruit.

For me it worked like this: I borrowed money from Omama and bought goods to sell in Poland, where I bought things that were not available in our country. Some of the goods I kept myself and some of it I sold back home. From the money I made through selling in our country I returned the borrowed money to Omama. The circle was closed and I finished up with goods I really wanted, all free of charge, and, if I was lucky, with some extra money.

The organisers called those trips sightseeing tours. True, in between black marketing we also did a little sightseeing.

I wish you were here Svetya. We would have so much fun. Walking through the shops and seeing the merchandise, I thought of that last trip when the District National Committee organised a three-day sightseeing tour to Poland. Those trips were good shopping, weren't they? Not even Yano objected. By the way, do you still wear that light-blue coat you bought in Kraków? No need for trips like that in Tasmania, I tell you. There are plenty of parkas, coats and everything at Myer.

Remember the night when, on the way back, we stayed in Zakopane in those small wooden huts with no toilets? And when the whole lot of us dispersed in groups into huts and we danced and sang and laughed? We laughed so much that everyone else wanted to come into the hut we were in.

And the wretched toilets, miles away from our hut, with huge queues in front of them? I will never forget how cold it was on that morning when we decided that we would not queue up but use the wastebin instead and wash it out in the snow afterwards. Remember? But there was no need to wash it, was there? Because the bucket had no bottom. But who knew? It was too dark in the room to see it. I still can feel the freezing wetness of the snow, as we carried it inside the room to scrub the carpet. I could do with those laughs now Svetya. Honestly ...

'You need to be among English-speaking people Yenni,' they advised me.

The Cadbury Chocolate Factory was and still is one of the biggest employers of Hobart's migrant and suburban population, and no skills were necessary. Nana put my name down and shortly afterwards I became a factory worker on the Cadbury assembly lines.

In those years, most of the Cadbury factory floor consisted of Russian and Polish migrants. They loved my pure Russian, unspoiled by English words. And in a few weeks working there my Russian improved remarkably, but unfortunately not my English.

I also learned that women who had lived for twenty years in Tasmania spoke only very basic English and could not help me with the translation of a simple horoscope in the *Women's Weekly*.

The horoscope was new literature to me, as back in my country at best it was unavailable and at worst a prohibited material. It was considered the para-culture of the 'decadent West'. After finding the horoscope in every Australian magazine, I attacked this particular column with great passion, not even bothering about the rest of the content of the magazine. I would go straight to the last pages, where I knew the secret of my future would be revealed. How exciting it was to find out the prediction of my fortunes for the whole week. I carried the dictionary in my handbag and, during lunchtime, tediously translated word by word the horoscopes in all the magazines I could lay my hands on. When I read about the week being hospitable, I was afraid, relating the word to *hospital*, for days.

The fact that I had Svetya to write to about my new experiences and reminisce about the old ones was a godsend.

Svetya, you will never believe me, but I am a factory worker now. A chocolate factory worker and, as a matter of fact, I am sick of chocolate. I smell it on my bra, on my undies, everywhere.

They dressed me in a white uniform and a white hat (I hate it) and I have my own locker in a huge hall, which is saturated by the smell of underarm deodorants and starch.

And one more thing I absolutely hate; they taught me to go to the toilet at ten o'clock in the morning. The first day the lady in charge tapped my shoulder and told me to go to the toilet. With the help of a Polish woman I explained that I didn't need to, but she insisted, so I went. Now it is the third week that they are sending me to the wretched toilet at ten in the morning and guess what I am doing every Saturday and Sunday morning at home at ten o'clock?

I also learned to drink white tea. You know the one we used to drink when recovering from an upset stomach? We are getting it free with biscuits.

A tea lady walks around in mid-morning with a trolley, while we are sitting down and having a morning-tea break, which is compulsory as well. A sheer luxury. I can also eat as much chocolate as I want to and, for a very low price, buy some prepacked ones to take home. So we are okay. Yano brings materials and I bring chocolates.

We live about thirty minutes' bus ride from the railway station. I am catching the bus every morning at 6.30. I tell you, it's no fun. I am the first one up in the house and it's cold. I would have never believed how cold it could be in Australia in July.

One morning I missed the bus and in my desperation hailed the first car that appeared on the road. When it stopped, I somehow explained that I wanted to go to the railway station. All in English, would you believe me? They must have understood, because they took me there. Very kind people, a lady and a man. At home I told Yanibachi about it. He was horrified and told me not to do it ever again, because people have been known to disappear that way, but I think he is just old-fashioned.

Anyway, the buses are heated and cosy and so are the train carriages and we can smoke there, which makes the time go faster. All the cigarettes have filters here, you know, not like those cheap cigarettes. The ones I smoke are called Viscounts and a packet of tens costs only 19 cents. Talking about passing the time, all the women are knitting here. I have never seen such a knitting nation. And the way they knit? To watch them keeps me amused during the whole one-hour journey to work.

I am convinced that this must be the prettiest train journey in the whole world. We are travelling alongside the sea. What do you think of that? Back home we could spend two or three weeks near the sea for a high price, but at the end we had to come home. Here the sea is everywhere.

You should see the city at night. From the train window on the way back from work it looks like a jewellery box with the flickering lights hemming the seashore and crawling up the hills.

On the mornings, waiting for the train and having a smoke, I like to stand outside the railway station looking at the mountain. The scenery from the railway station with Mount Wellington in the background with it's snow cap reminds me a little of the High Tatras.

Hobart is a cocktail of all the cities I have seen. Little bit of Riviera, a spoonful of English countryside, a pinch of Europe, shake well and, if served with ice cubes, it definitely feels like winter in Hobart, especially on the frosty July mornings.

By the way, do you remember that suitcase Mami lost back in Vienna? Guess what? Two weeks after our arrival Yanibachi got a notice from the airline to pick up a suitcase at the airport for Mrs Pokorny. The family silver has arrived!

Because Chopi had a university education, Nana found her a temporary job at the Geology Department at the University of Tasmania. Her boss was a Dutch gentleman, who could also speak German, which made it a little easier for Chopi.

Within one month of our arrival we were all employed, except Mami, though she had her work cut out for her.

CHAPTER TWO

On the Wave of Friendship

Omama and Opapa had been correct in their prediction. Mami was holding the family together by looking after the children, running the house and cooking for all of us. I knew that her job was the hardest.

When you are the cook you need to shop. What an experience! Imagine walking along the aisles, between parcels of goods wrapped in white or brown paper, or packed in cardboard boxes with large black, blue and red letters that didn't add up to a word you could understand or even vaguely recognise. 'What's in this one?' We would smell it and finger the parcel. 'It feels like sugar, or perhaps breadcrumbs?'

At home there were more surprises when we cooked a meal with the groceries and vegetables we had just bought. Everything seemed to cook faster in Tasmania than on the other side of the equator. When I had my first mouthful of fried pork it tasted like fish to me. Yanibachi said he couldn't taste it but maybe the pigs were fed with fish meal.

The biggest surprise came when I baked my first cake in Tasmania, following a recipe from my old recipe book, which I had managed to bring with me. This was the very cake that I couldn't get right in Košice for years. It always turned out to be a flat, dense chocolate cake – and for this was given the name 'The Spoiled Cake' – but had become the favourite of our family. When I made it for the first time out of Australian ingredients the cake grew higher and higher into a spongy consistency, just the way it was meant to be. *So, it was the ingredients all the time!* I mused. *And I always thought that I couldn't bake.* My triumph did not last long though. By turning out to be a perfect cake, it lost its characteristic stickiness and nobody liked it any more. I tried and tried to make 'The Spoiled Cake' as sticky and spoiled as it used to be but unfortunately it was perfect every time. The slices sat on the plate for days and no one touched them. So I stopped trying to bake the perfect cake.

The long process of assimilation had begun.

Ishtvan's friend Allan visited daily after school, patiently repeating English words over and over to Ishtvan and Zsuzsi. We were all learning from each other. Allan learned to eat our Hungarian and middle-European dishes and, in an attempt not to insult us, he never left anything on his plate.

'Good. Good,' I would say to him encouragingly, when placing the food in front of him, then when he had finished, 'Good?' I asked, in a hope to find out.

Allan's native vocabulary was widening each day in the necessity of describing an event or subject with as many different English words as possible, digging deep into his memory for expressions and hoping that we would recognise at least one of them.

This pale, blue-eyed twelve-year-old will stay in my heart forever for his patience, kindness and interest in other cultures. In his way he made an excellent ambassador for Australia.

At the Silk and Textiles factory Yano was taught his job by Tony, a good-looking man of thirty, with wavy light-brown hair, an expressive face and a heavy Yorkshire accent.

Tony's first visit happened unexpectedly, when one evening after six o'clock there was a knock at our door. The door knocker was a new experience too. Every time it was used unexpectedly the whole house echoed with its hollow sound and we jumped in fright.

The three of them, Tony, his wife Gail (with her even heavier English accent) and their six-month-old son Martin on her arm, all stood there smiling. Handshakes were followed by introductions, using our *new* names, and silent smiles as we sat around the large dining table near the kitchen. Now and then, when we ventured to communicate, the dictionary was passed around, with us corkscrewing out the unfamiliar words.

Avoiding eye contact as much as possible, we were trying to size up one another without being too obvious. For my part I thought Gail was a very shapely and attractive young woman. Martin, a round and healthy bundle, was surprisingly quiet and I couldn't stop wondering why he was not in bed at that time of the night. When the silence became uncomfortable I made coffee and tea in my newly learned way (that is, with milk) and then sat down again, sending out more silent smiles.

Without words the time passed slowly, even with more cups of white coffee and white tea. At eleven o'clock, with Martin sleeping in the arms of his mother, Tony and Gail got up and bade us goodnight.

The following evening at six the door knocker sounded and the three of them stood there again, smiling. Something had happened in the intervening twenty-four hours though. During the previous night while staring at each other we gained an experience to fall back on. They weren't strangers any more. We felt a friendly familiarity towards our new acquaintances. During that evening, as the night before, we began passing the dictionary between us, slowly at first, but all of a sudden we had so much to say. The dictionary passed from person to person like a possessed ouija board. Sounds of laughter, hmmms and aaahs, surprise and recognition filled the room, books and photos came off the shelves, and the hours became short. 'My God is that the time already?' and the English words started forming in our heads and our mouths slowly mimicked them.

In those first months we were drawn more and more into the social circle of Yanibachi and Nana. Most of our new acquaintances were either of Hungarian origin or English. Whichever nationality, they had one thing in common. They all wanted to help us through the hard beginnings. They were newcomers to Australia years ago and understood what we were going through.

Joy, a shapely and smiling girl of twenty, and the daughter of Yanibachi's English friend who was at the airport when we arrived, turned up at our home one afternoon.

'I will teach you English.' Her round face was radiating friendliness and confidence. And, just to make sure I understood, she mimicked some silent words, pointing to a book with a figure of a man in front of a blackboard drawn on it. 'I have parked my bomb in front of the drive. Is it okay?'

A bomb? A shiver ran through me. A bomb? My God! Such a nice girl, what would she need a bomb for?

Perhaps there would have been less confusion if I hadn't understood any words at all.

You have no idea what an international company of friends we keep here, I wrote to Svetya.

Last night we had in our living room a Dutch professor (Chopi's boss), an English husband and wife, an Australian girl, two Hungarians and a Slovak (if I take into consideration Yano's nationalistic feelings, ha-ha-ha).

To know what it is to be of a certain nationality, then live in another country and learn what the perceptions are there of that nationality can be very surprising, and sometimes hurtful. Do you know that most people here think that Hungarians are Gypsies? And that Slovakia is Slovenia and the capital city is Budapest?

After a month living in the house it became obvious that we had to move. It didn't suit two families and the rent was too high.

Yanibachi and Nana were there for us with advice and help whenever we needed them. They asked us to consider a house consisting of two flats. Our Hungarian friends Stephen and Elizabeth drove their Valiant through the city centre and turned into Macquarie Street. With some satisfaction I admired the architecture of the large sandstone buildings along the road. I thought it beautiful. *I will have to walk this way one day,* I promised to myself.

As we followed the long street the large buildings seemed to be shrinking to cottages, many unkempt and some weatherboard, with verandahs around them. By each turn of the steering wheel Mount Wellington became closer, tall and proud, silhouetting against the red sky.

South Hobart is one of the oldest areas of Hobart. We stopped in front of an old weatherboard house with a wooden verandah, its rear flat backing up to the soccer field in Darcy Street. It felt such a long way from New Town and the city.

I did not mind the street but disliked the house, especially the three-bedroom rear flat that was available for rent. The front flat was already rented out to a couple of Indian origin, but might be available to rent at some time in the future.

I was absolutely disgusted with the flat. In my mind I kept saying I knew it was going to be like this in the first months after our arrival. I kept reassuring myself. *I know that the flat will look much better when we move in, after we tidy up the rooms and light the fire in the open fireplaces.* The bathroom had a bath but no shower. The toilet was outside in one corner of a wooden shed and in the other corner was an old washing machine (which we couldn't use for the lack of space around it). The rooms in the flat were painted in cold grass-green and an even colder blue but the rent was much lower than the house we were living in.

So we moved. And it was a bigger move than we had anticipated. When we first arrived in Australia, Yano, the children and I together had three suitcases. Now we had to ask Stephen and Elizabeth for their help to move us in their station wagon. Where had all that gear come from in one short month of our living in Tasmania?

The rear flat became a home to us all. A few cardboard tubes used for the materials at Silk and Textiles were cut up by Yano and made into a standard lamp and a couple of wall lamps. I made the orange lampshades. Someone suggested we visit the secondhand furniture shop down the road on the corner. Never in my wildest dreams would I have considered buying furniture that had been used by strangers before me, unless they were bona fide antiques. But we bought an old bedroom suite, which most likely would fetch a small fortune now but back then had been thrown on the scrap heap at the back of the secondhand shop. I hated it for its dark, almost black, wood and for the shallow depth of the wardrobe. We also chose a couch and two armchairs. So we had our first pieces of furniture. All that for the savings from just one week's wages. We could never, never have done that back in our native country. Never! We would have had to save and save for months, perhaps years, before we could afford to buy furniture. And, while no one had secondhand furniture there, the furniture we bought here would do us nicely to begin with.

The bedrooms were divided between us. Yano and I had one, Chopi, Mami and Roman had the second bedroom and Ishtvan and Zsuzsi the third. The loungeroom and rest of the facilities were to be used between all of us.

Mami and Chopi lived on Chopi's wage. We all shared the expenses of the flat and the food. Mami, besides sewing up dresses, skirts and blouses for Zsuzsi, Chopi and myself, got busy with seatcovers, bedcovers, curtains and doilies, all from the materials in the Silk and Textiles parcel for a dollar. And when the family silver was displayed in the rooms I once again marvelled at Mami's skill in creating an elegant home from almost nothing.

After having arranged all that we organised a party and invited our new friends to extend our gratitude for their help and friendship. I cooked up two pots of authentic Hungarian goulash and Mami baked some cakes. The party was a huge success. We were praised for our effort and creativity. Yanibachi, Hedineni and Nana were relieved that the horror predictions of many, about newly arrived migrant families not appreciating the support given them, had not come true for us and we fed our hopes on their praise.

Ishtvan's dream to own his own dog did come true. A Hungarian couple was moving to Sydney and we inherited their two-year-old Zsofia, a beautiful sandy-coloured bottlebrush, a cross between a collie and something else. She soon became part of our family.

Even though, through the thin cracks between the weatherboards of our bedroom, we could see the bushes, somehow we came to like this place with its very private, grassy backyard and fruit tree, although we had no idea what it was then.

'Don't touch that fruit!' Mami ordered the children 'You might finish up with an upset stomach, or even worse.'

The following weekend the owner came to pick the fruit. He was a kind man.

'For the children.' he said, handing Mami a full bowl of fruit. 'The nectarines this year are beautifully sweet.'

It took a conscious effort to weather out the squabbles and arguments between Yano and me, Yano and Chopi, Mami and me, Yano and Mami. When people have to survive against the hardship of outside influences they stick together. Once all is settled and there is no immediate outside threat, they will fabricate problems between each other. So, it inevitably happened to us.

A parcel of my books arrived, sent by Pinki, one of Yano's sisters. Mami opened the parcel while we were at work and took out a few books, placing them into her part of the flat.

'I took my books out, Yenni,' she informed me on my return from work.

'What books? All the books are mine,' I insisted.

'How can you say such a thing? You took those books off my shelves back in Košice and never returned them.'

'That's not true!' I yelled.

'Are you saying that I am a liar?' Mami yelled back.

I shut the door between us with a bang. And, as I have done throughout my life and regretted later, I told Yano about it.

'I was waiting for something like this to happen, our being bunched up together. The "high society lady" came out with her true colours once again. How dare she open a parcel that is not addressed to her? How dare she? Just like with that silver cutlery,' said Yano, disgusted.

In Košice, while I was on maternity leave with Zsuzsi, Mami visited sometimes after work. I looked forward to her visits, waiting at the open door for her to climb up to the second floor. That particular afternoon she came through the door, brushing against me without the usual kiss.

'I never knew a woman so careless as you are Yenni,' she said, barely containing her anger, and then told me about the silver teaspoon, *her silver teaspoon*, which she found in the sandpit. 'This is from the silver service your father gave me.'

'Sorry Mami, I don't really know how it got there,' I said, feeling ashamed and disgraced.

'You don't know? What an excuse! Your son was playing with it in the sand, this is how. Well!' Absolutely inconsolable, Mami told me that she would take the silver cutlery home and buy me a stainless-steel set instead.

True to her words, the next day she turned up with a set of stainless-steel cutlery. The silver set, which was part of my wedding dowry, was polished up, as good silver deserves to be, and placed into Mami's sideboard drawer, wrapped in soft flannelette cloth.

I did not mind. The stainless-steel cutlery would do. Besides, I agreed with Mami. Silver is silver.

'What happened to our silver cutlery?' Yano asked while having his meal that evening.

I told him honestly, and once again regretted it.

'This is your mother all over! It was her present to us. The cutlery is ours!' Many years have passed since that incident, yet I haven't learned to hold my tongue about the disagreements between Mami and me.

Whenever Yano and I had an argument it was like reading from a historic calendar of our life together. We threw at each other everything we could remember that the other had done wrong going back years. Yano had a good memory.

The arguments die away, everybody is asleep. I look at my precious books scattered around on the floor, our very first consignment. The exchange of words with Mami leaves a bitter taste. I sit on the carpet surrounded by torn-up brown wrapping paper with lots of postage stamps stuck on it in continuous lines; all of them of the same colour, with the picture of our Tatra mountains, and deep in my heart I feel upset and guilty.

I look at the books again. Pinki chose well. Many of my favourites are here, among them Nazim Hikmet's *The Legend of Love.*

It was a present from the local tenor from the National Theatre in Košice, who had flooded me with books, records, poems and proverbs before I was married. I fondle the book's hard cover, made out of blue hemp-like material. Inside, on the first page, is a handwritten note:

For our eternity,
for memory,
for perpetual kind thoughts,
for youth, for beauty,
for love,
Remember ...

But there is no signature.

After the episode with the books Yano and I stop talking to Mami for weeks, while Chopi has to dance between us being careful not to take sides. Mami and I, as so many times in the past, finally patch up our differences, but Yano keeps out of it.

Mami got to know the Indian lady in the front flat. Her husband was a GP. She took a liking to Mami's polished manners and invited her in for a morning tea.

'How did you talk to each other?' I was curious.

'In English,' said Mami as if it would have been the most natural thing on the Earth.

O-o-oh yes? I thought to myself. Here we go again, Mami will never change.

They must have understood each other though, because the morning teas were repeated a few times until the family eventually moved away.

When the front flat became vacant Mami and Chopi moved in and all the squabbles were ironed out once again. The front flat was incomparable to ours, and well suited to Mami's silver and her flair.

And even though, years after, Mami remembered the time living in Darcy Street as the very best years of her life, back then she complained about everything: about the distance to the city; the flat, which was good, but could be better; about our working long hours; about her not knowing the language; the lack of money; you name it. And every lamentation finished with the same clause:

'If I would have known, Yenni, I would never have let you talk me into leaving my homeland. Never. This is all your doing.'

I often recall those words, because it was Mami, back in Košice, who told me to be careful about forcing Yano into emigration. She thought Yano would never forgive me if things didn't work out. He would make my life a misery by reminding me that it was all my fault. Strangely, Yano never mentioned any of it, although Mami frequently did.

The people we were introduced to became closer to Mami because of their ages. In a few months Mami had established a group of friends around her, which inevitably extended to Yano, the children and me. Elizabeth and Stephen, with their two daughters, were almost daily visitors at our place and, because they were teachers, during the school holidays they took Mami, Roman and often Ishtvan and Zsuzsi to picnics.

And then there was Feri, a middle-aged and quite good-looking

Hungarian man who married an Australian lady by mistake, meaning that he thought he loved her but later realised that he did not and never forgave himself for marrying her. Originally from Adelaide, Feri lived with his wife in Hobart for years without unpacking his private possessions.

'So, if we want to be truthful we could say, Feri, you haven't arrived in Hobart yet,' laughed Stephen when he found out about the suitcases under his bed.

Trying to distance himself from his wife, Feri loved his weekend and evening card games with us, and before long he became almost part of our family. To his credit he eventually introduced us to his wife, a very cultured piano teacher with whom we all sympathised and became friends with also.

Mami once again excelled as a hostess. Most of the get-togethers happened in the front flat because it was much more presentable than ours.

The old 1939 Voigtlander camera, which Yano and I originally borrowed from my mother-in-law for our honeymoon and which eventually became ours, was clicking furiously. The pictures were placed into envelopes and distributed to friends and members of our family back in the old country: 'Chopi and Roman in front of the house'; 'Mami with our new friends Xenya and Frank'; 'Ishtvan with Zsofia'; 'Around the table playing Canasta'.

Word about our arrival in Hobart spread and more people visited, introducing themselves, advising, offering help. We were truly carried on a wave of friendship in the first year of our settling in.

Yanibachi, Hedineni and Nana already belonged to the Hungarian Club and we also became members and made new friends. We became quite close with one family in particular. They were part of a very prominent and aristocratic family in Hungary, with ancestry reaching back centuries. *A true blue blood,* I mused when I found out their family name. *And, outside the Hungarian community, no one in Hobart knows about it.* They were just one of many migrant families. The son of this Hungarian count was working as a baker in Hobart. *That would have pleased the proletars,* I thought to myself.

When they were moving to the mainland, Christie's, the fine-art auctioneers from London, came to give a valuation, for insurance purposes, of their priceless furniture, collection of artefacts and antiques. While they lived in Hobart I truly enjoyed the grandeur of their home.

Before they left for Sydney Nana organised a farewell barbecue in her garden.

'What is a barbecue?' we asked.

'It's an Australian social custom,' Hedineni said. 'You can find a barbecue in almost every backyard.'

We found out on that sunny Sunday afternoon.

❦❦❦

In Nana's garden there are about twenty-five people, Hungarian, Australian, English, and they all know each other. The women move with an ease on the freshly cut grass with a glass of wine, the men group around the barbecue and with unusual utensils attend to the cooking while they keep drinking beer. The sun is smiling on this cheerful crowd, warming the salads on the table, which is pushed against the wall of the house and is covered with netting in an attempt to protect against the sun and the blowflies. I have never seen such large flies before.

'The meat is ready!' A call from the group of men activates the leisurely mingling crowd. Everybody moves in the same direction. They congregate around the table and, finding a paper plate, they load it with salads then proceed closer to the barbecue to choose their steak or a sausage. We are the last ones in the line, so we can watch and mimic.

'Have some chops, Yenni. They are nice,' Hedineni says.

'What kind of meat is it?'

'Lamb. Go on, it's nice,' she repeats.

The only time I ate lamb meat was during Easter, sometimes, when

Omama made a stew from a baby lamb, I think to myself, *but it would be interesting to try.*

We all look for a place to sit at to consume our feast. I find a long sleeper out of the sun and balance the paper plate on my knees. The large paper plate buckles under my chops and coleslaw. *Not bad,* I decide. The meat is a little tough and too fatty for me, the sausage has no taste. I would prefer lean pork or beef.

The closest thing to a barbecue in my native country would be when on occasional overnight picnics the lot of us would sit around a bonfire and make what, in a loose translation, means *The Gypsy Roast.* No salads or tables with netting, only a jar of mustard. We would cut a cross at both ends of a thick smoked sausage and then push a long stick, sharpened at one end, lengthways through it, adding perhaps a few rings of onion. In one hand the long stick with the sausage dangling above the fire and in the other a good chunk of rye bread with no butter. The heat of the fire would turn out the cut ends like the petals of a rose, making them crisp, and as the sausage sizzled we would drip the tasty juices onto the rye bread. There would always be one among us with a guitar or a harmonica and our songs would echo in the pine forest, travelling high with each leap of the flame, while the wine would make our songs more and more sentimental and melancholic.

I found it strange to turn up with my own meal when visiting. 'Bring a plate,' they would say. 'It's easier for the hostess that way.'

So, this is what Erzsike, my next-door neighbour, was trying to explain once, talking about her Canadian friends who told her this story while they were visiting Košice.

'You know they would turn up with their own food, or the richer families would pay for a cook to provide the meal. It would be served on paper plates and the table covered with a plastic tablecloth. When the party was over they simply rolled up the plastic tablecloth with everything on it and threw it in the rubbish. None of this washing up, what we are doing here,' she said, as I listened unbelievingly.

It was true that it made it easier and cheaper to entertain the way they did it in the west but the social etiquette of my native country was 'who invites, he provides'.

'Don't bring anything, all is taken care of,' I would say to my guests, and settle to plan the dishes and cakes I was going to make to show them my hospitality.

I didn't like my job at Cadbury. It made me feel brainless. So to use my brain I spent hours counting chocolates on the assembly line, working out the ratio between the amount of chocolates passing and the time it took for them to pass.

I also had a problem with my attitude and learned that the socialist idea of collective identity and enthusiasm for achievement for the good of the society did not apply in given circumstances, because I had nothing in common with the goals of the Cadbury chocolate factory or the people working there. We all, including myself, were there to make the weekly wage and this was all there was to it, but for me it didn't seem to be enough. To my surprise, in the freedom of the regime, I found myself missing the purpose I was used to so much: that of contributing to the development of my country by good work and achieving for the betterment of all. The motivation for getting up on early winter mornings and working from dawn till sunset was missing. The fact that I was making money did not raise my enthusiasm.

I was also bothered by my not being recognised as an individual. I came from a society where education was both a priority and the right of all citizens, and it followed that knowledge and grooming was utmost. Not that I had any skills to offer right then, but I had potential and so to be simply a number without motivation and without the quality of interaction with other people was to me almost unbearable. And, as banal as it might sound, in my desperation I started dressing in my best clothing, displaying my jewellery, just to be recognised as a person instead of a number on the assembly line.

There was an effort from Australian ladies to make me more familiar with other workers, as they kept introducing me to Yugoslav and Polish nationals and would smilingly watch us as we exchanged what to them were unfamiliar words.

One day, sitting in the line with others at morning-tea time, a lady I was working with dragged a young woman towards me.

'She is Czech,' she said briefly, then left the two of us to familiarise.

'I am Helena,' the Czech girl said smiling.

It was great. From that day on we travelled together to and from work and, through her Czech language interwoven with English, I began learning new English words.

There were other surprises too. How should I have known that when a man enters the factory floor and winks at me it means good morning?

When I was winked at for the first time my eyebrows hit my hairline and my nose turned towards the ceiling, pointing right to the sea of fluorescent lights. *How dare he?* I thought. *I am not a whore, just because I work in the factory.*

But all this lasted only three months as, unknown to me, I was just a relief factory worker, a filler for the busy pre-Christmas season. So one nice spring day, along with three hundred other women, I was sacked.

'Thank God for that,' I naively told Yano.

'What do you mean, thank God? We need the money. You promised me that you will work and help with the money.'

'Okay I did, but I don't want to work in the factory any more, Yano.'

'So where would you like to work with no English?'

The family once again came to the rescue. Nana knew an Italian restaurant down the street. She had a word with the owner, who needed a kitchen hand.

From the day I was hired I spent between 6 pm and midnight

with my back turned to the kitchen, facing a stainless-steel wall above the sink, scrubbing huge pots and washing up an endless numbers of plates, cups, saucers and cutlery.

But the proprietors were good. Most evenings I heard Phillipo's deep voice singing the *O Sole Mio*s and *Arrive Derchi Roma*s behind the dividing glass door, as he carried the plates of spaghetti lined up on his white shirt sleeve. And in between the orders his wife, Maria, would sit sideways on the corner of the stainless-steel table, with one leg touching the floor and a box of oysters in the crook of her elbow, sipping one after the other and dropping the empty shells noisily next to the box.

'Have one,' she invited me with a smile, and I understood, mainly because of her body language.

'Thank you,' I shook my head.

'Have one,' she repeated without success.

I had one though, without witnesses, later in the pantry. With a feeling of heroism I slowly placed the slimy body onto my tongue and encircled my mouth around it. Cold and slippery, I swallowed and, whoosh, the oyster was gone. I could not even taste it. I wrote to Svetya.

Guess what I ate yesterday? A real raw oyster. It tastes quite good, if you know what to expect.

By the way I had an argument with my boss. Actually neither of us knew what the other was yelling about. He argued in Italian with hands gesticulating somewhere around my nose, finishing near my knees. His face was going red and purple and for the life of me I couldn't work out what I had done wrong. When I had enough of that yelling I yelled back and emptied my heart completely as to what I thought of him, all in Hungarian. You should have seen the surprise on his face. At the end we both burst out laughing and to this day I don't know what it was all about, but anyway we are friends again.

And you know Svetya how we were taught to finish the job we have started. Well, this Italian man doesn't want me to work past midnight. I told him it does not matter to me, but he would not have it. We almost had another argument when he wanted me to go home, and I was not going to go until I finished scrubbing the oven. His wife had to come to my rescue and promise me that she was going to do it for me. It's a different world here I tell you and, when I checked the oven the following day, it wasn't done properly ...

Of course, I didn't know about union rules and award wages then.

Chopi's temporary position at the university finished too. Following my example, she found herself a job in the kitchen of a large, newly opened hotel-motel called the Town House, in Macquarie Street, only a few steps from the restaurant I worked in.

Mami once again had a good reason to rub in the fact that it was my idea to leave our country. 'Look where it got us!' and, 'Our income is much lower than Yano's and yours. I think you should support me, as you promised back home that you would. At least five dollars a week.' Feeling guilty about their situation and considering that she cooked for us, I paid her the five dollars out of my wages for more than ten years, never adjusting the sum, even though back in 1969 my weekly wages were only eighteen dollars. By the time I stopped supporting her, on Mami's request, five dollars was just peanuts.

While in Vienna, where we waited for months for our immigration to be accepted, Yano had taken over our family budget and the handling of wages. It stayed that way in Australia. In my mind he couldn't have done worse than I had in the past. There was no Omama to help me out and I would have had no excuses. It was also easier that way, no hassles. Because of the bickering that went on between him and Mami, for all sorts of reasons, I could never tell Yano about Mami's five dollars. I had no energy left for arguments or perhaps for an unsatisfactory outcome. So I chose to keep it secret from him and juggled the money as much as I could. Luckily the extra five dollars always rolled in at the end of the week for overtime. So everyone was happy.

When Zsuzsi started school at South Hobart Primary her teacher told Hedineni that she was two years ahead in knowledge in comparison with the syllabus for the same age group in Australia. If she could speak the language she would have progressed two grades. It was a big drawback that she couldn't speak English. *(Didn't we all know?)* The teacher strongly advised Zsuzsi to stop speaking her native language and concentrate on her English.

How could it be done? How could we communicate with our children in English when we ourselves couldn't speak it? Didn't the teacher know that in most European countries languages are taught parallel with the native tongue? Didn't the teacher know that people are paying to learn other languages?

In 1945, when I was nine, one morning, without taking a step outside our home, I woke up in a different country from the one I was in when I went to bed the night before.

That morning I had gone to school with many others and the language now taught there was Slovak, which we could not speak or understand. Children learn fast, so it took only a short while before we mastered the new language, so very different from our mother tongue. The following year the Russian language became compulsory. Through all my years of living in my native country I had been using three languages parallel with each other and, in addition, could understand at least two more, even though some languages were more encouraged than others for political reasons. Our young generation was intimately exposed to the folklore, history, literature and music of at least three cultures; four, if you consider that the Czech culture and history was different from the Slovak. We were proud to speak many languages. There is a saying in my country that you are as many times a person as the number of languages you speak. The native language is the identity and history of a person. So what does the teacher mean by letting Zsuzsi forget her own language?

I realised though that all the suggestions were made in good faith, in an attempt to help. The teacher allocated a Yugoslav girl from the class to translate for Zsuzsi. Eva lived round the corner from us and, even though those two never saw eye to eye, Zsuzsi had someone to relate to and sometimes to play with.

Ishtvan, after much consideration and advice from Stephen and Elizabeth, went to Taroona High. We were told the same at his school. Ishtvan was a couple of years ahead in knowledge compared with the syllabus for his age group in Australia.

Ishtvan was a quiet and placid boy. From his own initiative he enrolled in a regular English course, informing us of his decision, and every day walked there after school, finishing in the evenings. Because there were no boys of his own age living in our area he spent most of his spare time at home reading, playing with Zsofia and Roman, and sometimes with his new friend, a Dutch boy he met through the English course. I know now that for the children to grow up isolated from their peers wasn't a desired experience. This was just one more price to pay for our emigration.

But Allan was about. Not daily, but at least weekly he would make the pilgrimage from Lenah Valley to South Hobart to be around Ishtvan and Zsuzsi.

After our moving we stopped attending our English course because of the distance to the school, and because Chopi and I were working at night. For a short while Eva's Yugoslav parents organised an English teacher to come to their home once a week, so we all went. Just like at our first course, there too we did not get much further than: 'I am, you are, we are.'

A six-week crash course in English was offered to Yano by the Immigration Department. The course was to be conducted during business hours with financial support provided by the government, though much lower than his wages. We decided it was of utmost importance for Yano to learn English in order to use his skills as a draughtsman. There was no other way; I had to find a better paid job.

The word about my looking for work went around the Hungarian community. A Hungarian man, manufacturing cottage cheese and yoghurt on a trial basis, heard about me and he needed someone to wash the returned yoghurt jars.

At four-thirty the morning found me standing in front of our gate waiting to be collected by my new boss to start work at five. On the property of the only milk factory in Hobart – Baker's Milk in Lenah Valley – he had rented a large space adjacent to the laboratory.

I still feel the shivers of morning after cold morning as we pulled up the roller door and entered the cemented interior of this grey structure with its long lines of stainless-steel troughs containing the tightly packed yoghurt jars, which were covered with cold water right up to their tin lids. Two huge cement baths were filled with dirty, returned yoghurt jars, which were covered by water saturated with caustic soda. In front of them was a wooden pallet, and on it a pair of legs in gumboots and a body wearing a long rubber apron weighing a ton. The mouth belonging to the body was blaring out songs of various origin, their tunes hitting the grey cemented walls, then flowing back with lesser intensity and finally drowning in the water covering the yoghurt jars.

'You happy, Yenni?' he asked me.

I was. Really, knowing this was only temporary and I was never scared of hard work. But to forget about my job and environment, I sang. I sang my full repertoire of Russian folksongs and marches, including the Russian anthem, then the Hungarian songs, including the anthem, and the Slovak songs, throwing in a Czech or Polish song as well, and when I exhausted my knowledge I started from the beginning.

I considered it fair to work hard, because my boss and the other Hungarian woman who was working with us did the same and they were treating me as part of the family. They regularly packed up a box of yoghurt and cottage cheese for the children and my wages were good and regular.

My English went down the drain along with the water and caustic soda, of course, as I spoke Hungarian all day and enjoyed the gossip of those two about other members of the Hungarian community. It was almost like being back home.

I kept my restaurant job also, finishing in the yoghurt factory at five at the afternoon and starting in the kitchen at six. I had just enough time to catch the bus from Lenah Valley to the city, walk into Coles, straight to the hot-food bar, point to a warm Chiko Roll wrapped in white paper and, enjoying my snack, walk to Elizabeth Street.

'You will get fat,' a lady in passing smiled at me. I smiled back with satisfaction. *I understood what she said and she took me for an Australian,* I thought to myself with a feeling of victory.

With my contributions and Yano's government subsidy our savings were increasing. I remember those times as physically the most demanding.

On Nana's suggestion we all joined private health insurance and regularly contributed to it, but had no idea about its application or the benefits we were entitled to.

It did not help that I kept my problem secret, even from Yanibachi, when my cuticles got inflamed because of the type of work I was doing. It was so bad, that the pus was pouring out behind all my fingernails and I did not dare tell any of my bosses about it, worrying that they might sack me. I kept my wounds clean by applying methylated spirits and some old cream I found in my basic first-aid kit, which I had brought from the old country. But it hurt. Many nights I would wake up with a throbbing pain in my fingers and the only relief would be an application of nail-polish remover. To this day I have no idea if it was the right thing to do but the acetone helped with the pain and by morning it had dried out the pus until I dipped my hands into the caustic soda and the water seeped through the small holes in the rubber gloves again.

In those months I lived in a haze of exhaustion, like a money-making machine, contented by the growing earnings but completely unfocused. Sunday mornings, lying in bed with sheets – oh, how I hated those sheets and blankets – tangled around my thin, skin-and-bone body, I listened to the voices in the next room. Then with an effort I lowered my legs onto the floorboards covered by a mat.

Sunday mornings were washing mornings, when in the bath I hand-washed the whole week's laundry for our family. Most of the morning I spent down on my knees squeezing and rubbing the shirts, sheets and underwear until my cuticles hurt and rub marks showed on my knuckles. The soapy detergent made them stink.

Despite our squabbles Mami never stopped working with all her strength to keep us all fed and make sure that the children were well looked after. To improve the financial situation of their small family she found herself a job minding our new friend's little boy of Roman's age.

And, knowing no better, we listened to anyone's advice and abided by it like it was from the Bible. And there was a lot of it, some better than others. Prompted by one useful piece of advice we applied to the Housing Department for a house for the four of us. Mami and Chopi applied for a flat.

CHAPTER THREE

A Summer Christmas

Christmas was nearing and with it the long-awaited summer. In the central business block garlands were drawn across the streets from lamp post to lamp post, with snow-capped bells and white reindeers, and the shops were filled with lights, Christmas carols, shoppers and an absolute abundance of merchandise. For the first time in my entire life I could afford Christmas shopping for everyone.

It was a challenge to wander through the interconnected shops, stopping to touch and feel, search for the right presents, forever surprising myself with the street I walked out onto.

My mind drifted back to when I was eighteen. This was the first Christmas after leaving school, being employed and almost having enough money for Christmas presents. Chopi and I decided to surprise Mami with the dress material we thought she had pointed out to us one day in passing. For weeks we had kept an eye on the display window, observing, hoping that the material would remain there until we had saved enough money. Yes, yes, it was still there. Excitedly we walked into the shop and bought the material.

It did not work out quite as well as we thought it might, and it left

Chopi and myself disappointed.

'Ah-a-a-a-ah,' Mami remarked. 'Very nice. I don't think the colour will suit me though. Didn't you see the material next to this one in the display window? That's the one I wanted.'

Year after year on birthdays or other occasions we never seemed to quite get the right present for Mami. Later the pleasure had gone out of present buying and it became a chore. Chopi and I agreed, it doesn't matter what we buy, Mami will want the thing next to it.

What should I buy Mami this Christmas? She didn't need material, that was for sure; we had plenty from the Silk and Textiles parcels.

Walking in Liverpool Street with a cardigan thrown over my forearm I kept repeating to myself: 'Tomorrow is Christmas Eve,' and I couldn't believe it. Christmas with the sun warming my arms and face, Christmas in summer?

❦❦❦

It's after midnight. This is a normal time for me to come home from work. A narrow pathway alongside the building leads to our flat. Passing the dark loungeroom window I walk through the shadows of the trees, which like arms reaching for the moon are stretching out their long leafy branches. All is quiet; everyone is asleep. Exhausted, I flick on the light in the sitting room. In front of the window is a ceiling-high Christmas tree, sparingly decorated with some paper cuttings, obviously by the children. The tree is almost bare. Yano must have bought it this afternoon. *At least he kept to the ceiling size as we are used to,* I observe, and think disappointedly that, having no Christmas decorations, he has let the children do it up the best they knew. The tradition we had preserved in our family with so much anticipation for children and adults was abandoned already.

This is nothing like what I remember, our beautiful Christmas tree lit up by candles, chocolates wrapped in silver and gold paper, decorations of fairies and huge shiny balls hanging on silver threads. I searched everywhere for such decorations this afternoon. They are not a tradition in Australia, I was told. *And the salonky?* 'What are they?'

So what do you hang on your tree? 'Cut-out paper hangings, flickering lights and such, and we decorate the rooms with balloons and paper streamers and with the Christmas cards.' It's too late anyway, they told me; the Christmas trees are standing in loungerooms at least two, three weeks before Christmas. *Why?* I wonder. We decorate our trees on the Christmas Eve, behind closed doors so no one sees it before the little angel rings the bell and the family is allowed to walk into the dark room, lit up only by the candles on the tree. We feel the magic of Christmas as we congregate around the tree and sing our Christmas carols in unison.

The low-voltage ceiling globe is throwing a sluggish light onto the pea-green walls of the room and is making them look almost grey, cold and unfriendly.

I sit in the armchair and tears of sadness roll down my cheeks for the very first time since we left our native country. Is this why I wanted to leave our homeland? Is this all I can offer to my children? We are working so hard, I have two jobs, we have money, but what is it good for? The true picture, the emptiness of materialism, is marginalised by the false sense of fulfilment, by the opulence of luxuries. I have no time to spare with the children. I can't even create a feeling of Christmas similar to what they are used to. How much more can we cut down on our cultural standard and our family life? How much more and for how long?

Remembering the cardboard box from Cadbury's with chocolates kept for *later on*, there and then I decide to make this Christmas tree as good as I can and mimic our traditional *salonky*, wrapped chocolate-covered fondants. I wrap up everything I can get my hands on, hang up biscuits and chocolates on long white knitting yarn, cut up a strip of Alfoil into shapes, twisting them. They shine between the rich-green needles. Right. This looks beautiful now.

It is four o'clock in the morning; I'd better have my bath and get ready for work.

That day above the concrete baths I thought with a smile of Yano and the children waking up and walking into the sitting room, finding this *new* Christmas tree. Almost as in my childhood, the little Jesus and his angels came down from the heavens to decorate it for us.

What a lovely Christmas it was after all. We made a long table to accommodate the new members of our family, Yanibachi, Hedineni and Nana. The windows were covered by thick blankets so that the sunshine would stay outside while the room was bathed in semi-darkness, mysteriously revealing the shape of the parcels and enabling the candles to shine. Everyone loved the tree. The sitting room was warm, the house smelled of our traditional sauerkraut soup, chicken, fish and potato salad. Yanibachi and Hedineni could not get enough. The last time they had this traditional Christmas dinner was years ago, back in Europe. And Mami's cooking was highly praised, and she deserved it. Everyone liked their presents, even Mami. The best thing though was that I had three days off. Three whole days.

It's 26°C on Christmas Day.

'Chopi, let's take the children to the swimming pool.'

We were told about the Olympic pool on the Domain, the Queen's Domain.

'Why do they call it the Queen's Domain?' I question Yanibachi.

It's simple; the land around the Botanic Gardens belongs to the Queen. But why? The Queen lives in England, doesn't she? True, but Australia is part of England. I thought Australia was a federation of six states, each with a premier and a federal prime minister. Yes, but the head of Australia is the Queen. She has a representative in each state. The governor of Tasmania lives next to the Botanic Gardens, in that castle-like building on the Queen's Domain.

So, we are living in a monarchy? No one had ever told me that, even though I wondered about the pictures of the English queen in offices and on documents. I feel good about it, almost proud. We couldn't have got further away from socialism than this.

Chopi and I are impressed with the swimming pool. The cleanliness of the building, the large expanse of the pool, the grassy patches covered by colourful blankets and brown bodies, and lots of shade-giving trees. Roman loves the small pool, even though the attendant complains to Chopi about him being naked. 'He is only two,' Chopi laments. 'It doesn't matter; he is naked,' the attendant says. Okay, I will dress him in his undies, Chopi decides, and all is good.

Splash, splash, the sun-warmed water whirls around Roman. Ishtvan and Zsuzsi are in the big pool, which is filled with blue water, children and laughter. Lying on my back on the soft grass, listening to the sounds and splashes of water and smelling the suntan oil around me, I am transported back to my childhood. Was I four or five? I am in Miskolc.

I see myself standing in front of the bedroom window and feel the excitement of the summer morning. Seeing the blue sky I know we will go for sure: we will catch the bus just around the corner and after a short ride will arrive at Tapolca, where the swimming pool is.

There I jump off the bus and look back for my father's hand. The relationship with my father is natural and easy. I trust him. No harsh words or discipline, I recall only his kind blue eyes. The trees are enormous and shady and I happily carry my little basket with my swimsuit. The familiar smell, the mixture of Nivea cream and pool water drying on the wooden sunbeds spread around the side of the pool, reaches my nostrils. My excitement culminates. In my mind I can already feel the coolness of the water and see the children playing on the grass. The medley of noises, people chatting and laughing, assures me that we are getting close.

There is another swimming pool in Tapolca, with naturally warm mineral water. That place is exciting too but a little scary for me because of the large stones and rocks around, as well as above me. And there is no sunshine because it's inside a cave. I can play only in some parts of the cave because of the depth of the water. I much prefer the outdoor swimming pool warmed up by the sun. It's magic.

How far in years and miles have I come from that memory?

A deep-blue flag with the southern cross and the Union Jack in one corner is fluttering against the clear blue sky. I squint in the bright sunlight up to that fluttering flag and smile. It looks beautiful and I feel secure and contented under it.

On Boxing Day we are invited to visit Yano's English teacher. What a privilege! Tony is going to give us a lift to Mount Stuart where the teacher lives.

When we enter the lovely old home, set against a backdrop of the sweeping views of Hobart, every seat in the loungeroom is taken by a person of a different nationality.

All of us sitting very upright, hands in our laps, we are aware of our differences in the colour of our skins, our outfits and the languages we speak. There are Chilean, Vietnamese, Russian, Polish, Yugoslav and us, Czechoslovakian emigrants, and their families.

The large table, covered by a lace tablecloth, is pushed into the corner to make room for all the chairs. It bends under the weight of plates with ham, a selection of cheeses, meats, cakes and wine.

The hands of the teacher, Mrs Helpern, and her husband are busy with the distribution of Christmas presents, which were carefully selected and wrapped for each family. Our family is presented with a set of fruit bowls of Bohemian crystal. I am overwhelmed. This is the third time that my eyes fill up with tears, tears of happiness and gratitude for the kind-heartedness and thoughtfulness of this Australian lady.

My dearest Yenni

Thank you very much for your letter. We received the $5 and I thank you very much that you thought of us. We don't wish for you to support us, because even though the situation is very difficult here, there is only the two of us and we have enough for what we need.

... the house is very quiet. This year I could not visit even the cemetery

before Christmas, because of the huge snowfalls. There is no day without me thinking of you all. How are the children? And how is my little grasshopper Roman? I can imagine how big he has grown since I saw him last …

My hands are paining, I can't write much more, love, your Omama.

Slowly, the centre of the city becomes familiar. The place I catch the bus from is in front of a park called Franklin Square. Two statues flank the bus stop. One is wearing a waistcoat and seems to be from the last century; the other is a bronze statue of Edward VII, *The Peacemaker*, says the writing on the plaque. They watch over the people whirling around the arriving and departing buses. I like this park. A little elevated from the street, it has seats under the large floppy trees and a fountain, in the middle of which stands another statue, that of Sir John Franklin, a navigator, rear admiral and once the governor of Tasmania. It was erected in his memory by the colonialists of Tasmania. While I am waiting for the bus to arrive, I walk around the statues and read the bronze plaques on each. I learn that Sir Franklin lost his life in 1847 attempting to discover the North-West Passage in the Arctic. Some of the writing I don't understand but what I do gives me a vague idea of the history of my new home. There seems to be so much history in this new, under-aged country.

The buildings surrounding the square are quite beautiful, most from honey-coloured sandstone and in Georgian architectural style, unusual to me. By now I know that the building on the corner of Elizabeth Street with steps leading to large arches and a corner tower with a clock on it is the main post office. From a small bronze plaque I learn that the land on which it was built was granted to Mr Lord in 1818 by the governor of New South Wales, Lachlan Macquarie. *One of the Queen's representatives,* I think to myself. So, this is where the name of Macquarie Street came from. Around the corner, almost opposite the Post Office, is the building of the Hobart City Council, in a similar style but much grander.

The three buildings I really like the best are opposite my bus stop.

One has a sign, ANZ Bank, the second belongs to Mercantile Mutual and seems to be the oldest of the three, unrendered as many old buildings are, it is built from grey stone. My favourite is the third one, next to the church park, the building of National Mutual Insurance Company. The cornerstone was laid in 1906, says the writing. Even though it has some Gothic elements, I can't work out its architectural style. The Gothic in buildings in Tasmania surprises me, because I know it to be used mainly in the Catholic culture of Europe from the twelfth to the sixteenth century.

Visible from my bus stop, on the corner of the street, St David's Cathedral sits majestically in the shade of large trees. One day I will venture inside it. I am yet to get used to the square towers on churches; I prefer domes and spires.

Rounding the corner at St David's Cathedral is Murray Street. To my left it stretches down to the wharf, which is surrounded by the blue waters of the Derwent River and the Tasman Sea; to my right it runs the lengths of the city, climbing up to outer suburbia. On this street, walking behind a man, I notice him kicking something gently, steering it towards the wall of a building. Suddenly he stops, looks around and picks up the twenty-dollar note from the footpath. Twenty dollars! It is more than my weekly wages. If it were me I would have gone to Myer and bought stuff for Svetya.

From that day on I keep walking the streets with my eyes pinned to the footpath and the contents of my imaginary parcel change, according to the shops I have just come out of.

Svetya, I still can't believe that it is summer here in January. Our new friends told us about the bushfires back two years ago in Hobart. They said that the whole of Mount Wellington and half of the city was burned down, about 1400 houses, and that lots of people died. That day is called Black Tuesday here. They advised us to hose down our house and the roof, because yesterday it was a hundred degrees Fahrenheit. Don't ask me what it is in Celsius, it sounds a lot though, doesn't it? They all thought it was a scorcher but, you know, since we arrived in Tasmania I feel the cold so much. I feel it through my whole body, right inside my bones. Perhaps because I lost all that weight, or perhaps because we missed out on summer last year. I don't know.

We applied for a house. Most people have their own houses here. Can you imagine us applying after such a short time in Tasmania?

Regarding my job, I don't like it all that much, but I like the people I am working with. They are incredibly friendly and helpful. Sometimes I think perhaps I should find a better job, but what kind, if I don't speak the language? There is a delicatessen in the centre of Hobart called The Gourmet. Apparently a Hungarian man established it but he has gone to Sydney and the shop was sold. All the staff speak Polish. I thought perhaps I could work there but so far have had no courage to ask for a job. This shop is the only place where I can get some smallgoods similar to what we are used to.

Talking about the language, you should listen to the radio here. The music is all right, even though I find it unfamiliar, but there is not one tune I can sing along with. But the way they speak! It sounds like the flow of a river. Can't tell the beginning or the end of the sentence. The very first radio broadcast I ever heard was incredibly fast. When I described it to Yanibachi he laughed. 'That was the horseracing, you silly,' he told me. They actually broadcast the horseracing here. He told us that when we understand what they talk about on the radio without concentrating on it, this is when we can say that we understand English. Right now I believe that time will never come.

This is for your ears only, Svetya. Sometimes I fantasise that I am working in the bank in Košice as an English translator. Perhaps some foreign correspondent needs help with a translation. (Remember that story I told you about, when Dubcek was negotiating on the Russian border and the city was full of foreign correspondents and they had to fetch someone from the university to speak to them?) I think I could handle it. Last night I had a trial run when everyone was asleep and I think I could translate some basic words already. So how's that?

With all the unfamiliarity around me, funnily I don't feel homesick.

Many people do, you know …

'There is a job vacancy in the laboratory,' my Hungarian boss tells me. 'What do you know about chemistry, Yenni?'

From the oblivion of my student years, Franklin, my hated chemistry teacher grows to life size. My answer is noncommittal. 'U-m-m, I have learned chemistry right through my matriculation college.'

This does it. He goes and speaks on my behalf to the factory manager and, on his return, with a huge smile he informs me that he has organised a job interview for me. 'Now,' he says.

I undo my leather apron, tidy my hair and walk the few steps around the corner to the office of the factory manager. I know that he is of German origin and the familiarity of the mutual social ethics is comforting.

He smiles when I symbolically, as good manners in my country dictate, knock on the door, which is ajar. A handsome man in his early forties, in his suntanned face are the most vivid blue eyes I have ever seen. He stands up in a grey laboratory coat, which is unbuttoned above his gumboots and offers a handshake only after my hand stretches over first.

I feel nervous and take only brief notice, more of an impression, of the square room with corner windows, where everything around and on the desk is laid out in perfect order. When he points to the empty chair I sit down and the interview starts.

I tell him my name and with this out of the way the rest of the questions to me are the biblical tower of Babel. I have no idea what he is asking and because there are only two possibilities I alternate between yes and no almost at random, guessing from familiar words the possible meaning of the whole sentence.

When he stands up I understand that the interview is over, we shake hands and I trot down into the greyness of my workplace to resume my position in front of the cement baths.

'So?' asks my boss.

'No idea.'

He wants to find out, lights a cigarette and disappears for a long while.

'You are hired.' He comes back grinning. 'You start working in the laboratory tomorrow morning at eight o'clock.'

'It must be a mistake. I didn't understand a word at my interview,' I object.

He clicks his tongue and repeats just to make sure. 'You start working tomorrow at eight in the lab, don't bother waiting for me in front of your gate at four thirty in the morning.'

It hits me like lightning. From tomorrow on I will have the civil job of a laboratory assistant in a nice clean and bright place and my working hours will be from eight in the morning. H-u-r-r-a-a-h!

'Dear Mr Ferenczy. Thank you. Thank you.' I jump up and down on the concrete floor for a while and then circle my arms around his thick neck and kiss his cheeks about five times. He suffers through this ordeal with a wide smile and gently places my arms where they belong, alongside my body.

'Okay, okay, okay. Calm down for God's sake. It's only a job.'

'What are you going to do without me?'

'I will manage,' he smiles.

❦❦❦

During my journey to my other workplace at the Astor Restaurant as a washer-upper that afternoon I was in a state of absolute euphoria.

I don't mind the downsides of life, as long as there are also moments like this, I thought and realised straight away how easy it was to say it, when I happened to be on the upside.

Starting from the top end of Liverpool Street going towards the city I danced and skipped through the whole length of it and on my way bumped into Elizabeth and Stephen. 'I have a job in the laboratory, I have a job in the laboratory,' I repeated, not quite believing it myself.

'It's fantastic, you deserve it,' they assured me after my lengthy story as to how it all happened.

Parting, I hugged them, wanting to hug the whole world, but mainly this great place Tasmania, my new home.

A large gravelled yard; in it the milk factory with the front and back ramps where the milk vendors loaded their trucks at three in the morning, the workshop, the carpark and the grey garage-like building, the yoghurt factory. Opposite the milk factory was a square besser-block building painted white, with long windows stretching through the length of it in a narrow strip. There was a concrete ramp from the yard leading to the door. Inside the square building were two rooms, divided by a short passage that branched off to the change room and toilet. The smaller room was the office of the factory manager, where I had my interview the day before. The other room, much more spacious and full of light, was my new workplace, the laboratory.

Next to the lab was the tipping bay, where farmers stopped their trucks, loaded with twenty-litre aluminium cans packed tightly next to each other, lifted them off the truck and placed them one by one onto a conveyer belt with screeching metal rollers. The cans rolled in a long line to a man who lifted the lid of each, stuck his face into the can, almost disappearing in it, smelled the contents and then tipped the milk into a hole lined with stainless steel and connected to a pipe leading to the factory. The empty cans continued their slow roll on the conveyer belt back to the truck.

The tipping bay was accessible from the lab by a door, but its side was open to the gravelled yard, into which the trucks, cars and vans pulled up with farmers carrying their produce to sell.

I walk into the lab and stop at the door. The whole length of the wall opposite is occupied by waist-high built-in cupboards, their sliding doors pushed half open, exposing measuring glasses, Petri dishes and other lab equipment. The white bench continues round the corner to form a writing desk. One part of the bench is a sink, just like any kitchen sink, along the rest are a number of water baths with thermometers and other machinery I have never seen before. In the far corner is a large, white and round creation, which I find out later is a centrifuge. Above the benches are shelves with pipettes and testing bottles of various sizes. To the left of the centrifuge is another sink, above it a distiller bubbling away, then the door to the tipping bay.

On the other side of the door are some more stainless-steel water baths. Under the windows is a large writing desk with books leaning against the wall, sheets of paper, a calendar and pencils. Continuing from the desk are the two incubators, each as big as a fridge; the second one meets the door in front of which I am standing. The middle of the room is taken up by a huge table covered with a white melomite top and on it some more machinery. To my right another door with a big handle. I found out later that it is the coolroom. Next is the passage connecting the lab with the office of the manager.

The floor is covered with dark-brown lino and the walls are light blue. It looks professional, friendly and deserted. The only person in it is me. The humming of the machinery inside the lab and the sounds from the factory coming in through open windows fill my ears with a medley that in the next ten years will represent a sense of familiarity and security.

Spoken words are getting closer to the door, I take a few steps towards the large table and the door flings open. A man talking with a heavy German accent and wearing a white lab coat and gumboots walks in carrying a bottle of milk and hurries towards one of the machines. He is followed by another man with a dinky-dye accent, a great grin and a head topped with curly light-brown hair, also in gumboots and wearing the grey overalls of the factory worker. I don't understand a word they are saying.

The German finally notices me and talks, first in English, but when he realises that I don't understand him he tries German. With my thumb and forefinger almost touching each other I show him that I can understand only a little German and even less English. He shakes my hand; his name is Otto and he is in charge of the laboratory. The other man is Roy. Later I find out that he works in the tipping bay and everywhere else. When Roy realises that I don't understand, he picks up an empty sheet of paper from the desk and draws pictures. I laugh and draw pictures back.

I am given a white lab coat and a grand tour of the factory, walking on the steel floor through the maze of conveyer belts and stainless-steel vats as in a dream, meeting many men and saying many hellos.

My grand tour finishes inside the canteen with a cup of coffee and hot scones with jam and cream. From that day on I pester Mrs Bowden, the lady in charge of the canteen, for her recipe for scones and other things I really like and have never heard of before. And Mrs Bowden, even though not very partial to New Australians, takes pity on me and writes out some of her recipes, which I eventually try and with surprise realise they work. I am also told with a friendly smile that I can call myself Australian only when I learn how to make good scones and a pavlova. *I will, I will,* I promise them and to myself.

Some smart person once said: 'There is no other reality except the one that is contained within us.' I was trying to live simultaneously in my two cities, the one in my memory and the other in my present reality. The size of Hobart and its population was approximately the same as that of Košice. My native city gave me a yardstick to define and measure Hobart. Each day I found something unusual or different in the, to me, still new place and considered it to be quite beautiful. But it felt just like looking at a painting that doesn't belong to you. The only thing you have in common with it is how much you like it. The people were welcoming too and wanting to help. Even the weather was good. But the isolation, that was the most difficult burden to bear.

When we left our native country with our idealised view of the west, where all our problems would be solved, we took into account all we would have to endure; the new and unknown political freedom, our lack of English and hard financial times at the beginning. One thing we never counted on was the human element. It wasn't only about the language. It was the need to belong. To identify with a group of people of the same tradition, familiar culture, history and interest. The need to share mutual memories. It was the past we missed.

The tragedy of exile. We had more than enough social interaction by meeting people of our own nationality, other immigrants and Australians who were willing to make friends with us. But the people of our own nationality had been living in Australia for years; many came after World War II or in the early 1950s. They had no idea about our life behind the Iron Curtain. Their perception was influenced by their own post-war experiences and by the American spy movies. Like a citadel of righteousness, they repeated the recent political propaganda about our country.

'Get on with your lives,' they advised.

'No politics, no religious debates,' our Australian friends told us.

So, what do they talk about? We wondered. Politics is the reality of life.

There were no memories to share or reflect on, nothing to fall back on, nothing to refer to in our new friendships and we had to reinvent ourselves, make our case each time we met new people. Our life in the native country, the hardships and achievements, had to be explained from the very beginning, over and over again. *Do they believe us?* I wondered as I was struggling to find my place in this new society.

In shops, buses, banks, at work and in our everyday lives there was this wall of unspoken words. People had so much to ask and we had so much to tell. But the words were missing. The words, which would bring closeness to a casual relationship, which could tell about our gratitude to the ones who helped, the words that would help to share our feelings.

Still, there was nothing wrong, nothing that we could express comprehensively, even to ourselves or to each other, to fill this big hole left through our departure from the familiar, the space that used to be occupied by the secure and reassuring feeling of belonging.

During working days Yano and I saw each other only for a short while, in the early mornings and sometimes when he waited up for me at night. Sundays were for our family, washing, house-cleaning and everything-else days, and days of doing things together with Mami and Chopi. Yano was a reliable husband, handled the budget trusted into his lap very well and shared the care of Ishtvan and Zsuzsi together with Mami in my absence. Besides some bickering between him and Mami there was not much to worry about, or was there? It wasn't so much about Yano, more about me. My jealousy was always my problem even though Yano contributed to it from time to time in big chunks.

CHAPTER FOUR

Tasmanian Tourists

I am walking on the footpath of Macquarie Street towards South Hobart. It's warm.

Mount Wellington looks dark and mysterious against the red sky. It stands almost two-dimensional, like large props on a theatre stage, and as I walk towards it the mountain seemingly gets bigger. I can never grow tired of looking at Mount Wellington; it always looks different, as if a painter had changed the colours of his subject every day. I think of the words of one of the first English books I bravely ventured to read with the help of the dictionary. It said that God employs a different heavenly painter every evening to paint a sunset; this is why sunsets are so different from each other.

The toot of a passing car disturbs my thoughts. From its open window a hand extends in greeting. Was it for me? I have a second look. It's Roy.

For a short second he takes my heart for a ride in that car. I was recognised by someone! I am not only a number in the population but a person walking on the streets of Hobart and I was recognised. My steps become lighter as I walk home.

❦❦❦

Repeatedly I was told by various people that I looked tired and should pack in my evening job. After talking it over with Yano we decided I would finish working in the restaurant. Fantastic! All my dreams were slowly coming true.

When I told Phillipo about my decision to quit we had another dramatic scene. His ruddy face turned darker still. He wagged his finger in front of my nose.

'You can't leave now! For months you were no good but I paid you and trained you. You want to leave now, when we are in the middle of the summer season?'

I considered what he said and thought it was fair.

'When will the season be finished?'

'In a couple of months.'

'Okay I will work for you for a couple more months.'

But I loved my job at Baker's Milk and all the people I worked with, including the farmers and the inspectors from the Agriculture Department.

Each morning, opening my eyes and realising that I had to get ready for work, a feeling of excitement and expectation spread inside me. I made the bed, packed the lunches for the children and for Yano and, with a kiss, saw them out the door one by one. Then it was my time to get ready.

Otto would often send Roy to drive me to work, in between the milk trucks' arrivals. Roy, in grey overalls and gumboots, with light-brown curls stuck to his skull, would pull up in front of the house in an old beaten-up Holden, walk around the front flat and knock on the window pane of our kitchen door.

'Hi sex-e-e-e. Came to getcha,' he would greet me with a wink, which by then I knew meant good morning.

Roy became a special friend and was always there when I needed him. From the first day of me working in the lab, he started presenting me with little gifts of comical heads. Some were rubber heads with faces of various expressions, used as pen or pencil ends; others were small plastic heads made for who knows what purpose. I had a whole collection of faces and heads placed in line next to each other sitting on the shelf above my writing desk, looking down at me, grinning with dubious smiles, making my day brighter.

My drawings became more precise. These I used as the last resort when I couldn't find words to explain something to anyone who came in contact with me.

They were also a way to amuse myself during my lunch breaks, sitting at my desk with a cup of coffee and a packet of cigarettes at my elbow, munching on my sandwiches.

❦❦❦

The door opens wide and a stocky man, about sixtyish, with his shirt sleeves turned up to his elbows walks in with long noisy steps.

'Where is Otto?' His strong and loud voice fills the lab.

I tell him in my English that I don't know. He comes closer, inspects me, then the contents of my desk, reaches for the packet of cigarettes, picks it up and lowers it into his pocket, saying, 'You don't need them,' and walks out of the lab.

Well! My blood boils. *How dare he? Who does he thinks he is?*

When Otto turns up I tell him, half German, half English. The more upset I get the fewer English words I can find.

'That was Mr Baker,' Otto says and he has no time to tell me more, because the very man walks through the door, straight to my desk and places a large bag of chocolates in front of me.

The chocolates are instead of cigarettes, Otto translates. Mr Baker can't stand people smoking; it's no good for their health.

'Was it Mr Baker, the millionaire?' I can't identify Mr Baker with millionaires I used to see in movies, leaning back in heavy leather chairs, feet on mahogany writing desks, with a cigar between their teeth. What kind of a millionaire is he with rolled-up shirt sleeves? I can't wait to tell this to Svetya.

I met my first true millionaire. His name is Mr Baker and he owns the milk factory where I work. He is nothing what you think a millionaire should look like, Svetya. I heard when he married all they had with his wife was a small patch of land and a cow. Before long Mr Baker started selling milk, distributing it to his neighbours on a small cart. And, you know, he never stopped working since, even though by now he doesn't have to. On Saturday mornings if the factory is short of a man Mr Baker with turned-up sleeves takes his place in front of the assembly line, watching the empty bottles passing, singing his heart out, dragging the factory workers into his jovial mood until everyone sings.

He loves to use his public address system, sometimes summoning people to his office, or singing a Happy Birthday song to one of his workers. We have an 80-year-old man in the factory who has worked for Mr Baker for almost forty years.

Anyone wanting money for a new car or something else would see him first before the bank manager and the money would be loaned with no fuss. He knows how to keep the morale and the friendship. Even though they all call him by his first name, everyone respects him. He is like a grandfather to me …

My letters to Svetya were dripping with contentment.

You have no idea Svetya how good they are to me. I think I must be the luckiest person in the whole world. When I left the Department of Social Security in Košice I thought I would never find a job I would love so much and, on the other side of the world, on this small island, I found it.

Last week I was taken to a real Australian farm. One of the inspectors from the Agriculture Department took me there. About an hour's drive south-east of Hobart is the Peninsula, which has good pastures and many dairy farms.

Even though I still can't speak English very well, somehow it doesn't seem to worry anybody and I feel that they understand me.

The farmer at Bream Creek invited us into his house to have morning tea with him. I met the whole family, including his five children. They were running in and out of the kitchen with muddy gumboots, eating sandwiches spread with butter and Vegemite. You can buy this Vegemite in jars. It's a dark-brown, almost black-looking spread with a salty taste, which supposedly is very good for you. I quite like it myself; Mami and the children like it too. Someone told me it is made from yeast and is rich with vitamin B. They said that you can only get it in Australia. Everyone eats it here. Would you like me to send you a jar just for the fun of it?

The golden point of my excursion came when Lewis, that's the name of the inspector, took me down to Marion Bay. Wow! The beach is covered by the whitest of white sands, the huge surf crashes noisily onto it and behind the froth is the deepest blue sea you can imagine. I am convinced if I had a pair of binoculars I could have seen Antarctica, or most likely New Zealand, because the beach is really on the south-eastern side of Tasmania. It was so wild and magical. And you know Svetya, Lewis packed a lunch for both of us to have on this deserted beach. People are so easy, so nice …

The days blended into weeks and the weeks into months, and the summer of 1970 was fading into a glorious autumn. The suburban gardens were at their very best, filled with an abundance of colour and foliage. The assortment of bushes, trees and plants, ranging from European to native Australian, looked to me exceptionally beautiful.

Not far from the centre of the city is St David's Park. I found it the first time I walked down Macquarie Street. *Smaller, but as beautiful as the park in Košice,* I thought. The sounds of my steps were absorbed in the mass of fallen leaves, as I walked on a soft carpet of gold and deep red under the branches of centuries-old oak trees that hung above me like huge umbrellas obscuring the blue sky.

St David's Park contained a cemetery from the nineteenth century. The pompous gravestones erected for the Tasmanian elite were scattered randomly in the park, and at one end was a wall displaying, I supposed, the tombstones of the ordinary Tasmanians, people who came to this country to start a new life just like I did. It seems they had been moved when it became a public park. The stories on the stones told me that Hobart in her not-too-distant past was a dangerous frontier town to live in.

That evening Tony and Gail visited. 'We are going to Port Arthur this Sunday. Would you like to come?' They explained that Port Arthur was the original penal colony.

'P-e-e-n-a-l colony?' I repeated with a question in my voice.

Tony crossed his hands at his wrists.

'A-a-a-ah!' Now I knew what a penal colony meant, in English.

The day is brilliant. It is my birthday and, because it's a Sunday, I don't have to go to work. This morning I was woken up with a kiss from Yano, 'Happy birthday Csitri,' he said and cuddled me. Then the children burst into our bedroom and were all over me.

I feel so happy.

We pack a picnic lunch for the four of us and also for Mami, Chopi and Roman. Elizabeth and Stephen are coming too. It is great that their station wagon is so spacious; we can all fit into two cars. The children sit in the back of the Valiant.

Tony, standing in front of his Holden organises our picnic basket and the rugs.

'It's a long drive.' To make sure that we understand, he stretches out his arms in front of him, showing the lengths. 'Maybe two hours.' His little finger and ring finger shoot up in the air.

The cars are leaving the city and we are nearing the bridge. It looks spectacular, like a boomerang, so high in the middle, so steep. I wonder quietly, *Has any car ever rolled back on it?*

A couple of weeks ago, one night after sunset, Stephen and Elizabeth drove us across the bridge. Then he explained that the bridge was quite new, was 50 feet tall and about 4600 feet long and it was opened to the public in March 1965 to replace the old floating bridge. Before that the Eastern Shore consisted mainly of farms, pastures and seaside shacks built alongside the spectacular beaches. Since the new bridge was built, the population of the Eastern Shore had doubled and was still growing. But the shopping and business was still on the western side, in the city, he said.

'So how high is 50 feet in metres?' I asked then. Stephen couldn't tell me (the metric system was still relatively new to Australia).

I looked over the side of the bridge and saw the deep, deep darkness of the water below. Whatever it was, it was very high.

'Over there to your left you still can see some remains of the old bridge.' He pointed as he drove. 'And up on the hill in front of you, to your left, is Rose Bay High School. This is where Elizabeth teaches chemistry.'

Once off the bridge he drove a little further and turned the car.

'Where does this road lead to?' I wanted to continue our journey.

'It goes through the Eastern Shore,' Stephen explained and drove us back to the city. This is the road that leads to the airport so I must have crossed the bridge when we arrived.

'Remember?' asks Elizabeth.

'Of course I don't. I was dead to the world almost as soon as we got off the plane.'

The houses we are passing are just like the ones on the western side, some even bigger, more modern. There are large gaps between the settlements, which Stephen calls suburbs. In those gaps the road is thinly hemmed with trees, which create stripes of shade and sunlight on the road, just like the back of a zebra.

Passing the turnoff to the airport we drive down a small hill. The rocky hillside and bushes obscure our view. Suddenly the horizon opens wide on both sides and the cars continue on a long, narrow stretch of road, kind of a bridge, almost floating on the shimmering water to our left and to our right. 'This is beautiful!' I take a deep breath.

'Wherever you are in Tasmania the water is never too far. The township up on the hill and this causeway is called Midway Point.'

'Did the convicts build it?' I ask

'I don't think so. I think it was built during the Depression,' Stephen tells me.

We are passing men and boys with fishing rods standing alongside the handrail. On the low swells, far in the distance, small boats are rocking gently. I can't see it but I assume that inside each are men and boys with fishing rods. What a perfect summer's day.

More spectacular scenery. There is a lack of green colour; even the low hills folding into each other on the horizon seem to be bleached out by the sun. Small settlements and lonely farmhouses sit amid the yellow-coloured pastures dotted with sheep or cattle. Hills with curly vegetation and bays with deep-blue waters meet us around the corners. Trying to absorb and express the unfamiliarity and beauty of this island, many unfocused thoughts float in my head. There is an overwhelming feeling of peace. A picture of peace around me.

Another small settlement called Copping. A badly made life-sized statue of a mermaid hints to the passers-by that this is *not* a fine art exhibit. On the side of the road is a sign *Convict Collection.*

'What is the connection between the mermaid and the convicts?' I ask hoping for a romantic explanation.

'Nothing,' Elizabeth says. It makes me curious.

We all climb out of the cars and walk into the sanctuary of this fascinating collection. The large shed houses thousands and thousands of items: machinery from a bygone era, car number plates, teapots, kitchen utensils, tools and other implements from the nineteenth century and recent times. An incredible heap of junk and memorabilia in an organised disorder. We are all entertained and learn a little more about life in Tasmania as it used to be.

More driving. We pass a large sturdy building, which is laced around with a wooden verandah. Someone says that we are halfway to Port Arthur. *Dunalley Hotel,* I read the sign.

The cars stop. Everybody out! *Pirates Bay Lookout.*

'You've got to see this. Get your camera ready,' Tony says. Out comes our inherited Voigtlander from its well-worn leather case.

For a second I let my eyes slide over the huge expanse of water into hazy remoteness, where the line between the water and the sky is obscured. My gaze takes in the ragged coastline, which slopes down to a long beach with pure white sand. In long lines the frothy surf is hurling over the turquoise waters. It is different from anything I have ever seen. It is uniquely beautiful.

'Is this the ocean?'

'Yes it is and far out in the sea, where the horizon is darkened, is Antarctica. Down there below us the beach is called Eaglehawk Neck.'

We learn that Eaglehawk Neck is part of Pirates Bay, that the thin line of land was the dreaded Dog Line, where vicious dogs were tied to barrels preventing the convicts from escaping.

'They had no chance,' Elizabeth remarks. This piece of land explains why the Tasman Peninsula was so well suited to become the home of the convicts.

A short drive. Between people congregating at the sides of the Blowhole we stand mesmerised and witness the thunderous rush of the incoming tide spilling into a narrow gap between rocks. When the water splashes around, Tony tugs on my sleeve.

'Stand back,' he says, 'This is dangerous. A few years ago a couple on their honeymoon were swept into the sea, never to be found.' He points to a stone with a plaque on it. 'This was done in their memory.'

Following the rugged coastline we drive through Doo Town, where the lovingly restored shacks have names that all include the word 'doo'.

'*Doo* Come In.' 'Thistle *Doo* Me.' 'Didgery *Doo*.' 'How *Doo* You *Doo*?' I read on polished boards hanging above the entrance doors.

This town is a crash course in Tasmanian humour. I am loving it.

Over a million years the wild seas of the Great Southern Ocean sculpted this coastline and created formations of natural wonder, which were named fantastically the Devil's Kitchen, Tasman Arch.

We are climbing up, following the narrow path around those formations. I hold onto Ishtvan's hand on one side and Zsuzsi's on the other. Even though the deep drop to the sea is surrounded by a wire fence, it still doesn't feel quite safe. The scenery is breathtaking but I feel relieved when we finally settle back in the car.

It takes only twenty-five minutes to the Port Arthur penal colony. Driving inside the grounds, it looks like a picnic area between the ruins. Under huge oak trees are trestle tables with benches and barbecue facilities. The grass stretches under the trees and is covered by colourful rugs with families sitting next to their Esky coolers, laughing and eating while the children run around.

The air is full of laughter and birdcalls. How incredibly fantastic that people transformed this area of suffering into a place that provides pleasure and relaxation and, at the same time, a good lesson in history to anyone, for free.

We learn about the suffering as we walk around the ruins. Despite all its natural beauty this was a cruel place for the 12,500 convicts transported here. Stephen is the teacher and is in his element explaining the history. They were not only poor English, Irish and Scottish deported from the motherland but also other nationalities, Canadians and Americans who had fought the English Redcoats in Canada.

There is so much to learn, so much to see. In a weather-beaten wooden house in keeping with the times is a small display of some convict memorabilia. They also have pamphlets with a short history of Port Arthur. I pick one up. *Will read it at home with a dictionary,* I think to myself.

After lunch we all walk down to the Remarkable Cave, similar to the blowhole opening to the wide sea. Another wonder of nature.

My birthday concludes with a drive into the sunset. I am exhausted. *I had a great day,* I think to myself smiling.

* * *

'The Hungarian Club is organising a bus trip to Orford. A picnic,' Yanibachi informed us.

Orford is a seaside place on the Eastern Shore of Tasmania, with magic beaches and good picnic grounds.

It sounded good. Even though everyone was telling us that it was autumn, the weather was still steadily warm.

At work I mentioned the picnic in Orford.

'Orford?' laughed Otto. This was the place where he and his family spent most of their Sundays. His daughter was water-skiing there. Most likely he will be there with his boat that Sunday too. If I like I could try out my water-skiing skills then.

❦❦❦

'Quick Mami, I need a pair of bathers. The ones I am wearing to the pool don't look very nice; they are stretched out on me.'

'I can't help you with the bathers. I have no idea how to make them.'

In the following days the free hour I have between the two jobs are spent in the city walking from shop to shop, looking for bathers.

'Excuse me,' I say to the shop assistant at Sussan's, 'bathers?' I found the word in the dictionary the night before.

'What size?'

'Eighteen?' I tell her, unsure.

'Are they for you?' Her eyes run up and down my body questioningly.

'Yes, yes, you see it's big.' I sweep my hands around my hips and backside.

'I don't think so.' She mumbles, goes to the rack and picks up a two-piece. The blue-and-white chequered number appeals to me immensely.

'Try them on.' She ushers me encouragingly to the change room.

I look great. The bikini looks great.

'Thank you.' I place the garment on the bench.

'Good?' She figures the fewer words she speaks, the better.

'Yes, yes.'

'They are only size eight, you know.' She says when she hands over the parcel.

Svetya, I am size eight. That's really small. No matter how skin and bone the mirror shows me, I think of myself as being a well-padded big woman.

We went to a Hungarian picnic last Sunday at a place called Orford. It was 26°C. The bus drew us along the bays with blue waters surrounded by blue hills. I have never seen blue hills in my life. Someone told us it's because the eucalyptus trees send out some kind of a vapour, which makes the hills look blue from a distance. The small settlements of wooden houses were surrounded by dry, golden-looking pastures dotted with cattle and sheep. It was very pretty, so different to European countryside. I wish you could be here. But to me the most picturesque part was entering Orford where the narrow road was running along the dramatic-looking tall rocks to our right and the slow-flowing river to our left. It reminded me a little of the Rumanian mountains when we were on our way to Bulgaria. Now that I am writing about it that stupid Bulgarian donkey came into my mind. Remember? When the sun boiled the water in our company bus while it was trying to reach the top of the hill?

'Everybody out!' the driver said and we hung around in our bathers. The heat rising from the asphalted road was almost unbearable and when the bus still wouldn't start the suitcases and tents came down from the roof-rack. Remember how we cursed those wretched heavy tents?

I tell you, the bus we went with to Orford was much superior to the one we were travelling on in Bulgaria and it was air-conditioned.

And that donkey pulling the cart! Do you remember the man in the cart? I am laughing even now when I think of him as he was bent down whispering into the donkey's ear and trying to push his backside up the hill.

'Da, da,' he said when our driver asked him to help with our luggage. All that work, us loading that small cart in 42°C heat and the bloody donkey wouldn't move; no persuasion helped. The donkey was nobody's fool. Remember how we ended up unloading the cart and carrying everything up the hill ourselves? The whole forty of us, all in bathers? What a sight! And, when we unloaded the cart, the donkey moved.

Nothing like that happened on Sunday. It was a great day, Stephen and Elizabeth were there too. My boss has a boat and I have tried to water-ski and spent most of the time submerged under the water while trying. Now

I know that water-skiing wasn't invented for me.

My negotiations with Phillipo about leaving my job in his restaurant were never ending.

'Not yet,' he kept saying every time I brought up the subject.

Past Easter Phillipo and I finally made a deal. Actually it suited him as well, because he was going to close his restaurant for a few months while visiting Italy, his homeland. Thank goodness it was all over and I was left only with my day job at Baker's Milk.

Dear Yena and family

I hope this letter will find you and all your family in good health.

Svetya's letters always started the same way, like a preprinted memo. The good bits followed only after this official part.

As from the sixteenth of August you are a godmother. I did not tell you that I was pregnant, because I wanted it to be a surprise. We have a lovely and healthy little boy called Richard. We call him Ricky.

Regarding the island you are living on, we were looking at it on the map and it looks really small. We wonder, how you can turn the car around there (ha, ha, ha).

I run over to Mami and stick Svetya's letter under her nose.

'Look. I am a godmother. He is my first godchild.'

When Yano comes home I am still excited. What should we send him? Perhaps a little outfit and of course a pillowcase and a lovely small soft blanket. What you think Yano?

'As long as you watch the money,' he remarks, half as excited as I am.

'So how much can I spend? Twenty dollars?'

'Twenty dollars? That amounts to your weekly wages! Okay, but not a cent more.'

Finally I fulfil my long-time ambition. I walk into Myer and from one department to another, looking, touching, then walk back to the department I just came out of. Which one is nicer? The yellow or the blue one? I suppose he is a little boy, so the blue it is.

I put together the parcel with some gorgeous babywear and other beautiful fluffy things for my new godson, carry the parcel to the post office and with a feeling of satisfaction post it.

❦❦❦

In those first years in Tasmania my life was like a concertina door. Each fold labelled as *one month* and pushed against the wall had so much hidden in it that when stretched out it would have filled years with excitement, good and bad.

Not long after Svetya's letter another arrived to my name, this time an official letter.

The Slovak Ministry of Justice
In the name of The Slovak Socialist Republic
Eugenia Miloshova, born 1.3.1936,
was found
GUILTY
of unlawfully leaving the country.
In the name of the law No.5/T 126/70.
Because of this criminal act, the Court decided to inflict the punishment of loss of freedom lasting fifteen months unconditionally.

On the sitting of The City Court, etcetera etcetera …
in Košice, 20th November 1970.

In the course of the month three similar letters arrived, for Yano, Mami and Chopi, all with the same contents. Each of us were given a different sentence. What surprised me was how the authorities in Košice knew our address in Tasmania? We had moved not long before from New Town to South Hobart. Would they have pressured Opapa or Svetya into giving them our new address, or perhaps they obtained it by some kind of innocent-looking trick? Anyway, from now on we all had a criminal record in our native country.

The job of the laboratory was to ensure the hygiene of the factory and the good quality of the milk. Relying on the skills and the judgement of the workers and the staff of the laboratory, quality control was a very hands-on task.

It started in the tipping bay with the sample of milk from each twenty-litre can that rolled off the farmers' trucks. There were written reports about farmers as to the quality of their products, which were followed up if necessary by the two inspectors of the agricultural department who visited the lab two, sometimes three times a week to advise and liaise between the firm and the farmers.

The laboratory was also essential to production at the factory level. We took samples of milk and cream from the holding vats before pasteurisation, after pasteurisation and on the hour during the process of bottling.

It was the responsibility of the laboratory to check the cleanliness of the lines and all the machinery that came in contact with the milk each day after the production was finalised. I found the laboratory work very satisfying, varied and interesting and, out of my own initiative, became intimately involved with the process of making milk products.

Every hour I trotted down to the factory, took a bottle of milk from the line and tested it for the butter-fat content and any other test that had to be done. Needing only a small quantity for the tests, the rest went into the coolroom, where it was collected for a couple of days until I had enough for a good batch of butter and cottage cheese. The experiences that I gained in my childhood while living in the village during the war came in handy. Digging from my memory how to make butter out of unpasteurised and slightly soured cream, I set out to make enough butter for our family to last at least a week. Otto and the factory manager watched in amusement the large Kenwood mixer filled with cream, which they knew was turning sour, therefore in their minds no good, until the whey separated from the fat and the fat became a lovely fluffy butter.

'Taste it,' I challenged their dubious smiles and tried to explain in *my English* that the unpasteurised milk and cream is not rotting by the souring process, only undergoing a chemical change when the milk sugar turns into lactic acid.

'It tastes good, try it. I was raised on sour milk and look at me.'

They tried it. It tasted great, just like real butter should.

Our family had a regular supply of butter out of the cream, which used to be washed down the drain. From the unused milk I made cottage cheese.

CHAPTER FIVE

Choices

No matter how hard or unpleasant a task, it makes a huge difference when you do it because you choose to, not because you have to.

Chopi was still working during the evenings and weekends in the Town House restaurant. One weekend she was asked to look after room service for the hotel on her own, as the other girl had not turned up. She phoned me. Would I help her out? From then on I became part of the kitchen team and was working again at nights, sometimes weekends. Even though the work and the hours were almost identical to my previous restaurant job, it was okay. I did not have to but chose to work in the kitchen.

My job is to operate the big industrial dishwasher. It is my first night working there. From the column of dirty plates I peel off a pile and carry it from one bench to the other. I slip. One foot in the air, the other can't find the floor. I sit heavily on my backside and watch the plates hit the wet tiles, coming down around me one by one. Everybody stops moving. The staff, including the chef, stares at me in quiet sympathy, with the sound of sizzling steaks in the background. It takes a while for me to disentangle from the fragments of smashed crockery and get up from my horrified position, first onto my hands and knees, then upright. Laughter erupts around me like the wave of an incoming tide; first gently then with full force. They all chip in sweeping up the kitchen floor. This creates an instant camaraderie between us.

Returning from work past midnight, I crawl into bed, stretching out indulgently, when the bedside lamp comes on at Yano's side. He is still awake. In the orange glow of the lampshade his face is lit up with a huge smile.

'I bought a car,' he tells me quickly as if not able to hold the secret any longer.

It takes us hours to get to sleep. We talk and talk about this car, which is still with the previous owner, a Hungarian man working with Yano in the factory. It isn't a new car and cost only $160, but it will do us for a while. Tony will help to bring it home and he will also teach Yano to drive.

❦❦❦

In my childhood it was a huge thing to sit in a car, let alone travel in one or own one. The bottom flat in my grandparents' house was vacant for a long time after the war. One day workmen moved in and started renovating. When they finished, a Czech family moved in. They had three daughters, but most importantly they had a large, dark-green sedan, which was kept in our garage. The space we called *our garage* in it's long existence had never held a car before.

Knowing what time the man was coming home, I would hang around the gates and pull them open on his arrival. For that I would score regular rides to the garage, lasting one full minute. I also remember my only real drive in that car, the feel of the soft leather seat in the back with his three daughters. We watched the road disappear in the distance through the narrow back window.

In my mind the car was something very special; to own one was an achievement, proof of our rising living standard.

The car Yano bought was a 1948 Vauxhall, similar to the sedan of my childhood. It had well-preserved leather seats, a small oval rear window, maroon in colour with a black roof, and it looked like an old London taxi. For a few years everyone in Hobart knew where we spent our weekends. The car was one of a kind in the age of sleek Valiants and Kingswoods.

Long ago I was told my fortune by a Gypsy woman, a client of the Social Security Department.

'I will tell your fortune, if you make my pension good,' she said.

'I will make it good.' I pushed my left palm under her nose.

In the full glory of her colourful skirt and back-knotted scarf she stood in front of me, her finger pushing the skin in my palm as she haggled about her pension.

'Missus, you are going to have a car that no one has in the city,' she told me then. Even she would be surprised how accurate her prediction was to be.

Click, click went the old Voigtlander camera when the car was brought home by Tony, and the photos were distributed to friends and family in the old country.

'So, how's that for an achievement? Our first car,' we wrote proudly on the back of the photos.

Those photos though weren't taken kindly to by one of our friends. The answer came swiftly: 'Anyone can stand in front of a car and take a picture of it.'

For people in our country it was hard to believe that after a short few months living in Tasmania we had managed to buy a car, regardless of how old the car was.

Driver's licences. 'Both of you, or at least Yano,' Nana said. 'You need a driver's licence and to get one you will have to sit a driver's test.' *Not yet,* I thought, *how am I going to learn all the theory in English? Besides, Yano will never agree with me driving.*

I was always the one when it came to official dealings. To pick up the form for the learner's licence for Yano I went to the Transport

Commission. After much gesticulation, eye rolling and half-finished English sentences the man understood that I needed a learner's licence form for my husband.

'Do you have any identification on you?' came the routine question.

I rummaged in my handbag and lay out next to each other my passport and my Czechoslovak driver's licence, only because it had a photo of me.

'What's that?' the man picked up the pink plastic booklet.

I did not realise that the licence I had obtained in 1967 after a very dramatic disagreement with Yano was indeed an International Driver's Licence. The Transport Commission of Tasmania recognised it and issued me with a Tasmanian licence without me sitting the test. So, there I was with a valid licence from the Tasmanian authorities, though not recognised by my husband. When it arrived by mail to my name Yano snarled, 'The idiots.' This was the end of the matter, and my driving hopes.

From that day on, after work Tony regularly turned up to take Yano for driving lessons. Yano was a technical engineer and it did not take him long to get the feel of it. And, even though I did not use my licence to drive, it came in handy. On weekend mornings, Yano in the driver's seat and me next to him acting as his instructor, we set out in our 1948 Vauxhall, with a large L sign stuck on the left-hand side of the windscreen, to drive on the streets and highways of Hobart at 40 kilometres per hour, while the other cars overtook us impatiently.

'Don't worry Yanichku,' I encouraged him, 'let them all kill themselves, you just drive slowly and safely.'

Yano got his licence. What a great day it was. The following Saturday we all piled into the car, me next to Yano, the children in the back with the well-worn and much-loved Viennese transistor radio between them, and with Olivia Newton-John singing *Let me be there in your mornings* … we drove half way up to Fern Tree. Reaching the tavern, after a few unsuccessful tries, Yano managed to turn the car to face the city, worried that we had driven too far and might not find our way back home.

Our Sundays became the driving days.

❦❦❦

It's Sunday. We are just driving from one street to another while the transistor radio plays on the back seat. *Clank.* The car stops near the GPO. It does not move and the rain is coming down heavily. For a while Yano and I sit in the car in complete shock. How could this happen? What are we going to do? How are we going to get back home?

'Are you all right?' A smiling face with dark curly hair bends down to our open window.

'No. Not all right,' we tell him the best we can and try to make him understand that we have no idea what to do.

The young man takes over. He opens the bonnet, looks here, looks there, orders Yano out of the car and tries to start it up. I sit in the passenger seat looking through the windscreen at the drenched street, observing the rain. There is a sudden stillness, with heavy drops of rain making bubbles on the ground. *It's going to rain for a while,* someone told me back in my childhood. *It always does when the rain makes bubbles on the ground.*

The car would not start.

Okay, it's not working. He drives his car from the other side of the road in front of ours, ties a rope from his boot to our bonnet and pulls us through Macquarie Street to the top of Argyle street, down Campbell street, looking for an open service station. We have no idea where we are most of the time.

In those years only a few service stations are open on Sunday afternoons. The ones that are open can't help. Finally the young man finds a workshop and makes a deal on our behalf. He gets a notebook from his car, writes down the address, phone number and the name of the mechanic, tells us that the car can be picked up by tomorrow afternoon, piles us into his car and drives us home.

By that time it is dark.

'Come on in,' we invite him.

'No, no,' he says with his palm lifted in protest.

We do not take no for an answer and persist. To us we have to do something to thank this man for his kindness. And he gives in to our persuasion. Once inside Yano offers him money, but he would not take it, so I make him a cup of coffee.

❖ ❖ ❖

This episode left us with hearts full of warm feelings, wondering what kind of young man would spend his Sunday afternoon driving for hours from street to street with a family of New Australians who know very little about cars and even less about the English language. Thank God for young people like him.

Everything of our daily routine was a big deal. The smallest tasks – how to get to places we had to go to and what to do once we were there – had to be thought out in minute detail, sometimes written down in English by Nana or a friend.

'Have you been to get your X-rays?' Nana enquired casually and told us that it was compulsory for everyone to get X-rayed once a year. They had eradicated tuberculosis of the lungs in Australia by keeping the population regularly checked.

Obeying Nana's instructions, one afternoon after work I walked down near the wharf, into a seemingly temporary white construction with a large sign: X-Rays.

There were none of the expected long procedures and, to my surprise, no need to get undressed.

'Take your chain off and stand behind the screen,' came the friendly advice with the finger pointing to my gold chain. Clank, clank, went the machine and all was done.

'What's your name?'

I told her.

'Could you spell it please?' I did, with great difficulty. The nurse found my name on her sheet in the long list of names.

Who put my name on their list? I had been living in Hobart only a few months.

Itca and Freddy were a Hungarian couple about our age with two teenage girls. We met in the Hungarian Club and were instantly drawn towards each other. They had been living in Tasmania for eight years and knew the hows and whats of Hobart. Freddy was working as an accountant; they also were proprietors of a small grocery shop, selling fish and chips on the weekends. Itca was a shapely blond, independent and well informed. She negotiated her Valiant station wagon on the narrow streets of old Hobart with skill. *All the qualities Yano admires in women,* I thought to myself.

On Sunday mornings Itca would pick the four of us up and take us to their home, which I found out was already fully paid for, thanks to the good little business she was running. Another feather in her hat. The usual Sunday handwashing of our weekly laundry, the house cleaning and anything else was shifted to other days or not attended to for lack of time. We spent our Sundays in Itca and Freddy's garden, sometimes in their shop helping to peel potatoes for the chips. Yano was a good-looking young man, slim, suntanned and handy. There were always things she absolutely needed to have done.

'But you know my Freddy …' her voice would trail away. 'I suppose he will get around to it one day.' She would throw her hands in the air.

'I'll do it.' Yano volunteered every time. The accolades about Yano's capabilities flowed right into his perceptive ego.

Between the two of them Freddy was the quieter partner. It was always Itca who was cracking jokes, advising on finances, on shopping, on building a house, and then cooking up a meal for us. After all that she would drive us home in the warm Sunday sunsets. Yano talked about her with great respect.

As I observed, at each Sunday's pick-up, Itca's shorts getting tighter and shorter, I became suspicious and quite jealous. *Here we go again.*

I thought in Australia I wouldn't have to face this feeling of inadequacy. Look at me. I faced myself in the mirror. *I need a complete change of appearance. Less conservative, more exciting and desirable as a woman, perhaps more tarty looking. Everyone adores Marilyn Monroe.* I pursed my lips to my image in the mirror. That was what I needed. I decided to go blond.

'Mami, in what percentage do you mix the peroxide and ammonia for your hair?' Mami, a born brunette, had become blond after my father's death and had bleached her hair since I remembered.

'What do you want to know that for?'

'I want to be blond.'

'Yenni, don't be silly, it wouldn't suit your complexion.' Mami tried but she knew it was a waste of time. 'Okay, this is what you do …'

I followed her instructions and my dark-brown, almost black hair became a touch lighter, kind of rusty looking, at each colouring session. I observed the change in my looks impatiently. It still wasn't the colour I wanted. I imagined myself as a sexy blond with billowing hair around my face. Keep trying, Mami suggested. My hair lost all its shine and after many tries became the colour of a not-quite-ripened tomato. My rosy-cheeked complexion, which was so well suited to my dark hair, now had a tinge of blue, kind of purple. I could wear nothing I had in my wardrobe, it all clashed with my hair colour. In the lab Otto laughed unashamedly and the boys from the factory smiled politely.

'You are mad Yena. What was wrong with your original colour? At least it was shiny.' Yano looked at me thoughtfully.

I had enough of trying; I was going back to my old colour. With that decision I visited the pharmacy to purchase a bottle of dark-brown hair colour.

'What did you use for bleaching your hair?' The pharmacist asked, luckily. I told her. She said the bottle was no good; it might turn my hair green. The only way I could go back to my original hair colour was with the help of a hairdresser. This was all I needed, an extra expense.

The factory manager's wife had a hairdressing salon in West Hobart, at the end of the steepest street in the city. I made an appointment.

'Yano, could you take me there, please?' I confronted Yano on the following Saturday.

Yano drove the Vauxhall to West Hobart. Halfway up the steep street the engine cut out and the car started rolling backwards. The fact that Yano was pressing the brake to the floor was of no help; he had to use the handbrake as well. Uncomplimentary words filled the interior of the Vauxhall. The driving, the steep street and the hairdresser who established her business on top of this hill were all my fault, not to mention that madness with my hair. A car behind us stopped. It had to because for a while we were sliding towards it. A young man jumped out and offered his help to drive us up to the top. He did manage to get our car there with Yano driving, discreetly coaching him to drive in first gear.

'I am not coming back to pick you up, that's for sure. You have to find your own way home.' Yano was quite adamant and rolled the car down the hill to Macquarie Street.

Back to my normal colour and with an extra good hairdo, out of the hairdresser the rain started, and it poured. By the time I got home, stepping slowly and very carefully down the steep wet street, my hair was dripping down my neck and there was nothing left of my great hairstyle but the colour.

Nothing helped though; the feeling of inadequacy persisted, until one warm Sunday, just before we all folded into Itca's station wagon, Yano looked deep into her eyes and, holding her hand, which was extended originally to say goodbye, he said:

'I dreamed about you last night, Itca.'

Oh! This feeling in my stomach, as if someone had punched me.

'All right Yano, I know you always dream about me. Let's go home,' I said and crawled into the back of the station wagon.

'You idiot, you,' I heard Yano muttering.

From then on I made sure that well before the Sunday I explained to Yano how very, very busy I was in the house and that it will be better if we stay at home this time, and the next time, and the next time.

In June the weather turned cool. Some days the rain came down all day. The house inside was cold, with the open fireplace in the loungeroom gaping at us black and unfriendly. Yano ordered a load of wood. It came by truck.

Before central heating became the norm in my country, carts with draughthorses used to deliver the coal or wood to houses. Since a little incident in my childhood with runaway horses, I had been terrified of them. Some pavements were so narrow that when a delivery horse turned its head towards the building it took up half of the footpath. I would walk to the other side of the street or sometimes even wait until the cart had unloaded and the horses stepped out to their next destination.

I thought about the Gypsies, family groups of eight or more – men, women, children – and their wood-sawing business. They were part of my autumn scene. They were equipped with a steel table-like construction on wheels, with a circular saw worked by a small engine. The cart was pushed by the oldest member of the family, the way one would push a pram, rattling on the cobblestone streets. The rest of the family, women in busy, patterned, colourful skirts and back-knotted scarves, walked alongside it. Autumn was their busy season. They would turn up in our yard, fill the motor with fuel and set out to push the logs through the saw to the required length, letting them fall to one side, where another man would split the wood fast and skilfully with an axe. The women and children tidied up the split wood and stacked it. Come lunchtime the whole party would stop, sit around the yard, men exposing dark sticky hair, with hats pushed back from their sweaty foreheads, women untying the large tea-towels containing their food provisions.

Here Yano carried the wood into the wood shed, stacking it in a neat pile, trying to save it from the soaking rain. The wood was saved but Yano developed a fever the next morning. Mami and I persuaded him to stay at home in bed. The following day his temperature climbed higher still.

'Nana, Yano is sick. Do you know a doctor around here who would come and see him?' We needed a doctor we could talk to, whose instructions we could understand and who could understand us.

Nana thought it would be best to take Yano to a surgery. To me it was unthinkable. He had a high temperature and was in no condition to go out into the cold and sit for hours in a surgery. The doctor should come out and see him at home. This was the way I was used to.

'Leave it with me,' Nana said and found a Polish doctor who was willing to visit the patient at home.

He came late in the evening, checked out Yano and diagnosed pneumonia. Yano was prescribed a course of antibiotics and bed rest for a few days. We understood each other, even though we had to speak very slowly. For a while he became our family doctor, especially for the children. The knowledge that we had a doctor to turn to if we needed him was a great comfort to us.

My dearest Yenni

Finally I got round to write this letter. My right arm hurts and I can do very little …

Opapa is on nine days' leave from work. I hope he will stop working before Christmas. You know everything is so expensive here, but, even worse, you can't get anything. Things are really bad here, even for potatoes you have to queue up; there are no oranges, no lemons. With one word, there is nothing. You can get sausages, but I assume they are filled with some rotten meat, so we don't buy them. This is how it looks here dear Yenni.

My dearest, beloved Ishtvan. I wish you from the bottom of my heart lots of health and happiness in your life. We are so happy for you. When your Mami wrote what a good student you are, we both cried.

From then on Opapa is carrying your Mami's letter in his pocket and is showing it to everyone he meets. And how is my little Zsuzsi? And my little Cricket Roman? I miss you all so much.

Lots of love, your Omama.

Baker's Milk expanded. With an awareness of tighter health regulations the practice in the lab become more sophisticated and demanding. The new testing machinery arrived and the need for more laboratory staff became obvious.

When I mentioned Chopi and her degree in chemistry there were no more questions asked.

I can still see Chopi in high-heeled courts tiptoeing through the gravelled yard, her miniskirt brushing against the black pantyhose, as with a smile she appeared for her interview. That day she stayed on, borrowed my lab coat and became part of this happy working environment. Roy turned his never-fading inquisitiveness onto Chopi and gave me rest from his attention.

The following days and months were filled with contentment and happiness between all of us at work and all of us at home. In those days I would tell everyone who would listen that I had never met a person in Tasmania I disliked. To me they were all angels, everyone was just great. On the mornings when Roy was too busy at work to fetch us in his Holden, Chopi and I would walk down to Franklin Square to catch the bus.

'Baker's Milk, please,' I would say holding the small change in my outstretched hand.

'Where to?' The driver would ask.

'Baker's Milk,' I repeated, knowing it would not click.

After some more interrogation the driver would say, 'A-a-ah, Baker's Milk.'

What's the difference? I thought.

After work we caught the bus back to the city, where in the hour left before starting our shift at the Town House restaurant we would explore the department stores. Arm in arm Chopi and I would happily walk the streets of Hobart talking and laughing.

The subjects to talk about never dried up. If it was possible, we grew even closer to each other than that day back in my teenage years when for the first time I confided in Chopi.

'Swear that you won't say anything to anyone, not even to Dyuri.'

'I swear,' she said with the wisdom of the seven-year-old.

In minute detail I told her about my first boyfriend. After intensive attention it was her turn.

'I tell you a secret too Yenni, but swear that you're not going to tell on me to Mami.'

'I swear.'

'Yesterday, when passing Mami's portrait above the antique chest of draws, Mami in the picture wagged her finger at me.'

'It's only a painting, Chopi.'

'I know, but her finger wagged. Honestly, Yenni.'

Just the day before this confession Chopi scored Mami's anger when she turned up with wet pants. I was sure the wagging finger in the picture had to do with Chopi's bad conscience.

Since those years we shared many secrets. Chopi to me was the closest friend and confidante I had ever had.

I was not sure if it just happened that way or it was one of the smart moves of Dick Baker that the company was employing whole chunks of the same family. In the factory the father was working next to his son while the wife was in administration *up in the office.*

After the initial training Chopi and I were given a free hand in our working routine. This we recognised to be trust in our conduct.

In different cultures freedom means different things, depending on where the norm lies. We are all confined in the straightjacket of our tradition, beliefs, family values, needs and daily routines. The requirements of freedom are specific to each person, the borders are mostly of our own creation. I was lucky enough in the past and throughout my public life that I was able to express my opinions freely. Because of this, freedom of speech wasn't an issue for me. It was important that I could give the way I wanted and when I felt the need for giving, and to be appreciated for it. The balance between the amount of giving and taking was the freedom.

I also was finding out that the many times repeated and misused phrase *to belong* had nothing to do with language. It mostly had to do with how much you were willing to give, with the way you were giving and how your giving resonated with the needs of the person or community you were giving to.

In our mind Baker's Milk became our own company and, like in the old country, we worked for the good of the whole, passionately keeping to the highest standards. The fact that we were paid was an extra benefit, a bonus. We would have worked anyway. There was a purpose for us being there, our ideas were listened to, and we felt needed and appreciated.

It was no use for the factory manager to explain about the regular coffee breaks, lunchtimes and leaving at four thirty. Whatever time, the task had to be finished. This attitude led to a mutual reliance and accountability on both sides. We felt secure in our jobs, did our best in contributing to the success of the company and looked after the lab as after our home.

With great care the lino was swept with a wet mop when too many gumboot marks were visible and everyone was made to wipe their feet at the door when entering the lab. The scratch marks on the large table in the middle of the room were painted away and we washed the large windows when the raindrops marked the dust sitting on them.

'You don't have to do that,' the factory manager said amazed. 'The window cleaner is calling in next week.'

'It's okay, he doesn't have to come,' we said, proud of our diligence and in complete ignorance of the system.

What a surprise it was when an employee of Telecom called in with a small suitcase, placing it on our large table, and took out a pressure can and a tissue to spray and wipe clean the telephone apparatus in the laboratory, and proceeded to do the same to all the phones in the office. And she did this every two weeks.

'We could have done that,' we said.

Our work, we felt, was exciting and very important. We mattered.

There was an atmosphere of incentive, trust and security as this curiously fabulous mixture of hard-line capitalism and the naivety of socialism blended. And it worked for everyone.

The word about 'those two in the lab' spread beyond the boundaries of the factory and seeped through the fences at the top of the drive into the grey square building where the offices were.

'Jenny, come up to my office, please!' I hear the voice of Mr Baker through the public address, which is installed in the top corner of the lab. *What have I done that he is summoning me up?* I wonder as I go.

'What do you drink?' he asks with his usual commanding tone at my entry into his sanctuary and pushes the wall-like sliding door to uncover a huge bar.

I have never seen a built-in bar of this magnitude in any office. To make sense of my new life I automatically relate my new impressions to my previous experiences. The pre-Christmas parties and everything-else parties at the Social Security Department in my native country, especially the 'name-day' parties, which can't be kept secret, as each day in the calendar is marked by a name and all Johns, Margarets and Helens celebrate on their marked day in unison. Deep inside my memory is the image of the large conference table covered with bottles of various liqueurs, half-filled water glasses and overflowing ashtrays. The bottles of pharmaceutical-grade spirit we obtained from the nearest pharmacy on prescription from our departmental doctors and hurriedly made into liqueurs behind the screen, out of sight of the clients during business hours. The shared cigarettes, the jokes told when all of us are crammed into the smallish office of our supervisor. That is another type of belonging and bonding, and it creates warm feelings in my heart.

In Mr Baker's bright and elegant office the mirrors behind the glass shelves reflect the light through the number of colourful bottles of top-shelf quality.

'Brandy, please.' I barely dare to move from the door.

'What do you have it with?' he asks as he goes about filling the glasses with ice.

'Just brandy. Please.'

'Neat?' He laughs and from that day on everyone in the factory and in the office knows that I like my brandy neat.

Mr Baker wants to talk to me about my superannuation. 'So, what is this superannuation?' I ask. He explains that it is a kind of pension scheme. *So what?* I think. *We have a pension scheme back in the old country too*. Little do I realise what an extraordinary gesture it is in 1970 when the women's rights movement is just unfolding in Australia. The superannuation scheme is a faraway future agenda in the minds of some union leaders, and the dream of many workers. Here I am, a New Australian woman barely speaking English and completely ignorant about everything, being offered superannuation from Mr Baker, the millionaire.

❦❦❦

I drank my brandy and thanked him for my superannuation, which at that time I did not think much of.

During the times Chopi and I spent in the tipping bay taking samples from the incoming milk, Roy had a chance to explain all our questions regarding anything and everything. His expertise was wide and dubious, but always creative. Nothing was too much trouble. Through him I learned about and came to like and respect the *true Australian character*. During lunchtime he got hold of us both, walked us to the canteen and ordered our food with no questions asked.

'Two Australian meat pies,' he smiled, then plunged one of the tall plastic bottles sitting on each table deep into the middle of the pie, smothering it with tomato sauce.

'Good?' He sat there observing our reaction.

'Not bad,' we said, 'Thank you, thank you. It's good Roy.'

Another day Roy made a small fire in the paddock behind the tipping bay and fried up sausages, eggs and tomatoes in a frying pan and carried it into the lab.

'An Australia barbecue,' he said and laughingly dished out the food on paper plates for us to try.

Roy isn't alive any more, even though he was several years younger than me. He died from an incurable illness of his heart.

Every time I think of him it is with a warm heart and a smile on my face.

'Could you send us some Australian recipes?' requests the letter from our friends Yuray and Zsuzsha in Košice.

Dear Zshuzsha and Yuray

This is the recipe for scones. It's fast and delicious and the Australians make it in the blink of an eye when an unexpected guest arrives for the morning tea.

1 cup of flour …

Another letter arrives.

The recipe for the scones is delicious. Zshuzsha makes it with chocolate and the children are loving it.

Chocolate scones? I wonder if Mrs Bowton in the canteen knows that recipe.

Otto had a top-of-the-range magnetophone resembling a fancy shiny square suitcase. Under the lid were the control knobs and two large reels. On one reel a ten-centimetre tape was wound.

His favourite music filled the lab – the sweet love songs of Engelbert Humperdinck and Dean Martin – from the collection of reels he carried with him.

'You can talk into the microphone and listen to your own voice.' He smiled indulgently.

When I did I couldn't recognise my voice. Reassuringly he told me that at first no one recognises their voice.

Till now I associated the magnetophone only with playing and recording music. Suddenly the door of possibilities was thrown wide open. If I can listen to my own voice, everyone else could. To send a spoken message back to the old country suddenly had a fair chance. I knew that Svetya and her husband had a magnetophone; we often listened to the music recorded from the Luxembourg radio station. If we send a reel to Svetya with our message for Omama and Opapa, she could take her magnetophone to them and they could listen to it. Once the idea formed in my mind there was no going back.

Could Otto come to our place and record our messages? Please?

The following Sunday he turned up and spread his treasured music box on Mami's dining table. We all congregated around the table and talked into the microphone with tears in our eyes and voices trembling with emotion.

Košice 5 February 1971

Dearest Marta

We have received the tape with your voices. Svetya and her husband came over and played it on their magnetophone. I was amazed by the excellent quality of the tape. We recognised each of you without delay, heard everything very clearly, only Omama cried all the time. The little Cila [Roman] already speaks very nicely. The people, who were here while we were listening to your message were Etaneni, Annaneni, Mancineni …

Following this letter a small parcel arrived from Svetya. It was a magnetophone tape. Mami phoned me at work to tell me about it. Could I ask Otto again to Mami's place next Sunday? We could barely wait till the weekend.

Around Mami's dining table the tear-filled words of Opapa and Omama penetrated deep inside us. They sounded so close, as if those two old, lovely people were sitting at the stretch of a hand, just a warm touch away. Svetya and her husband finished the session with a medley of popular operetta music.

Under Yano's management our savings were growing and in a short year and a half we had saved $500. Yano thought of his grandfather's advice: *When you have money buy land, no one can take the land away from you.*

Because the old man died before our country became part of the socialist bloc he couldn't know that his advice would not have worked under socialism. The government did take away private land, nationalised it and blended it into the Kolchozes-collective farms. That of course was on the other side of the world; it could never happen in Australia. Yano had a desire to buy a block of land that he could call his own.

A Hungarian friend knew about a good block in Springfield for only $2500.

'It's an excellent price,' he told Yano and looked for a lawyer who would be willing to loan the remaining $2000 to a migrant family who was unknown, had no history of borrowing but had two incomes and were good and trustworthy people.

'Honestly,' the friend assured the lawyer.

In those years the lawyers and banks were less suspicious and the deal was struck. We turned up to sign the contract, shook hands and became the proud owners of a block in Springfield with a beautiful view of the city.

From then on the weekend activities were enriched by regular visits to our block in Springfield. We would stand in the middle of the block mesmerised, admiring the view, then take off to one of the Jennings display homes. Hoping to build our own house, we completely forgot about our application to the Housing Department.

If I thought of the houses of our friends as old fashioned, not quite to my liking, I was enchanted by the display homes. The pinks and blues of the wall-to-wall carpets, the walls with prints and oil paintings, the wall units made from light wood with books on their shelves and potplants dotted under the airy windows were the closest so far to what I wanted for myself.

'We don't have to build a house on our land, Yano. Lets buy one of the Jennings houses,' I suggested to him, completely taken by the one we had just walked through in the suburb of Howrah.

'Are you mad? Do you have any idea how much it would cost?'

'No, but I can enquire and if the price is reasonable we can think about it and plan towards it. See that sign?' I pointed: *Display home for sale including the contents. Enquire at the front desk.* In my mind there were no boundaries in this new country, we had done so very well already.

At the front desk we were told it would cost us $12,000 for the three-bedroom house with the furniture, and of course the outdoor furniture in the courtyard is also included.

'Oh, $12,000? Thank you,' I said to a person at the desk.

Twelve thousand dollars!

Shortly after, Zsuzsi's schoolmate Eva's father paid us a visit. He heard that Yano was a draughtsman. He wanted to know if Yano would draw up a house plan for him. Yano tried to explain that he was a technical draughtsman, his skills had to do with machinery, but Eva's father was not easily persuaded. He thought a draughtsman was a draughtsman. He himself was trained as a shoemaker and now he was a builder, even though he didn't know much about building. So what? Anyway, this was where the money is.

Yano declined, telling the man he couldn't do it because he thought it unethical. The whole episode only reinforced our suspicion of how little education and skills were required in those times in Tasmania. For many less scrupulous, Australia was truly *the land of opportunity.*

CHAPTER SIX

The Learning Curve Snakes On

Every day I was made to realise that I still had a lot to learn about the Australian way of doing things. The learning curve snaked through each hour in many of my days.

When Mr Baker's son-in-law, a director of the company, walked into the laboratory he stretched out his hand.

'You must be Jenny.'

How humiliating, I thought. I did *not* give him permission to call me by my first name and he didn't even wait until I offered my hand, as would be the case in sophisticated circles in my country. What a rude and very good-looking young man. I was going to pay back his disrespect at once, director or not.

'Hello Glen.' My hand stretched across to meet his warm grip and my proud, straight stare confronted his smiling face. My intent didn't work though; he obviously wasn't offended by me calling him by his first name.

The same day I walked up to the paymaster and on the way stopped in the front office to admire a long amber-coloured vase full of flowers.

'Beautiful.' I pointed at the vase and smiled at the lady sitting at the desk.

'You like it?' She returned my smile.

With many relevant and irrelevant words I attempted to explain that our family was not in a financial position where we could buy luxuries like vases. Not yet anyway.

The next morning the same vase full of fresh flowers was sitting on my desk in the lab.

'Margaret wanted you to have it,' Otto explained.

What can you say when your heart is overflowing with gratitude, not for the vase but for the thoughtfulness and kindness? A simple thankyou seemed so inadequate. This act of kindness made me think about the difference between the people I used to associate with and the people I was associating with now and realised that in every country of the world most people had the same desires: to be kind, compassionate, to give and receive love. They breathe, they feel sorrow, battle though life and love the same way I do. The difference was in the political regime. It was the regime that brought out the best or worst in people.

A few days later a thin wooden-veneer postcard with an image of the High Tatras burned onto it arrived from Svetya.

Dear Yenachka

Thousands of kisses from our first schooling in the High Tatras without you. You are greatly missed.

Under the signatures of my colleagues many personal remarks were written. Olga, the legal adviser of the Social Security Department wrote:

Yenni, I often think of you and wish you and your family a good life in your new home.

❦ ❦ ❦

Elizabeth stands with her back against the glass pane of our kitchen door with her arms plaited into each other at her waist. She is tall, blond and attractive, a woman in her late thirties. Her blue eyes observe the sink, where my arms are submerged in the soapy water up to my elbows. Relaxed after the evening meal her family and ours have eaten together, the conversation is easy. We talk Hungarian, continuing on the subject we started earlier on.

'So, where did you learn about the palm reading?' I stop rattling the plates in the sink.

'I did this really interesting course. Also about horoscopes and other things.'

'Can you do a course on horoscopes in Australia?'

'You can do a course on anything in Hobart,' she smiles.

'And can you tell the future from one's palm?' I place a pile of washed-up plates on the drying board.

'I have a fair idea.'

'Can you tell my fortune then?'

'Show me your left palm.' She steps closer to the sink, unfolding her arms.

I lift my left arm out of the suds, brush my palm against my skirt and place it in the cup of her hand. She observes the wrinkled skin for a while.

'You are going to meet a man in the not-too-distant future.'

'A man? Here in Tasmania? I wouldn't understand what he is talking about,' I laugh. 'Anyway, what kind of a man? An English man?'

'Seriously. He will become a very important person in your life.'

'What else can you see?'

'This is all I am going to tell you for now.'

My learning curve snaked on. The inspector from the Agriculture Department suggested I should try to get my ticket in milk grading and milk testing.

After a lengthy explanation I did get the drift of this *ticket* business. All I had to do was to sit an exam. The material was written in a textbook of more than two hundred pages, all in English. I would have two months to learn the material and then go up to Launceston, where the written, oral and practical exams would be conducted by the representatives of the Agriculture Department for students from milk and cheese factories all over Tasmania.

'But I can't speak English well enough,' I objected.

It was okay not to pass, but I should try, they told me. In any case I should take the textbook home, read through it and at the end of the two months say if I felt confident enough to sit the exams.

I took the book home. That night I waited until everybody was in bed, dragged the small single-bar radiator into the kitchen, made myself a cup of strong black coffee, lit a cigarette, set myself next to the table and looked through pages and pages of English words. *Where should I start?* It was bad enough that it was all in English but even in my language I had no idea about anything relating to farms, or feeding and milking cows.

A breathless urge to know, to learn, to prove to everyone and to myself got hold of me. Night after night, sometimes after midnight on returning from the Town House restaurant I sat in the kitchen with the mug of coffee steaming in front of me and the ashtray filling up with cigarette butts at my elbow. With the help of the dictionary I translated all the English words from the textbook into my native language one by one, writing them into an exercise book. The small kitchen filled with cigarette smoke and the radiator could barely hold the heat in the early autumn mornings. Through the glass pane of the door to the backyard, beyond the bushes huddling tightly at the fence, the sky started losing its darkness. I thought of the electric blanket that I had turned on just before midnight, tidied up the table, emptied the ashtray and washed it in the sink. *This will do for tonight, I have four hours to sleep,* I thought and unplugged the radiator.

After many early mornings I finished the very first step. All the English words were translated into my native language. Reading through, many times they made no sense even in my language, but still I gained a basic understanding about the farms, the cows, the pastures, the composition of the milk, the process of pasteurisation, of various tests, keeping quality control and other related issues. All this was new knowledge to me. I had to learn it by heart. When I organised the words into some kind of order that made sense and filled up my brain with that knowledge I put together an extract, still in my language. The autumn turned into cold winter, the thought of the bed warmed up by the electric blanket was hard to brush away. With the small radiator almost touching my heels and with the help of the dictionary, I translated my extract, word by word, back into English. The hardest part came when I had to learn all those strange words by heart, repeating them with eyes closed, trying to memorise them by relating the words to sounds, colours and objects in my native language.

Even though my intentions were simply to learn about the material for the exams, my English skills also benefited. In the process I got to learn some spelling and my vocabulary widened. After the two months, when asked at work if I wanted to sit the exams, the answer was an emphatic *yes*.

❦❦❦

It is 1971, an early and very cold July morning, almost two years and a month to the day of our arrival in Tasmania. Yano drives me to the Red Coach Lines terminal where I catch the bus for the three-hour trip to Launceston, where I am to spend the next five days preparing for and taking the exams.

As soon as the door hisses closed in the comfortably heated and upholstered coach, a feeling of absolute loneliness descends and lies on me throughout the whole journey. I observe the strange countryside, the small houses and the streets empty of people, with no emotional response.

Stepping out of the bus at the depot I wander through the empty streets of Launceston, dragging my overnight bag, having an argument with myself while looking for the Tasman Hotel. Confused thoughts keep my spirit down and won't let my eyes enjoy the unusual or the picturesque.

What am I doing in this strange city? How could I ever think that it is a good idea? Only I could be that silly and ambitious to think that I actually can pass the exams in English. In English? Hah! Why on Earth have I come here to feel alienated and utterly cut off from everything meaningful and familiar just when I am starting to get used to Hobart? Haven't I had more than enough excitement in the last couple of years of the new and unknown? It's easier when you share it with the family. But on my own? Now it is too late to think this way. I will never change, I will never learn. At the next turn I will do exactly the same.

The Tasman Hotel is an old and very European-looking multi-storey building of grey stone. Inside I find it quite pompous in a kind of 1930s fashion.

Receiving the key, I climb up to the second floor. Not bad. Basic but clean, warm and comfortable.

There are no other days in Launceston as quiet as Sunday afternoons. Through the window of my room I observe the totally deserted street.

Ring-ring. The phone.

For me? I think and lift the receiver: 'Hello?'

'Welcome to Launceston,' a male voice speaks in perfect Hungarian. He is phoning to invite me to join him and his wife for a good Hungarian dinner. Who is he? How does he know about me speaking Hungarian and being in Launceston, in this hotel? That's easy, he is the manager of the hotel and was expecting me; Dick Baker had asked him to look after me.

Should I burst into tears, blurting out thankyous, every time I am overwhelmed by a kind gesture? Or should I finally get a grip of my emotions and just be thankful for the kindness and gracefully turn up for this Hungarian dinner? It's hard to suppress your true self. As usual I burst into tears and am barely able to thank the manager for all, whatever he was going to do for me.

The middle-aged Hungarian manager and his wife, who was also the cook at the hotel restaurant, were exceptionally friendly and welcoming. After a good dinner and a glass of wine I realised why I had been so very depressed earlier on. To lose the ground of belonging is the hardest thing. By meeting those two they put me back on familiar ground, at least partially.

Almost happy, I had looked around at my new surrounds, checked out the bathroom and the comfortable bed, when someone knocked at the door. A slender young man with a mild and cheerful manner, seemingly unsure of what to say, was standing there.

'Sorry to be so late,' he started, not knowing how to continue.

I knew Michael. He was in charge of the Launceston laboratory. For a short time, while Otto was on holiday, he had worked with us in Hobart's lab.

Michael said that he was here to help with my learning. He would also provide transport to the school every morning and then back to the hotel every afternoon.

Suddenly an image formed in my mind. As if something truly magic would happen if I waited long enough; little elves and fairies unseen by human eyes were running around in front of me and behind me, working hard on my behalf. Without me knowing, a network of people were plotting together to make my time away from my family as pleasant as possible and trying to increase my chances of passing the exams.

This particular 'time fold' in the concertina door of my life was filled with a mixture of deep loneliness completely balanced out with the warmest feelings of thankfulness and exaltation.

For a whole week I had a chance to experiment with the Australian menu. The breakfast cereals and toasts, the lunches of white sandwiches, to me fluffy and quite tasteless. Dinners – unlike in the Town House restaurant where I was dishing out the medium–rare steaks and lamb chops for other people, here I could consume them, taste the watery vegetables, chasing the peas with a fork turned the *wrong way around* as I have seen people do and wondering why on Earth the fork was scooped if not for shovelling the food onto it. I wasn't accustomed to the large slabs of meat with the small servings of vegetables. Our native dishes were mainly tasty vegetable stews with a small portion of meat and a good chunk of rye bread. Just the same, I learned to love the Steak Diane and found myself ordering it more often.

After the hard slog of the restaurant shifts in the hot and busy kitchens, I enjoyed my evenings, when I could dress for the occasion, descend from my room, choose a table, figure out a meal from the menu and expectantly wait for it. *What is it going to taste like this time?*

Michael came every evening. The two of us comfortably spread out on the carpet of the hotel room surrounded by books and sheets of paper. Evening after evening we talked, drew pictures, discussed the milk and everything related to it, while this shy twenty-eight-year-old man was siphoning out all my knowledge and patiently explaining my questions over and over, until he was sure that I understood.

Around midnight he would depart and turn up in the morning to take me to my school. There I mingled with many people, all of them Australian, men and women from various Tasmanian milk and cheese laboratories and factories. We were there to revise what we had learned, to question what we did not understand and to prepare for the exams.

The morning of the exams. Michael walks into my room with a bottle of brandy.

'Confident?' He smiles.

'H-m-m-m.'

'Here.' He unscrews the top of the bottle. 'Have a sip.'

I take a sip and in the hotel carpark I climb into his yellow Charger.

The Agriculture Department is an old building, with high ceilings, long cold corridors and a large hall with desks alongside the walls. There are about fifty of us, some I know from the lectures, some are new people who had just arrived that morning to sit the exams. The atmosphere is thick with tension. The steps of the two lecturers on the bare floorboards echo against the light-green walls around the hall. They walk from one desk to the other, placing the sheets, blank side up, in front of us. Then one sits behind the table elevated by the podium; the other keeps circulating.

'Turn over your questionnaires. Start writing now. You have two hours.'

I lower my eyes to the sheet. O-o-oh! I know that question. And the next one!

'Jenny,' I hear my name whispered as the inspector bends above me. 'Are you sure, you want to go ahead with this? Perhaps I can get hold of a translator for you.'

'Oh, no. Thank you. No need. I know it.' I smile into his face and all my nervousness leaves, as I start writing those English words that I have learned by heart.

The two hours are up. I am so proud of myself. I answered almost all the questions. I can't believe that I have actually had an English test. *Svetya, you should see me now.*

The oral exams are conducted in the afternoon on the same day in some kind of a laboratory in a different part of the city. It's a hands-on exam that also involves some milk testing. Much easier. I know the tests from my work. Face to face with the lecturer I can explain myself in many words and roundabouts while they all smile. I feel the luckiest person in the whole world to have all those friendly and well-wishing people around me.

'Have I passed?' I ask impatiently.

They will let me know in writing within a couple of weeks. But deep inside me I know I have, I know for sure.

Michael is going home for the weekend to his family in Hobart. Would I like a lift? In those two and something hours' drive I learn some more about Michael and I think he learns about me. I worriedly clutch the inside door handle and watch his speedometer climbing up to 150 kilometres per hour, as he cuts the corners of the narrow roads in his Charger.

❦❦❦

'You did all right,' said Otto encouragingly on my return.

How did he know? He heard from the inspectors of the Agriculture Department.

A few weeks later Mr Baker turned up in the lab.

'There girl. I am proud of you. You passed with 90 percent accuracy. Congratulations.' He shook my hand and gave me the certificate.

Department of Agriculture

Tasmania

The Dairy Produce Act 1932

Certificate as a Tester.

This is to Certify that

Jenny Milosh

has been examined in the theory and practice of testing milk and cream and is qualified for employment in the testing of milk and cream factories.

16th August 1971

signed by two examiners and the Director of Agriculture.

Otto was a great source of information. Somehow he knew a lot about other people and their private business. He knew that forty per cent of the class failed the test. Was he sure? They all seemed knowledgeable to me. There was no reason for them not to pass; their first language was English.

Košice 27/9/71

My dear Yenny

We received your letter and also the letters from the children. It was great to hear from you and learn that in such a short time your family was able to grow so much financially and in knowledge.

It is very important, that you get used to your environment and your working conditions, but I can see that you have already done it and mastered the English language so much that you could pass your exams. My congratulations. Now you have an English certificate about your skills …

With us things are not too good. Omama is still very weak, her back, her legs are aching, she can't go out of the house because she is too dizzy, she doesn't want to see the doctor and doesn't want to take any medicines.

I left my very good job in January, because I could not leave her in the house on her own, she is also very forgetful and …

Lots of kisses and cuddles to the whole family.

Opapa

In Omama's handwriting:

Lots of warm wishes and love to you all.

Omama

Stephen and Elizabeth were leaving Hobart for New Guinea. Stephen had applied for a teacher's position in Port Moresby and his application was successful.

I could barely comprehend the luxury of possibilities in my new world. Could you just decide which part of the world you wanted to work in and go for it? Wasn't New Guinea a tribal country where in some parts they were still practising cannibalism? Perhaps, but not legally, Stephen told me. There were a lot of Germans, Dutch and Australians in Port Moresby. By providing a skilled workforce and infrastructure the Australian government supported the civilisation and development of New Guinea. What would happen to the house in Hobart and to the girls? A-a-ah, the house would be sold, the girls would go to boarding school in Sydney and during their school holidays they would come to New Guinea. Easy as that. It surely was a new way of looking at things. As for me, I couldn't imagine my life without my children being around.

It's a lovely Sunday afternoon and it is Stephen and Elizabeth's farewell party. We are in the manicured garden in West Hobart, hemmed with beds of hybrid roses, full of guests and tables covered with good food and wine. From the garden the dark silhouette of Mount Wellington is almost at the stretch of a hand and down below on the far horizon the bridge curves above the glassy mouth of the river.

To me the place you live in is your home. This is where you create your memories and family traditions and you leave only when you absolutely have to. This cultural attitude stems from the country I came from, mirroring its values and limitations. Stephen's house will be sold and all what was before, the effort that went into making it a home, will be discontinued, lost as if the family living there before never existed.

At the end of the day, just before the sun drops behind Mount Wellington, Stephen, who has offered to drive us home, staggers to his Valiant parked on the street and looks for the hole in the car door to stick his keys in. After many tries he finally finds it, turns the key to open the door, flops heavily onto the seat, manages to find the ignition and turns the engine on. Chopi, Yano, Mami and I are sitting squashed together on the back seat, Ishtvan, Zsuzsi and Roman in the back space of the station wagon. One of the guests, a Catholic priest, who also lives our way, takes his place in the front seat, next to Stephen.

My hands clasped hard, I am glad about the priest being in the car with us. He is closer to God than any of us. Perhaps he can pray for us all.

❧❧❧

Our very first Australian friends had left and the days and months had gone by without their regular visits. A parcel with a small present for each of us arrived from New Guinea. I received a lovely necklace with wooden beads and a small carved figurine. Mami, being home, was the one who missed them the most.

As our family was trying to blend the old and familiar with the new, Zsuzsi became a teenager. For weeks I was preparing myself, looking for an appropriate opportunity to explain to her about the facts of life.

That afternoon I mastered my courage and sat her on my knee.

'Zsuzsikam. I would like to talk to you about adulthood. To tell you how is it to grow up and what will happen when you do.'

'O-o-oh I know Mami! You don't have to tell me, I know it.'

Good, I thought, but just to make sure asked, 'What do you know sweetheart?'

'I know that when I grow up I will get married, have to take care of my husband, cook, keep the house tidy and work really hard.'

'This is not …' Someone walked into the kitchen and Zsuzsi slid off my knees.

'I am going over to Eva's, Mami.' The story of Zsuzsi's and my life. She always knew it all. But Zsuzsi was only half the story.

'Did you talk to Ishtvan about the facts of life?' I confronted Yano.

Trying to corkscrew anything out of Yano never worked.

'Keep your mind on things that concern you.'

'But Yanichku, he …' Yano walked out of the kitchen.

It concerns me, I thought, and because I wasn't sure if Yano had talked to Ishtvan I visited the local newsagency, bought a couple of *Playboy* magazines and discreetly placed them on Ishtvan's writing desk. He never mentioned finding them and it made me wonder if it was Ishtvan who had found them or perhaps Yano before him?

Years later Ishtvan told me about the shock when he saw the magazines on his writing desk and how much he appreciated the information.

Chopi and I were doing night shifts at the Town House restaurant and I gradually got to know the staff.

'Cold drink, please?' I asked the chef.

'Ask someone from the bar, or wait, I will.' He opened the door connecting the kitchen and the bar and called in.

'Could someone bring some drinks for the kitchen staff, please?'

A tall man emerged balancing a round tray with two glasses of soda water on his palm and introduced himself to Chopi and I, in

Hungarian.'

In surprise I stopped feeding the big industrial dishwasher and wiped the sweat off my forehead. How did he know we speak Hungarian? How many Hungarians are living in Tasmania anyway?

'Not all that many, but you must have been lucky to meet them all,' he said smiling back.

From that day on we had no problems with cold drinks. The coldest and sparkliest soda water was supplied by George on the round silver tray twice a night, accompanied by a cheeky smile to the chef to curb his remarks about those two Hungarian girls. George lived in South Hobart, only streets away from Darcy Street and if we liked he would give us a lift back home every evening, no worries, he said. Chopi and I were on familiar ground once again.

'G'night.' The kitchen was tidied up and the staff left one by one. In the empty dining room with tables set up for breakfast Chopi and I were stepping from one foot to the other, waiting out George's shift. There was a piano. It had been years since my fingers touched the ivory of the keyboard. With a sudden urge to touch the cool keys, to run my fingers through, to produce a sound, I pulled up a chair and played a popular Hungarian Gypsy song. Before I finished there was a small choir circling around me. Chopi and George singing out the words and George's German friend Karl humming the well-known European tune.

From that night on I often played and they sung, sometimes accompanied by curious waitresses elbowing the highly polished piano lid. The transitory sounds of Hungarian Gypsy songs would float above the aromas that filtered through the kitchen door and were trapped in the red-carpeted dining room. But it was not easy to hold on to the sound; as soon as you heard it, it was gone and you were deposited back to the reality of the present.

'It's getting late, let's go home.' After those singing sessions Chopi and I crawled into George's new secondhand car and through the midnight streets were driven to our gate in Darcy Street. There we would sit inside the car for another thirty minutes in animated discussion, until Mami's head would appear in the window: 'Chopi! Yenni!' she would call out in half whisper. 'C'mon! It's past midnight!'

❦ ❦ ❦

'What happened to the twelve dollars missing from my wages?' I asked the chef in the kitchen.

'No idea. Perhaps union fees or something. You should see someone in the office.'

I go. They have deducted union fees, I am told.

'U-n-i-o-n? What kind of union? I didn't join any union!' *Oh! How can I find the right words to express my total disagreement?*

'Everyone is a member of the union. You understand?' The Townhouse Hotel badge shines silver and is proudly pinned to a lapel of the dark-blue uniform displaying the name of the office worker, Helen. She smiles. Reading off her name from the badge I think in my native language, *Listen Helen, don't patronise me, I am an adult person. I decide when I join the union or any other organisation.*

'No way!' I blurt out in English. I am caught up, agitated by this infringement of my understanding of freedom, not knowing what I know now, that the concept of freedom varies from one political ideology to the other.

I have come to the other side of the world, I am arguing inside me, *leaving my family, friends and possessions behind to be rid of unions and similar organisations.*

Helen tells me that I don't have to join the union but, if I don't, I can't work in the Town House Hotel restaurant. *So, this is also included in democracy?*

And George isn't working tonight; Karl, his friend, offers us a lift. He is just as good a friend to us as George is. A handsome man, I suspect he fancies Chopi. We sit in the back of his car as he pulls out of the underground parking lot and turns in the opposite direction to where we should be going.

'Karl, Karl!' we call out from the back. 'No good, no good. There,

there.' We try to point to the right direction.

'Don't worry. You will be all right.' Karl keeps driving.

We pass the sandstone buildings in Macquarie Street, turn onto the Brooker Highway and drive past many traffic lights as the car speeds up. The two of us hold each other's sweaty hands and sink deeper into the seat as we watch, horrified, the overhead lights coming and going in regular intervals. It hits me like a lightning bolt. This is what Yanibachi calls *hijacking*. This is what he was talking about when I told him about me stopping a car and asking for a lift to get to the railway station in the first months of us being in Tasmania. *Yenni, you silly fool.* The highway is getting darker, the lights less frequent and it is past midnight. Driving for over forty minutes, so far this is my longest drive in the city. With imagination running wild I see both of us tied to a tree, raped and perhaps even killed. Who knows? *If we manage to get out of this situation,* I keep promising myself, *I will never get into anyone's car. Never.*

The car slows down and turns a corner. If I was worried on the highway, right now I have three times as many reasons to be worried. The street the car turns into is unlit, the road non-existent, new houses, most of them dark, some under construction, dotted around the muddy terrain. *Oh my God!* This is the end for sure. The car stops in front of a new brick house. The light in the entrance door comes on. Karl turns around with a huge smile.

'C'mon girls, get out.'

Still holding hands, we get out as cattle going to the slaughter. The front door opens wide.

'Welcome. Welcome. Come inside. Karl promised me that he will bring you over one evening.' An elderly man in slippers and shirtsleeves speaks to us in the Slovak language. 'I don't meet many Czechoslovakians. It's very good of Karl isn't it?'

Baker's Milk employed a Czech man in the factory. I found out about him when Otto asked me to translate. Honza was stocky and young, with a great grin and a heavy walk, as if walking over a snowfield, typical of people living in the mountains. Honza, his wife and his little boy had just arrived in Hobart from South Australia and couldn't speak a word of English. Besides the language problem he also had one with Australian food. He couldn't stand it. None of it. Full stop.

One morning Honza called in through the small trapdoor cut out in the side of the laboratory building, which was used by the factory personnel to hand in various samples to be tested.

'Missus!' Even though I requested it, he never called me by my first name, not then and not in the many years of our friendship.

'Try this one.' He stuck his heavy arm thickly overgrown with blond hair through the small space. The corners of the paper serviette were folded around a large oval slice of a *true* rye bread. Gosh! I haven't seen rye bread for years. Where did he get this from? A-a-ah! An indulgent smile spread through his wide Slav face. He made it with his wife. 'Good?'

'Honza, it's excellent. Can I take a small piece to my husband?'

This was the beginning of a new relationship between Honza and his wife Yana and our family. I would have liked to call it a friendship, but not Honza. He told us that he didn't believe in friendship, that all relationships are based on some kind of need. This was a good observation but, even though Honza did not think of Yano and I as his friends, he and his wife always behaved towards us as if they would have been. He wouldn't give me the recipe for the bread but we could perhaps get together and discuss the possibility of a business baking and selling this very good bread?

Yano and Honza got together, emptied a couple of bottles of wine and decided that they have a lot in common, an observation based on their mutual liking of wine and a mutual desire to make lots of money. A business was a good idea. Glass after glass Honza kept calling Yano Pan Milosh (Mr Milosh).

'When you call someone a Mr and you happen to get angry with him it's harder to call him *you bastard*.' He smiled and never swayed from his principle.

Yano and I knew a Hungarian man who was running a grocery shop in North Hobart. It was a freehold business with a flat above the shop and a bakery in the backyard.

'Yes, of course you can rent it. I will not ask for much money; no one is using it,' said the Hungarian after a couple of glasses of wine. 'Come and have a look at it,' he said invitingly and gave us a grand tour of his house, his shop and the bakery. Great! The bakehouse was a large concrete space with an electric oven, a huge table in the middle, shelves around the walls and, the best part, an industrial pastry mixer.

'I don't know if it works; we bought it with the place and never used it.'

'It will work,' Yano said with the assuredness of an engineer, and rolled up his sleeves. After many afternoons spent in the bakery the mixer did work.

The bread business called for planning.

So how about that recipe Yana?

'Okay I will show you.'

We sat around their kitchen table until Yana made the dough. We emptied some glasses of wine while the dough rose, laughed and planned while it baked.

No good. It's too flat and heavy. Nothing like the one you brought to Baker's Milk. So where is the recipe?

'O-o-oh! It's up here,' she motioned to her head.

'Lets work on it,' Yano suggested.

More glasses of wine, some new ideas. Perhaps more yeast, or flour? Let's try again.

Life went on and the four of us tried to get closer to the perfect bread. Suddenly Honza, Yana and their little Mike were daily visitors in our home.

But bread here, bread there, the three of them had to live and for that they needed more money. Yana started working in a restaurant and Mami volunteered to look after Mike, who was the same age as

Roman. Honza was young and strong. Besides the new business he also wanted money to fulfil his dream of prosperity in the west. Chopi enquired at the Town House restaurant. Would they want a young man for scrubbing and washing those huge pots? Yes, they would. Honza had an evening job. From then on evening after evening he took his position in front of the big, deep sink, his wide face covered by droplets of sweat, now and then saltily dripping into the water.

'Whoosh! Did you see it Mrs Miloshova?' he called out in Czech.

'What?'

'Did you see those dollars whooshing past me just now? Next time I will catch them,' he laughed noisily.

'What's up Honza?' The chef wanted to be let in on the joke.

The three of us tried to explain but did the chef understand?

'O-o-oh yeah,' he said without a smile.

A letter arrived from the Housing Department. We were allocated a three-bedroom family home in the newly developed subdivision of Rokeby. When applying it was one of the three suburbs we were asked to choose from. Rokeby is not bad, Otto advised. It's a new housing development, the land used to be called Clarence Plains and later became farm land.

Tony loads us into his Holden for a trip to Rokeby. 'It's not too far,' he says reassuringly.

Through the metropolitan area, across the bridge, passing small mostly weatherboard houses in gardens, parks and more small houses in the suburb of Howrah. He drives and drives, and drives. *My God! This is as far, if not further than, living on the hill at Magnezit's quarry site,* I lament in my heart, thinking about the first-ever accommodation Yano and I had together as a husband and wife, and the following hateful year, which I do not care to recall. We get onto a seemingly long drive over a hillside covered by prickly bushes, no houses. On top of that hill a view of a magically beautiful valley, with curly hilltops and a vivid-blue bay stretching out in front of us.

'This is Rokeby,' Tony says.

There are only a few newly built houses alongside the road. A turn into a wide street, more new houses, a mixture of weatherboard and brick homes, some still under construction, some already occupied, with sheets stretched over the windows. The lots around the houses are dusty or overgrown by dry grass; no gardens, no trees, no birds – only dogs and cats wandering in the deserted streets.

At the intersection of an already bitumened road Tony's car stops. The house number of the corner red-brick building with a tin roof matches the address in the letter from the Housing Department.

Wow! We walk around, circling the brick house, looking in through the windows. What a beauty! White lacquered built-in cupboards in the pale yellow kitchen, with a dining area under the large corner windows catching the setting sun. It is love at first sight. Even though it's far out of the centre of Hobart, we will manage somehow with our Vauxhall, we are sure of it. Next morning we have to confirm our decision to the Housing Department in exchange for the keys. We can barely wait.

Mami and Chopi have a letter too. The flat they asked for is allocated to them in a block of flats at Stainforth Court, near the Brooker Highway. Just what they always wanted.

CHAPTER SEVEN

Our Dream Home

Once again we were at the very height of our contentment, full of ideas, dreams for the future and gratitude for all the good things we experienced in two short years living in Tasmania. A kind of Mills and Boon utopia got hold of us now that all our dreams were coming true and we were quite sure that we would live happily ever after.

Letters crossed the ocean to share our happiness with the ones left behind; the answers followed with the return mail.

… and if you also have a garden around your house, that's a big job. The garden needs looking after. I know, because for the very first time in my life I have tried it this year. I got sick of it soon enough though. This is how it goes when you don't have any gardening skills, like myself.

Once you furnish your house, you will feel at home again …

wrote Opapa.

The price of the house is $9000. We can either buy it or rent it, they tell us at the Housing Department. If we buy the house we will pay it off in monthly rental; no need for loans. It will take about twenty years.

Yes, yes, we will buy it.

'Sign here, both of you.' The short man with glasses hands over the form, turns around and from a pigeon hole takes out a bunch of keys. 'Here are the keys. We'll send you the contract with the mail in a few weeks' time. You can move in now.'

In the first week, after work Yano drives in the Vauxhall to the house every day to scrub and polish the floorboards. No, he doesn't want me there with him; I would be under his feet.

I am so impatient; can't wait to see the shiny floor and the inside of the house again.

At work I talk about nothing else. 'You know, in *my* new house we are ...' They are all very patient with me.

❦❦❦

A man in a suede lumberjacket, unbuttoned shirt, cheeky smile, with well-spoken English with a German accent, often parked in front of the lab to visit his countrymen, the factory manager and Otto. While there he would shop for fresh yoghurt and cottage cheese from the Hungarian cheesemaker. 'Healthy tucker,' he would say laughingly and would carry the box full of yoghurt jars, placing it on the back seat of his small beaten-up VW.

'He lives just past Rokeby in Clifton Beach,' Otto remarked. 'When you move to Rokeby, he could give you a lift in his German sewing machine.' The man smiled and spent some more time in the lab talking to us. He was about fifty and they called him Hans.

Mami and Chopi were busy with their flat. When Chopi was walking me through the empty rooms, still smelling of the fresh paint, we were both excited, like two kids preparing a tea party in their doll's house.

'Isn't it beautiful,' said Chopi as we progressed from room to room then up the stairs. 'This will be our bedroom and this will be Roman's bedroom.'

'And we have a balcony looking out on trees and a patch of grass.'

The only thing Chopi didn't like was the light-blue colour of the loungeroom, but that wasn't a problem. She took a day off to repaint it white. That day Hans turned up in the lab.

'On your own?' he enquired.

I told him about Chopi painting her new flat. What a coincidence! He also happened to be off work for a couple of days and wouldn't mind helping her.

'That'll be nice. I am sure she would like it.' What a nice man Hans was. 'Here is her address.'

You know Svetya I never thought it possible. We are here for two years and already Chopi and Mami were given, by the government, a beautiful flat. Yano and I have bought a car, and we are buying a block of land, which is almost paid for. We were also allocated by the government a three-bedroom house with land around it for a garden. We have a choice of buying or renting the house. So we decided to buy it and will be moving in next week …

I did not even think about the impression I was giving to Svetya and to everyone else who read my letters. My intentions were honest and naive. I wanted to reassure them that we did the right thing to leave for the west, that we were all right here. The contented letters were arriving in my native country when it was sliding down the steep hill of a corrupt economy, when people were queuing up for hours, considering themselves lucky to get something at the end of their long queue, with no money to spare. A car? Land? A house? All this in a short two years?

… There is nothing else you could possibly want. You must be living in a consumer paradise …

came the answer from Svetya.

But did I tell Svetya that our car was cheap and old, luckily with wheels still turning? Of course I didn't. Knowing that not many people in our country would consider buying such a car even if they had the money. Did I tell her that we needed the car, no matter how old, because of the long distances between the places we had to get to, daily? Did I mention that it would take thirty minutes by car to get to the centre of the city from our new home, another thirty minutes to

Baker's Milk for me and thirty minutes to Silk and Textiles for Yano, with no public transport provided by the government from Rokeby to the city?

When we start living in our new house Yano will take the car and I will catch the private bus that travels once in the morning to the city and once in the afternoon back to Rokeby, and I can't miss it because there is no way of getting back home unless I hire a taxi, which I can't afford. And did I realise at all that our Housing Department area and its occupants are looked down on by most middle-class Tasmanians? That our suburb is not what one would call a good address?

I did not mention any of those things in my letters simply because some of it I did not know and some of it I did not think of. Our financial situation was improving week by week, month by month. We were honestly contented.

I started wondering, though, why the government was building public housing for financially disadvantaged families so far out of the centre. Didn't they think about the transport? The families living there needed it the most. Nowhere near the suburb or within walking distance was a cultural establishment of any kind, a cinema, a theatre, not even a shopping centre. After two years living in Tasmania I still had a problem with the long working days, with the early morning starts and late afternoon finishes, the compulsory tea and lunch breaks that prolonged the time spent at work. In Tasmania my working life absorbed all my spare time, which back in the old country was allocated to socialising, spending time with the children or resting.

I could but wish for a three o'clock finish, a home within walking distance of my work and childcare facilities. Partly I blamed it on the way the city was structured, the remote suburbs and the lack of efficient and sufficient public transport. My day in the new suburb of Rokeby would begin by leaving home at half past six in the morning for an eight o'clock start and returning home after six in the evening to the domestic chores and to care for the children, who would be left unattended all afternoon. What could the children do? There was no chance of after-school activities; we couldn't provide transport for them to get back home. And I would have to give up my evening job because of the transport. There would go part of my wages.

All those questions bothered me before we moved out to Rokeby. Suddenly I was sorry to leave the Darcy Street house. It was so close to the city and after all it wasn't all that bad. Was it?

'What do you think Yano, about buying this house and selling the land in Springfield?'

'Are you mad? Two houses? Suddenly you want two houses, this one and the one in Rokeby?'

'No. You don't understand. We would not have to build in Springfield if we bought this one.'

'Who said we will be building in Springfield? We are moving to Rokeby, aren't we? And this house? You can see the blue sky between the boards in our bedroom. The back flat is terrible.'

'Okay, okay, I just thought it might be an idea.'

We started to organise the moving.

'Yena, find a furniture store and buy some basic furniture. We are not taking this old rubbish into the new house.'

'Do we have the money for new furniture?' I was surprised. Yano was saving but I had no idea how well he was doing it.

'Yes, of course we will be buying only the basics, you understand?' We will buy as much as we can afford. Yano didn't want any loans; we would be paying by cash.

'I do understand, I do understand. Come on Zsuzsi, we will go to Mather's in Liverpool Street. I need you with me to translate.' I almost skipped out of the house.

❦ ❦ ❦

Zsuzsi and I are squeezing through narrow spaces in between chairs, tables and settees in the furniture shop, touching, looking, stopping for a while, up the stairs, then down to see the window display. There is nothing I like. I want Scandinavian-style furniture. What is that? They ask. Scandinavian furniture is highly polished, made out of light wood, with slim lines, glass table tops and wall units, I explain to Zsuzsi, who explains to the salesman. Sorry, he has never heard of it. Do they have a valenda then? Zsuzsi, could you please explain in English what a valenda is? She tries. Sorry, no idea. Okay then. Which couch do you like Zsuzsi, the one upstairs or this one in the window? We choose a day and night couch and two simple armchairs, a colonial-style dinning table with four chairs, for Ishtvan a bed and a combination wardrobe, for Zsuzsi a three-piece pink and white bedroom suite. What do you think Zsuzsikam? And for us simple bedroom furniture with a double bed, two wardrobes and two bedside tables. In my eyes it is a huge shopping spree. From my purse I count out the money into the hand of a surprised shopkeeper.

The furniture that we had is sold back to the secondhand dealer on the corner of Macquarie Street. He comes with his truck, loads up everything he sold us fifteen months ago, including Mami's beautiful dinning table, seating ten, which would fetch a fortune now, pays us half of what we originally paid him and drives the truck back to his shop. Roy turns up with an empty milk truck and helps us to move all our belongings to Rokeby and then Mami and Chopi's to Stainforth Court. The new furniture is delivered the next day. Mami once again gets busy with making curtains and doilies out of Silk and Textile parcels for both households.

Now, with our moving finalised and out of the way, the bread business came back into our life. Many evenings in the new Rokeby home were spent with meals and bottles of wine between Yano and Honza, discussing new possibilities, while Yana and I watched the television. Little Mike was safely tucked in the back of Yana's new and very rugged-looking secondhand panel van parked in our drive, which they had purchased that afternoon when Yana's international driver's licence was recognised by the Transport Commission, to her and Honza's surprise, without the need to take the test. 'We will go up to Mount Wellington,' said Honza, after they pulled out from the secondhand caryard.

'I can't drive this huge thing, I have never driven on the left side of the road and drove only occasionally back at home,' Yana objected, but it was no good.

'I will help you,' said Honza, who couldn't drive because of a problem with his eyes, and off they went up to the top of the mountain. From then on Yana drove, and masterfully backed the van into our drive every time they visited.

Some more unsuccessful tries followed with the flat, heavy and sticky breads that were distributed to the family and friends. Those trying sessions were good fun for Honza, Yano and the owner of the shop, though. In the concrete-floored bakery filled with the sweet smell of yeast, each man with a glass of wine circled around Yana to watch her making the dough and then, with a fresh glass of wine in their hands, waited with expectation for the bread to come out of the oven.

'This one should be good,' they offered hopefully.

'Not quite. It seems still a bit heavy. What do you think Honza?'

Eventually Honza and Yana came up with a perfect recipe. They recorded it and from then on, at each baking, the bread turned out to be the same. For a while we had more bread than we could eat.

Not always but many times the baking started early in the morning, at 4 am. I was never really involved with morning baking because of the children, but also because Yano did not want me around. I could be of no help, he thought. Yana was an excellent cook, a smiling young woman with wide hips, a good dose of humour and a complete lack of organisation. Everything around her was disorganised, her finances and her household.

'Sorry Mr Milosh, I forgot the salt,' she said at four in the morning, when they were just about to turn the key to the bakery after the thirty minutes' drive.

'But there is salt somewhere inside the bakery, isn't there?' Yano asked hopefully.

'I don't think so,' Yana said with a wide smile.

So back to Yana's flat for a packet of salt, which had to be salvaged from under packets of biscuits, washing powder, tea-towels and whatever else. There went the precious time before Yano's eight o'clock start at Silk and Textiles.

Sometimes it was the salt, sometimes the flour and sometimes the key to the bakery. Despite all that, they managed to produce quality rye bread, which to begin with was sold in the front grocery shop.

'The bread needs to be marketed,' Yano and Honza thought, and dispatched Yana with a few loaves for tasting, for her to drive around all the grocery shops that she could think of. 'Um-um,' said the shopkeepers. 'Nice bread, we could try to sell it for …' and they suggested the price. Yana came back to the bakery with cheeks coloured rosy from excitement.

'We can't possibly produce bread for that price! The price is too low,' yelled Honza. Yano, Honza and Yana debated the question of the business and the price of the production.

'Okay then,' Yano and Honza decided, we will leave the bread-baking business alone, there is no money in this. We have had enough of early mornings anyway,' and they stopped making the bread.

Chopi also gave up her evening job at the Town House restaurant. There was no transport around midnight for her to get back home and she did not drive.

Hans became a regular visitor at Mami and Chopi's. He would drive Mami, Chopi and Roman around to weekend destinations. 'Let's go to Strathgordon, I will show you the dam,' he would say and load the three of them into his small VW. He had European manners, loved classical music and amused them with stories from the wide repertoire of his adventurous life. Besides, he was tall and dark, his eyes filled with sharp intelligence and an impish smile.

'Hans invited me to a concert tomorrow night,' Chopi reported at work.

I was thrilled. Just what Chopi needed, a partner to go out with.

Mami was less enthusiastic.

'He could be your father,' she lamented.

'O-o-oh Mami, he is just a friend,' laughed Chopi.

Hans was working for the Hydro-Electric Commission, the Hydro, as an engineer, and sometimes did shift work. His post was in Glenorchy and on his way home he would stop over at Mami and Chopi's.

During those evenings he would talk some more about his life and its unexpected twists until Mami got sleepy and hinted that it was time for bed, 'Tomorrow is a work day for Chopi,' bade Hans goodnight and went upstairs to their bedroom.

At one o'clock or sometimes a little later she would realise that Chopi and Hans were still downstairs, talking.

'Chopi-i-i!' she would call down from the top of the stairs, dressed in her nightie. 'Listen, you have to go to work tomorrow. It can't go on like this night after night!'

When I called in for a visit we talked about nothing else.

'What does this man, Hans think? We are a working family; we all need our rest. Yenni, can you talk to Chopi and make her understand that this is not the right thing to do?'

'Okay Mami, I will.'

'Yenni, it's okay. I am having enough sleep. If Hans wouldn't be there I would be reading till one, you know that,' said Chopi. 'It's not about my sleep and rest. Mami objects to his age and to the fact that sometimes he asks me out. Mami and I are having lots of arguments lately.'

At one of the visits Hans met Yano. They liked each other.

'Would Hans like to visit and have a dinner with us?'

'That will be nice, thank you very much,' Hans accepted the invitation.

He came, walked into the loungeroom, looked around and nodded. 'Very nice, very nice,' he smiled. It was a pleasant evening. The food was middle European and the atmosphere great. Hans approvingly commented on the family spirit of our small Housing Department house. He hasn't had a meal like this in at least twenty years, possibly longer, perhaps in his childhood back in Germany. 'A glass of wine?' Yano offered.

'No, No thank you.'

'So you are an abstinent?' Yano asked, surprised.

'Yes, you could say that, but it wasn't always like this.' He waved his hand in the air and dismissed the subject with a smile.

Hans was a skier. He and the members of the ski club were looking after the ski lodge at Mount Field. For years in winter he had been going up to Mount Field on Saturdays for an overnight stay.

'Does Ishtvan ski?'

'Yes, he did back in Košice but not since he came to Tasmania.'

'Would he like to come with me and spend the weekend up in the snow?'

O-o-oh, Ishtvan's eyes lit up, he would love it. It was a deal.

I felt that we were establishing a new friendship with Hans. Not only because of Mami but it also could be taken as a guarantee for her, regarding Hans's good intentions with Chopi.

Ishtvan went skiing with Hans and loved it. Perhaps they could repeat it if the snow lasted? Yes, yes, Ishtvan said.

When the snow melted on Mount Field, Hans invited Chopi to stay at his *really just a shack but it is home to me* for the weekend.

'What do you mean stay at his place on the weekend?' Mami lifted her eyebrows. 'What will people say? You can't just pick yourself up and leave us here. You have a child to look after!'

Another argument, another disagreement. 'Okay, I will take Roman with me. Hans doesn't mind.'

'The poor child. He is going to be taken out of his cosy clean home just to please an old vagabond. You just watch yourself and listen to his tales. Really listen. Do you know what kind of men were serving in the French Foreign Legion? They were mercenaries. All mercenaries.'

'Mami for God's sake. There is nothing in our relationship. It's not like I will be moving in with him. Honestly he is just a friend.'

'Don't tell me. I know men. Don't tell me he wants you just for a friend. You make me laugh.'

Chopi told me the story, cried and went with Roman to Clifton Beach anyway.

'Honestly Yenni, he is only a friend,' she said at work. 'Hans is a fascinating character. He can talk on any subject, has a great collection of classical music and a lovely rustic house right on the beach. The hill next to his house he calls the Hobbit Hill, he named it after reading Tolkien's novel *The Hobbit*. We walked up to the top and Hans almost made us believe that there was a hobbit hiding somewhere. Roman and I had a great weekend. Can you talk to Mami?'

I did and for a little while the emotions simmered down.

It is early evening. Hans is again at Mami's. The doorbell sounds. When the door is pulled open, Yanibachi's arms circle around Mami's torso.

'So how are you all?' He has come to check on Mami and Chopi. He hasn't heard from them for a good while. Are they all right? Explaining his unexpected visit, step by step he gets closer to the loungeroom.

Hans, stretched out leisurely in the large armchair, stops in the middle of his story to listen, and hearing the familiar voice his smile disappears. Yanibachi arrives at the door. The two pairs of dark eyes meet with an unfriendly stare and at Yanibachi's end the realisation comes with anger. No greetings, he turns on his heel and with fast furious steps walks back to the kitchen where Mami is preparing the evening meal.

'What is this drunken bastard doing in your home Marta?' He confronts Mami with a red face, hardly controlling himself.

Hans quietly mutters an excuse to Chopi, gets out of the armchair and with long steps measures out the passage to the door and departs.

Yanibachi comes out of the kitchen into the loungeroom, throws himself into the still-warm armchair, takes a deep breath and explodes into rage.

He knows Hans from the Hydro village. Everyone knew him there. It wasn't enough that he constantly threatened and chased his wife around the village but, when they moved back to Hobart, Hans was turning up at Yanibachi's place night after night blind drunk, making passes at Nana. One night they almost had to call the police.

'But Yanibachi, he is not drinking any more. Hans has not drunk for years.' Chopi tries but does not succeed. 'He told me all about it and how sorry he was for things he has done.'

'Don't tell me Chopi! I know the bastard.' And it continues. You can't change a person. Once a man is violent, he will remain violent, no matter what you do. It's in his blood. Hobart is a small town, many people know him. It would be wise if you stop seeing him altogether. Yanibachi's rage simmers down as he goes, leaving Mami and Chopi with a heavy load to sort out.

'I knew it, I knew it. What did I tell you?' Mami is wagging her finger at Chopi. 'I don't want to see him in my home ever. Never. You understand?'

❦❦❦

Chopi cried all night and the next morning did not turn up at work because her eyes were swollen from tears.

'Yenni,' she said over the phone, 'Hans told me about his past. He has changed. He is even friends with his ex-wife, she remarried and forgave him. Hans has three sons and they regularly visit him, sometimes even stay with him at Clifton Beach. I met them; they love their father. He is a different person to what Yanibachi knew of him. It was the circumstances in the Hydro village, that's all. I have no relationship with Hans. But honestly I can't see any reason to stop seeing him. It's a matter of principle. I will make my own decision about my friends and will not rely on gossip.' Chopi was pleading quietly, still upset.

The happenings of that evening ended the contented relationships between Mami and me, Mami and Chopi and, sadly, Chopi and me. Even though, years after, we made up, we never really recovered the closeness the two of us had shared throughout our earlier life.

Following this episode, when we finished work in the lab, instead of catching the bus back home to Rokeby I regularly walked with Chopi to their place. All other problems were pushed into the corner. The main worry in our family was Hans's soiled past and Chopi's insistence on keeping up the friendship with him. Day after day Mami, Chopi and I talked, trying to reason out the situation and when it did not work we yelled at each other, then cried, and cried. After two, three hours of this Yano would come and pick me up, the three of us totally drained, absolutely exhausted physically and emotionally. Hans lay above us like a big bad cloud.

Poor Mami. She wasn't going to lose her youngest daughter to anyone. Not even if it cost her and her daughter's happiness. No way was she going to support this relationship with this terrible man who, besides his dirty past, was almost old enough to be Mami's partner.

Chopi told Hans what was happening, and he wasn't going to take the insult without hitting back.

'Your mother asked me for money,' he told a stunned Chopi.

'But it couldn't be. She wouldn't do a thing like that.'

'Well, she did. She was crying on my shoulder about not having enough money and, even though she did not spell it out that she wanted me to help, she was leading up to it.'

'Hans told me that you asked him for money!' Chopi confronted Mami.

Mami sucked the air through her clenched teeth in outrage. 'That's not true! The liar!'

Mami developed health problems. 'Nerves,' said the GP and prescribed her Valium. 'She needs to avoid stress and needs to calm down,' he told us. Mami was losing a lot of weight.

'Chopi is going to be the death of me. Now I have heart palpitations because of her. The other day I almost fainted, had to lie down in the middle of the day,' she told me on the phone at work. 'What can I do? What can I do?' she cried into the receiver.

'I don't know Mami. Perhaps we should wait and see what will happen. I really don't know. Perhaps it is the way Chopi sees it. Anyway I can't discuss it now, I have things to do. We'll talk about it when we get to your place after work.'

'The way *she* sees it? Are you against me too? She is so naive; she has no idea. That vagabond, that drunken vagabond.' And she hung up.

Wherever Mami went, whoever she met, they all talked about Hans. Was it true that Chopi was going out with him? They all knew him. 'Hans is no good for Chopi, Marta.'

Yano thought that my mother was an hysterical old woman but Chopi should take notice of Yanibachi, and he did not want to see Hans any more. Yano had enough problems of his own.

'Chopi, perhaps Yanibachi is right, perhaps …'

'Listen Yenachka! Perhaps, perhaps, perhaps. I will find out for myself. You remember when I told you there was nothing in this relationship? Well, things have changed. Mami achieved one thing with her attitude. She tossed me right into Hans's arms. So, now I am in love with Hans.'

Hans, a man who had run away from home at fourteen and never experienced a close family life, not understanding the emotional ties of our family, felt that now, being in a relationship with Chopi, he had the right to express his opinion and say his bit.

What kind of a mother was she to Chopi? Chopi was thirty years old and could do what she wanted. Hans never heard of anyone of that age obeying an old hysterical woman who was only after her daughter's money. She was reliant on Chopi's wage. Besides, Chopi should look for a better paid position. A university degree in Chemistry and look what she was doing! A laboratory assistant. She should earn much more than she does. And that was not all. Chopi's mother didn't know how to look after Roman. He was spoiled and will grow up like a little sissy. Just look at him the way he was dressed, like a toy kid. He was already four, he should run around with boys, not walk hand in hand with an old woman. And he should be speaking English not Hungarian. What was that language good for? No one spoke it here. How did Chopi expect him to do well at school?

The arguments and the heartaches kept coming and Hans's cloud kept spreading wider and heavier.

As days passed Chopi started to see the situation through Hans's eyes. True. She was thirty; Mami had no say in her life. She didn't need Mami to look after Roman and, yes, she would apply for the position of laboratory analyst at the Chemistry Department of the technical college, which was advertised last Saturday in *The Mercury*.

Amid all this a letter arrived from Košice. Inside the envelope was a single folded sheet with a thick black border. Below a large cross printed in black ink:

Gizella PELKOVA, nee Dolyakova
passed away after many month of sickness
on the 5th day of April 1972
May your soul rest in peace.
The mourning family.

Omama had died.

I found Mami sitting in the armchair with red eyes, tears flowing uncontrolled; her shaky hand holding the announcement.

'My mother is dead,' she repeated in disbelief.

All I could do was kneel down to Mami, hold her hand and cry with her.

In letters that followed it was explained that Omama had never really recovered from her sickness, a combination of old age and various other complaints. Since we left the country she had talked about her great-grandchildren all the time and cried.

Omama's destiny was one of loss. I recalled the death of her best loved young brother, as a political prisoner in the early 1950s, and years later when her disabled son, my uncle Dyoszibachi, died suddenly from a stroke in his fifties. She cried inconsolably then too, for years, visiting the cemetery every weekend. Each time someone she loved passed on or moved away they would take a chunk of Omama's heart with them, until she had nothing left. The last was the loss of her much-loved great-grandchildren, and I was the one who took them away from her. From my Omama, who I adored.

Yet above the heavy clouds the sun had risen every morning. It made me take a deep breath and turn the focus onto my life and my family.

Ishtvan and Zsuzsi were attending Clarence High School. Zsuzsi's schoolmates teasingly called her a *true blue* because of her foreign surname, her accent and not-yet-good English. Ishtvan, who played soccer, was called *Jezza* after the then well-known footballer Jesaulenko. His nickname stuck.

The school bus picked the children up every morning and brought them home in the afternoon.

Zsuzsi became friendly with a girl from her class, Cheryl. On some weekends she would invite Zsuzsi to her home for a sleepover.

Cheryl's parents were Australians, warm and kind people of Yano's and my age, with a keen interest and curiosity about other cultures. Picking Zsuzsi up from their place we got to know them.

'Would you like to come for a Sunday breakfast?' they asked us.

That morning Fiona treated us to piping hot scones with cream and jam. I looked around the spacious, sunny and modern loungeroom. *What a treat!* I thought.

'… and what is your work Bruce?'

'I am an engineer.'

'A-a-a-ah! Yano is an engineer too, but here in Australia they don't recognise his university studies.'

'Not that kind of an engineer,' Bruce smiled. 'Not an engineer by title but by position.'

'Can you be an engineer by position without the university degree?'

'Of course you can; you start from the bottom and work your way up.'

'But what about the knowledge?'

'O-o-oh! It comes with the practice.'

I thought of a lady I had met socially. Her sixteen-year-old daughter had finished her education in the tenth grade.

'It's best if Mary looks for a job in administration while she is young,' the lady said. 'Every employer wants young, trainable people. Once you are twenty it's too late.' I observed this trend since we had arrived in Tasmania. Very few people I met had their matriculation or a uni degree, even though they were in executive positions. This was in direct contrast with the tendency in my native country, where matriculation was considered a basic education. I was taught to establish a base of self-worth through my achievements. Education provided experience to fall back on socially, physically and academically. It was designed to create a mechanism through knowledge, which would, hopefully, help to survive all circumstances in life. I had first-hand experience of that by working as a laboratory analyst without the knowledge of the English language to start with, because chemistry was one of my matriculation subjects and chemistry was international. *Come to think of it, I hated chemistry in my school years!* Ishtvan and Zsuzsi were going to get properly educated, I promised myself.

A friendship developed between the Barrets and us. Bruce and Fiona would regularly call in on early Sunday mornings for a cup of coffee on their way home from the Lauderdale tip.

❦❦❦

'It's only eight o'clock, sorry, Yano is still in the shower.' I try for an excuse after opening the back laundry door, which they use regularly instead of the front entrance.

'Don't worry, we'll wait. This is also an Australian custom.' Bruce smiles and places his large and tall body, covered by a sloppy jumper with several holes showing his white singlet, into our colonial chair, stretching out his legs in front of him, clear of the table. He obviously is at ease in our small dining corner, where the long, red homespun wall-hanging, Svetya's present, is fastened by small rings onto the back wall. Above it spaced out are four hand-painted plates with Hungarian motifs. The tall antique coat stand behind him, bought at a secondhand shop for five dollars and with Yano's skills repainted, is turned into a display of various Hungarian pottery and memorabilia. Fiona takes her seat on a colourful homespun cushion resting on the old chest, another good purchase from the secondhand shop, supporting her back against the red wall-hanging.

'The flowers look nice,' she comments pointing to the two macramé hangers on each side of the curtain rod, each containing pots of African violets.

Like an umbrella, their friendship stretches also over Mami and Chopi. During the turbulent, argumentative months about Hans, Fiona has Mami over for weekends, driving her here and there and treating her as if she were her mother, a member of her family. Upright and proud to be Australian, they do their best to introduce us to their way of life, while comparing it with ours. And, by some miracle these two very different cultures never clash, in fact they complement each other.

There was another loyal Aussie who kept visiting during the weekends. Allan from Lenah Valley retained his friendship with Ishtvan and Zsuzsi. He came by bus, with a shy smile, his sandy-coloured hair combed wet and tidy, his long limbs hanging at his side awkwardly, said his hello and spent the day with Ishtvan and Zsuzsi kicking the ball, walking Zsofia around the suburb or going down to the Rokeby beach, climbing fences through the paddocks.

At the end of summer the nights got cooler and I shopped for doonas. 'No such thing. What are they?' they asked at Fitzgeralds and Myer. I explained. They had only eiderdowns, kind of comforters, with polyester covers, a throwover on the bed. Sorry.

I looked at the merchandise. The colours were nice. *That will do, anything is better than those blankets*. I bought four, one for each of us. Mami once again became handy with her sewing. She made the white covers with a large oval cut-out in the middle, which she hemmed around with lace, to show the colour of the eiderdown. *A little thinner than the doona but with an electric blanket it will be sufficient,* I thought, contented.

❦❦❦

It's a beautiful evening. The sun has already set but the light lingers, shimmering in the air. We are sitting in the loungeroom after our evening meal. Through the window the breeze ruffles the curtains. *How unusual, it's still light even though the sun set a while ago,* I think. The pink light is penetrating the net curtains, colouring everything in the room with a pink tinge. Yano walks to the window.

'Come here Yena. Look at the sky.'

I get up and stand next to him. The sky is moving!

'They are not clouds are they?'

'No, they are not clouds,' Yano agrees.

Through the window we see people standing in front of their houses, watching the sky. Dave, our next-door neighbour, is there too. I like Dave; he works at the waterfront as a labourer. Sometimes he is called in at two in the morning to unload a ship. He likes his beer and at various occasions he would come over carrying a bottle to share with Yano. Dave is a devoted father. Many times we see him kicking the ball with his kids in his backyard. Last month he lost his driver's licence because he was caught driving with a high alcohol content in his blood. After considering his working hours the court has left him with a licence that allows him to drive to work and back. But a man with a family of three children has to go to the supermarket, especially when his wife does not drive. Dave is a resourceful man; he purchases a long blond wig and wears it when he has to drive outside forbidden hours. Now he is standing in front of his gate, shading his eyes, looking up at the shimmer.

The sky is still moving and as the evening descends it gives a dark background to this fantastic palette of green, pink and gold, the colours moving together in the vast expanse. *It's the end of the world,*

I think and with a pounding heart a panic sets in. In my mind there is no explanation. There is not one experience in my life that would come even close to this one. *It's the end of the world,* I repeat to myself and settle to make peace with the inevitable.

'Beautiful isn't it?' Dave calls over the fence. 'You can see it now and then in Tasmania but this is the best I have seen in my lifetime.'

'What is it?' I dare to ask.

'Aurora Australis.'

I look up to the sky again, standing motionless and staring at the colours. It feels as if the sky was still but I am travelling in space very, very fast. Absolute magic. Only then, reassured, do I start to enjoy the spectacle.

❦❦❦

The Department of Immigration wrote that we could ask for Australian citizenship if we could speak, write and read reasonable English. They also explained that when we became Australian citizens we would have duties towards our new country but it would also protect us and give us rights.

It had been almost three years that we had belonged to no country. Australia was good to us. We considered it to be our home. The time had come to make a commitment.

'So, what do we have to do to become citizens?' I asked in the Department of Immigration at the Commonwealth Bank building in Elizabeth Street.

Here are the forms, four lots, one for each of you. When you fill them in we can make a separate appointment for every person to sit the English test.

'How does it work? What is *reasonable English*?' I asked Nana.

Nothing to it. Her department conducted citizenship tests daily. She couldn't remember one person who would have failed or was refused because of a lack of English. We will be all right, she said.

The forms were filled in, the appropriate document was translated and attached to the forms and the appointments made separately for each of us.

When my turn came I walked into the warm vestibule of the bank, to the counter of the Immigration Department and explained what I was there for.

'My name is Mr Cooper, I was expecting you,' said a short friendly man who shook my hand. 'Come into my office.'

I found myself in a bright cubicle and was seated behind a desk.

'Here,' he said. 'Read this article from the newspaper,' and he handed over *The Mercury*.

With a trembling index finger I followed the lines and to the best of my knowledge read out the small letters.

'That will do,' Mr Cooper said.

'Good?' I asked nervously.

'Very good,' he smiled, shook my hand again and walked me through the door to the large vestibule, which at every visit to the bank created in me a feeling of awe and respect.

We all passed the test, Yano, Chopi, Mami and I.

The naturalisation ceremony for Mami and Chopi was conducted in the city. For Yano and me, because we lived on the Eastern Shore, it happened in the Bellerive Library.

It is a cold Tuesday afternoon, 23 July 1972. I keep fussing about Zsuzsi's dress, Ishtvan's hair, his tie, and my blouse, several times confronting the mirror for assurance that I look all right on this very special day, until Yano puts an end to it.

'C'mon Yena, it's time. We have to go.'

There are a few of us. Among those present are two more Czechoslovakian families, one being the family of my schoolmate from Košice. None of us would have believed when wearing the corn-blue shirt of the Union of the Czechoslovakian Youth back in our student years that one day the two of us, on a small island called Tasmania, with trembling voices and in unison, would recite our allegiance to the English Crown and its Queen, all in the English language.

I, Eugenia Milosh, swear my allegiance to Her Majesty Queen Elizabeth the Second, her heirs and successors, and swear that I will observe faithfully the laws of Australia and fulfil my duties as an Australian citizen, become entitled to all political and other rights, powers and privileges, and become subject to all obligations, duties and liabilities to which an Australian citizen is entitled or subject, and have to all intents and purposes the status of an Australia citizen.

Handshakes and well wishes from the chairman of the Clarence Council and other officials whose identity I have no idea about. An exchange of awkward smiles with our countrymen leaves me with confused feelings. *So, from this moment on we are Australians,* I think. Now we belong to a great and prosperous western country, which places its values on individualism and self-survival. The culture of my native country grew out of an agricultural society. In its not-too-distant past individuals were not able to survive on their own, relying on the collectiveness, mutual solidarity and obligations, creating bonds, quality interaction within their community and concerns about their disadvantages.

Have I sold my soul? Have I sold the souls of my children and their children? They will grow up not remembering or knowing the sounds of the everyday life, the smell of food, in their native country. Their children, my grandchildren will never know about the traditions, the songs that were created about life as a repository of history, carrying it from generation to generation. They will belong to this country, to me still a very unfamiliar country, and as its citizens they will adopt new values and will help shape its future. *As for me,* I think to myself, *I can't denounce my geographical nativity but I am free to choose the country where I want to belong.* We all have the right to a secure life; our intentions are honest and solid.

I sigh and look around the hall that is almost deprived of furniture, with the shiny bare floorboards and the picture of the Queen on the wall. All is unfamiliar. *One feels more at home where one's spirit is,* I think to myself.

A photographic crew gets hold of us.

Stand over there please. Yes, this is good. and you young man, just behind the young lady, and you sir, right at the back. Good. Now could you just hold that paper in your hand and all of you look at it as if you are reading? This is great. Click. One more, stand still, click, click.

Three years after our arrival we become citizens of Australia and have a country to belong to.

Arriving home from the ceremony the phone rings.

'Congratulations. This calls for a celebration.' Bruce's voice sounds cheerful. 'We'll come over.'

The bottle of champagne and a beautifully illustrated book of Tasmania are placed on the table.

'For you to remember this very special day. Where are the glasses?'

The next morning the Milosh family was plastered over the front page of *The Mercury*. The picture was titled 'Eight take oath'. 'Two Clarence High School students watched the naturalisation ceremony with unusual interest ...'

Two days later another letter came through the mail addressed to Miss Susan Milosh, with a copy of the photo from *The Mercury* 'as a memento of a very special occasion. With warmest regards and our congratulations to your parents'.

A warm, fuzzy feeling spread inside us all. The long-lost and much-desired feeling of belonging was slowly creeping back into our lives. People around us cared, we were not only numbers in statistics. We were Australian citizens.

CHAPTER EIGHT

Finding Purpose

Mrs Helpern, Yano's teacher, took a liking to our family and kept in touch after he graduated from the English crash course. She thought that Yano had learned English very well and it was time for him to look for a position suitable for his education.

Influenced by his own thoughts and her encouragement, Yano applied for a position advertised in the Saturday *Mercury*, that of a draughtsman at the manufacturing firm called Stanley. His application was successful and this provided him with much-needed self-esteem. Yano barely had time to settle in his new job when the workers of the company went out on strike.

'I am not going to work tomorrow,' Yano said that evening. 'The workers want higher wages.'

What will happen now? Will you get your pay anyway? No, Yano did not think so, but we will manage, it was only for a day.

The day after the strike he went back to work. The union demands were met, wage rises granted. The new wages took their toll though. Before long some employees were sacked, Yano among them. Last hired, first sacked. Some colleagues tried to drag Yano's self-confidence up from the dumps.

The hard times hit emotionally and financially and the happy days of our contented life were slowly sliding away.

Yano wasn't entitled to unemployment benefits because of my wages. Very low wages. But, no matter how hard he tried, he could not get a job. For a couple of weeks he lived in denial about the fact that he was unemployed. He got up early in the morning, had his shower and started working around the house. He dug the garden, polished the car, paved part of the backyard, built a bookshelf in the loungeroom, as well as the much-needed fence for Zsofia, who we often looked for all around the neighbourhood on our return from work. With the fenced backyard she had a large and safe area to run around in. Zsofia was the fifth member of our family. I still can see her circling the clothesline in a mad whirl when our car pulled up in the drive. Then she would find a leaf or a twig, carry it to the paling fence and with her front legs marching rapidly on the spot she would try to fit it into our outstretched hands. Before going into the house our first stop was always the backyard and Zsofia.

In our minds unemployment was for people without a trade or education, or for the ones who did not want to work. Yano was never unemployed before and we both found it hard to live with the stigma. This time Yanibachi or Nana could not help. Some people advised Yano not to take on *just any job*, the way they had done it – and look what kind of work they were stuck in now. 'You should wait until you find the job you want, otherwise you will be digging the streets,' they advised.

Yano read *The Mercury*'s employment column daily and one Saturday he found an advertisement he thought interesting. They wanted fruit pickers in the country, outside Hobart, in Woodbridge.

Yano thought about it, talked about it and slept on it. Then he decided and went fruit picking.

'Too far to drive back and forth,' he said and stayed there for five days, returning home for the weekend.

Yano surprised us and himself. He loved his fruit-picking job. The fresh air and stress-free life suited him well. He met international students, slept on the bunks in the same barn as many others and had food in the local pub. He loved the outdoor life and talked with deep admiration about the beautiful valleys and hills of Woodbridge. On the weekends I welcomed a deeply tanned, happier and more relaxed Yano, no comparison to the thin, pale man with the dark stare. In years to come he often said that those were the good days.

The biggest problem though was the money. The two low wages barely covered the expenses of our family.

Mrs Helpern called in one evening.

'So, how are you?' she enquired. 'How's Yano's new work?'

'Not the best right now, Yano lost his draughtsman's job and is fruit picking in Woodbridge. It is very low paid labour. Most of the money is going towards the petrol and his upkeep, because he lives away from the family.'

'Wait a second! He is a very knowledgeable young man and his English is good too. The government is in an election year; this is the time when you earbash your local MP and ask him for the impossible.' She would look into the possibility of Yano's employment as a public servant.

'Leave it with me,' she smiled, 'and don't worry too much.'

A-a-ah! So those kind of interventions existed not only in socialism but also in capitalism? I was told otherwise by Yanibachi.

'You are not in Košice. In Australia you don't have to push and shove,' he said, a little annoyed seeing me intervening for a faster outcome in a number of instances. 'They know about your case; when your turn comes you will be seen to.'

Obviously even in Australia one had to count the human element. In my experience people were all the same anywhere in the world.

Many silent weeks followed, filled with anxiety. Day by day I caught the bus to the city, from there another bus to Baker's Milk and after work the two buses back home, carrying bags of groceries.

Again and again I railed about the distance of our, to me, very beautiful home, to the city and to my workplace. Again and again I railed against the loneliness of the Housing Department estate and suburbia. I bitterly missed the friendship and closeness of neighbours in the grey, prefabricated blocks of flats of my native country. I missed Svetya's calls under my window on Saturday mornings: *Yena, you want to come to the market?* The knock and the head of a friendly neighbour in the half-open door and the *Wouldn't mind a cup of coffee* greetings. This was seemingly impossible in the new three-bedroom houses separated from each other by immaculately mowed lawns and fitted out with the latest washing machines and fridges. In my mind this kind of living was good only for the accumulation of goods but a definite deprivation of family and community ties. It wasn't giving anyone a higher standard of living, only more things around them. Why did people mistake money for a better way of life? In stead of calling in to see my family I had to make a phone call, an appointment to see them.

I thought of Lydia and Ivan, back in Košice, and about the moral and emotional support we had given to each other.

Lydia was a teacher and Ivan a university lecturer in chemistry. Their little girl, not quite one year old, was sick, dying of leukaemia. The bone-marrow transplants hadn't helped, her little body was rejecting them and she was deteriorating each week, spending most of her short life in hospitals and Lydia with her.

Through the thin wall dividing our kitchen from theirs we heard Lydia singing sad lullabies and witnessed the little girl's first word, Mum-m-m-a.

How difficult it was to see your child developing mentally, giving you the joy of her first words but deteriorating physically? How can parents live with the knowledge that their child would not live to see their first Christmas? How hard was it to live with heartache like that?

Each week the hospital stays had become a little longer, till one night on the other side of the kitchen wall we had heard a heartbreaking cry.

I knocked on their entrance door. Ivan's eyes were red from crying. There was no need for explanation. We all cried. Lydia's head against my shoulder now and then shaking in fits. Ivan also needed a shoulder to cry on; he came over to talk to Yano. After an hour, when Lydia and I walked into our flat we saw Yano and Ivan sitting at the kitchen table, in front of each man a small glass of rum. Ivan's head cupped in his hands, he talked absently, almost in a whisper.

'People don't understand how I could laugh at work. They thought I wasn't sad enough. What would they know? How would they know how sad I was?'

The only car we possessed between the seven of us was with Yano, parked in Woodbridge.

From the whole lot of us Yano was the one who was most contented, and with good reason. The daily family duties, the ever-present family bickering, my lamentations about the relationship between Chopi, Mami and Hans became a distant memory for Yano.

There was no money for luxuries. Because we had no telephone I couldn't take part in Mami and Chopi's daily life and heard the one-sided, rebellious version about their arguments from Chopi at work.

But, despite all that, the sun shone, moved across the sky effortlessly, set behind Mount Wellington, and on its way it warmed the dining corner of our kitchen through the large windows. Then the orange disc was replaced by a bright moon, making the summer nights silvery blue, transparent, almost unreal, until the thin strip of the bay visible from our bedroom window coloured bright red once again from the waking sun, and the days went by.

Since my last meeting with Mrs Helpern I counted those days impatiently and when I couldn't stretch my patience any longer I trotted down to the phone box on the main road and dialled her number. Is there anything new? Did she talk to any politician?

No news yet, but do I have any documents about Yano's education? Are they translated into English? Yes they are. Okay then. She knows about a position for a draughtsman in the Department of Building and Construction. She will approach the local MP tomorrow. Yano is a very capable man, and he deserves a better job than what he is doing.

'Give me a couple of days and then ring me again.' I heard the smile in her voice.

When I rang Mrs Helpern again she said that yes she had talked to the local MP and he thought it was possible for him to help Yano to get that position.

I excitedly threw my arms around Yano's neck on his return from Woodbridge and told him the news. He might be a public servant, a draughtsman shortly. But Yano wasn't all that pleased. 'Just calm down for God's sake,' he said. He didn't mind fruit picking for a while longer and why am I bothering other people with our problems? But okay, if Mrs Helpern could help he will go along with the whole thing. Of course I will have to take care of the lot, take a day off from work and see to Yano's documents and whatever else is necessary because he had to go back to Woodbridge, they were counting on him.

I have never had a problem talking to people in authority, not even then, when I knew that my English was far from perfect. As a rule throughout my life I made sure that I always talked to the person who was in charge. Regarding Yano's employment as a public servant he needed to prove that his education prior to arriving in Australia was on the level required for the job of a draughtsman. At work I asked for a day off and made an appointment with the head of the Hobart Technical College.

The first impression counts, I think to myself, and, acting on my experience from Europe, I take great care with my dressing. *Perhaps I will wear the black tight miniskirt.* Satisfied with the result I catch the Rokeby bus to the city, walk to the college, up the stone stairs to the first floor and knock on the dark-brown door. The principal is a tall middle-aged man wearing glasses. 'How can I help?'

'I need in writing that my husband's matriculation and four semesters of university are on a level with the Hobart Technical College education.' *On a level with this school?* I think to myself. *A technical college? Yano has a university education.* 'Here are the reports about his university studies, all translated into English and here are the original documents.'

Yes, he can look into it but it will take a little time, perhaps a week.

A week? I think and tilt my head looking at him sidewise with the biggest eyes I can master. 'But I need it this afternoon, you see my husband …' I explain the situation.

The head of the college is a kind man; he doesn't even let me finish my long speech. He measures me from the tip of my toes up to the highly piled dark hair with his glassed stare and he says, 'Okay. Come back after lunch, about two o'clock.' He smiles. 'I will see what I can do.'

Too far to travel to Baker's Milk. I decide to wait out the lunchtime in the city. I walk into the newspaper shop in Liverpool Street, buy myself an astrology magazine, cross the road to the corner milk bar, order a salad and impatiently turn the pages to 'Your love life, business and health'. *This is going to be a good year.*

With a smile on my face I turn up after lunch in front of the shiny dark-brown door on the first floor of the college.

'I have had a meeting about your husband with the representative from the Department of Technical Engineering at the University of Tasmania. We think your husband's education is adequate for the job of technical draughtsman,' he says. 'The documentation is very good. Would you like a cup of coffee?'

'Oh, no thank you, I just had one.'

'Well then, here is the letter of recommendation.' He shakes my hand with a smile.

Thank you. Thank you very much, sir. Thank you very much.

Yano became a public servant, a technical draughtsman at the

Department of Building and Construction with the state government. His office on the eleventh floor in Murray Street overlooked the whole dock area of Hobart and the Derwent River, where it met up with the blue sea.

In later years Mrs Helpern moved with her family to the mainland and we lost touch with, but never my gratitude to, this great lady.

Hungary, as many other European countries, had its fair share of fights for freedom during the thousand years of its existence. March 15 is still celebrated as a Hungarian National Day, related to the 1848 war of independence from the suppression of the Habsburg monarchy. The second, more recent, day of national importance is 26 October 1956, the day of the Hungarian uprising against the occupation of the USSR.

This uprising was the reason why most Hungarians present at the solemn service on that day in 1972 were congregating around the cenotaph on the Domain in Hobart instead of in Parliament Square in Budapest. As any respectable club would have it, after the ceremony the members met in a hired hall, where they reminisced with lots of friendly back slapping, handshakes and tears, and sung in harmony familiar melancholic melodies while consuming large quantities of homemade cakes, washed down with many glasses of wine.

In those years the Hungarian Club of Hobart existed, but only just. Once a year they organised a picnic, where they would cook up huge pots of goulash; some would even turn up with a gramophone and old Hungarian folk and Gypsy LPs, and while the wine flowed the annual financial report about the club's finances would be read out. 'This is it then, for another year.'

There was a nucleus of ambitious members who did not mind working hard, had the will and the necessary skills to shake off the dust of complacency.

One weekend a red Holden pulled into our drive and Piri, one of those energetic members, stepped out from the driver's seat.

'We are thinking of establishing a Hungarian Dance Group,' she said confidently. Would Ishtvan and Zsuzsi be interested? Piri had a whole heap of Hungarian folksongs, her mother knew the steps, her husband played the harmonica and Latzi could play the violin.

What a great idea! I thought. Yano went along with it and Zsuzsi, by now a teenager, did not mind being part of the group.

The Saturday-night dinner-dances in Hobart's Polish Hall served as fundraising venues. The Polish Hall and the dinner-dances, which were organised there by various ethnic groups, were a popular part of Hobart's social scene and were patronised by a wide group of migrants and Australians, as well as by politicians. They were truly multinational get-togethers. There the tunes of well-known melodies from a variety of nations were played by the live band, consisting of German, Hungarian and Yugoslav musicians, and were danced and sung to in unison by members of all nationalities.

Suddenly Yano, Mami, the children, Yanibachi, Hedineni, Nana and I found ourselves in a social whirl of regular Saturday-night dinner-dances with a real purpose.

On one of those nights, with the sounds of the accordion and drums spilling into the entrance hall, I met George and his wife.

'How nice to see you George. Are you still working in the Town House restaurant?'

'No-ho-ho-ho,' laughed George. 'Meet my wife Pauline, we have just come back from Hungary a couple days ago.' He pointed to an elegantly dressed, tall and slim brunette with a short fashionable haircut.

'How did you like it?' I asked the attractive Pauline.

'It was all right.' She smiled, not giving much away, straightened her belt and looked up to George.

I did not realise then that I had just met my first close friend in Australia. Pauline and George's daughter, as well as her two boys, George Junior and Stephen, also joined the dance group. This was a good enough reason for Ishtvan to join in. Yano and George found in their repertoire many Hungarian folksongs to sing out loud together and also shared their mutual liking of a good wine. So, we got involved with each other, our family with Pauline and George, then with their social circle, then the whole lot of us with the Hungarian Club.

'Come and have a barbecue with us,' invites Maggie, a childhood friend of Pauline, who we had met recently.

'They bought a large building block in Sandy Bay,' Pauline says with a meaningful smile.

'What's so special about Sandy Bay?'

'It's the suburb of rich people,' Pauline explains, coming down to my level of understanding.

Yano drives us, following George's car. It feels a long way from the city. The block stretches from the road down to the beach hemming the mouth of the river. At the far end of the block is a great big bonfire circled by many people we don't know. Halfway up from the beach is their house. A house? *More of a shack,* I think.

'C'mon I will show you around,' Maggie tells us and we all follow her up the steep block.

This house is worse than our Darcy Street home used to be, I think. An old, dark and cold wooden structure. *That poor woman, Maggie, she has to live in this, this …* With a feeling of sympathy for her I think of my beautiful new house with its clean walls and sunny kitchen and I can't understand Maggie's enthusiasm.

Later Pauline tells me that they will demolish the house to build a new one. *I would,* I think to myself, and it makes me feel a little better about Maggie. But of course it will happen only after their return from New Guinea, Pauline says. What are they doing in New Guinea? I thought she was an Australian. Yes, of course, but many Australians work in New Guinea; you see they don't have to pay taxes there. *Is New Guinea part of Australia?*

Yanibachi reached retirement age with Telecom, where he had worked for the last ten years. With the retirement money came the fulfilment of his dream. For the first time, after twenty-five years in Australia he could visit the place he carried deep in his heart, the city where he was born and grew up. Yanibachi and Hedineni left on the *Marco Polo*, an Italian liner, for the three-month trip around the world. Our mailbox kept filling up with postcards from Acapulco, Florida, Germany, Hungary, Czechoslovakia and Spain, the country he fell in love with during the few months he spent there in his younger years.

A staunch anti-communist and an outspoken person, Yanibachi had much to criticise in Czechoslovakia and Hungary, the way he saw the country and the political situation, and had many disagreements with almost everyone he came in contact with. On his return he reported to us about those with a passionate fever.

'Bloody communists. The things they have done to my country. I understand now. You have done the right thing to bring your family to Australia, Yano.' He patted Yano approvingly on the back.

On their return Nana organised a small welcoming party. In her cosy, sunny sitting room the deep, comfortable armchairs were spaced out in the corners. There Hedineni pressed into my palm Omama's earrings.

Omama had always worn them. I was told about their value: one large diamond and a smaller one in each, set in white gold and platinum. *One day, when I die they will be yours,* Omama used to say. *Oh, Omama,* I protested then.

'Omama wanted you to have them. It was her last wish on her death bed,' Hedineni said. 'When Yolineni, Omama's younger sister, visited the hospital, Omama pointed to her earrings. 'Those are Yenni's, remember Yolan. They were always hers.' She made Opapa promise to get those earrings to you somehow.' Hedineni held my hand clutching the earrings in her palm. 'Look after them Yenni.'

As if someone had grabbed my heart and squeezed, my eyes filled with tears. It hurt to hear of Omama's last days. I wear those earrings at all important occasions but not a day goes by without me thinking of Omama, not one day for all these years.

Opapa, even though he was still alive, sent over his thick gold ring. He wanted Ishtvan to have it. Mami received Omama's gold wristwatch and Chopi some other jewellery.

In 1973, at work, I was given another book of two hundred pages to learn. In June of that year I attended the exams again in Launceston. This time it was to get my Milk Testing and Grading Certificate. By then my English had improved and I had a blueprint of how to learn the English text well enough to pass the exams. It was a repeat from 1971 but with less trauma. I felt almost at home; I knew Launceston, the hotel, the hotel manager and his wife. I knew Michael's way of teaching and his way of driving from Launceston to Hobart, this time in a VW hatchback.

The only new thing was a visit from our new Australian friend at my hotel room one evening.

'John! What are you doing here?' I exclaim, glad to see Yano's friend when I answer the door.

He is on business in Launceston. Would I like to join him for dinner? Of course I would, gladly. How lovely of him. We dine in a good restaurant, plenty of good food and laughs. Have another glass of wine Jenny, John encourages me. I do. It's lovely. Another one? No, no thank you.

He walks me up to the second floor of the hotel, straight to the door, and then behind me walks into the room.

But what is happening? His hand encircles my waist and his face gets close to mine, brushing my cheek. I smell the pleasant mixture of alcohol, tobacco and aftershave.

'No. No. No,' I object, and think to myself, *and he is Yano's friend?*

'Why? No one is going to know.' He is still very close. His head with tight golden curls bent above my face, his grip around my waist.

'No thank you,' I say as politely as I can and my palms flat against his chest I am trying to apply a gentle pressure.

'It's either you absolutely hate men or I am the ugliest bloke around.' His grip eases, the smile disappears from his face.

'No. You are not ugly, only I ...' What can I say? I don't want him. His hands drop to his side; now he towers above me a head higher, looking intensely into my eyes. For a while I look back but then I feel intimidated so I lower my stare. He turns towards the door and walks out of the room mumbling goodnight.

'There my girl, here is your certificate. Congratulations.' Mr Baker smiles and taps me on the shoulder.

As a holder of two certificates issued by the Tasmanian Department of Agriculture , I became a laboratory analyst and was very, very proud of my knowledge of English and, of course, of my accomplishment.

... *I am so proud of myself Svetya. I have just passed my second exams in milk and cream testing, all in English, and achieved the title of a 'Laboratory Analyst'. Sounds good? I had to travel again to Launceston, a city in the north of Tasmania. I really like it there, even though the city is smaller than Hobart. There are lots of specialised boutique kinds of shops and it has a different atmosphere to Hobart.*

Of course it wasn't anything like the schooling seminars we used to have in the High Tatras. To begin with, I did not know anybody in the class; they came from all over Tasmania. You see I look, walk and try to eat like Australians and am all right while my mouth is shut. But one has to talk. In the end everyone was very helpful.

I just found out something interesting. Do you remember that time when we bumped into an English-speaking film crew in the foyer of our hotel in the High Tatras? I can still see those model-like girls in the ski gear we could only dream about and in the midst of all that fashion the good-looking and quite arrogant hero, Tony Sponar. Do you remember how I gave him my last 100 korunas to autograph it because I had no other paper on me and how I had to cash it in to buy the train ticket, because I spent the rest of my money? I always thought of him as an American skier.

Well, I tell you what, Tony was a big impostor pretending that he could speak only English, because in fact he was a Czech skier who won an Olympic Medal in 1948 then emigrated to Australia, where he worked on the so-called Snowy Mountains Hydro Scheme and later helped to build and develop a ski resort in the Australian Alps called Thredbo. Actually, when we saw him in the High Tatras he was making a commercial for that place. If I had known I wouldn't have been so upset for having to cash in the hundred korunas with his autograph …

The winter passed. At the beginning of September the gardens looked lush after the winter rains. The huge rhododendrons paraded in light pink, red and dark mauve under the yellow pompom-like flowers of Australian wattle trees, stretching above the footpaths like a golden umbrella. The spring had just started and with it the winds that arrived inevitably every year.

'We'll meet you at the Prince of Wales at five thirty,' Yano phones.

With a feeling of satisfaction I walk from the writing desk to the other side of the lab, to the bench covered with small samples of milk and cream. It has been too long for Yano, not knowing the people he is working with intimately, not knowing the rules of etiquette, not belonging to anyone or anything. Perhaps the ice is finally broken now that he is employed as a draughtsman in the public service. Perhaps the people he works with now see him as a person, past his foreign accent and his not-quite-perfect English. He deserves an afternoon in the pub with the men.

At four thirty I hang up my lab coat, call out *See-ya* (the saying I copy but still hadn't figured out) and walk up to Lenah Valley bus stop just in time to see the state Minister for Immigration, Mr Miller, bicycling past in his pinstriped suit and a tie. He knows me from the Hungarian dances in the Polish Hall.

'Wanna lift?' He smiles and cycles on.

Just how close are the politicians to ordinary people in Tasmania? I wonder with gratitude for his friendliness and recognition.

Following Yano's directions, I walk to Battery Point and stop in front of the large square building with the pompous name. That's the one! The sign above the door says Public Bar. I poke my fingers into my hair to tidy it up and push the door.

Even though the sun is streaming into the room, the lights are on. The haze of dust and smoke in the shaft of sunlight stretches between the windows and the bar. The saturated smell of cigarettes and beer hovers above the heads like a blanket. A few men are elbowing the towelling runner that lies on top of the bar loaded with glasses of beer at assorted levels. Some men are sitting at the tables near the walls. The room is filled with a mix of country and western and the murmur of conversation. In that second when the door closes behind me the sounds cease to exist, the heads turn towards the door, eyes pinned on me; only the music plays on.

'Excuse me please, my husband …' I start, and stop, looking for the words in my limited English vocabulary.

'You are not allowed in the bar.' The man behind the counter is annoyed.

'Why?' And after a while, 'My husband told me to meet him.'

The man behind the bar looks around.

'Can you see your husband anywhere?'

'No.'

'You can't stay in here.'

'Why?'

Leaving his post he gets hold of my elbow and swings me towards the door.

'But my husband said to come here.' I dig my heals into the floor in defence.

'You are not allowed in the Public Bar, lady. You have to look for your husband somewhere else.' Then as an afterthought, 'Perhaps he is in the Saloon next door.' He opens the bar door and I find myself on the street.

Why can't I be in the bar? I think of the many involuntary afternoons spent in pubs of my native town during the first year of our marriage. I walk around the building again and come across a door with the sign Saloon.

There is a group of men sitting, conversing, Yano among them, to look at him, just like any other Australian man.

On the way home through the car window I see the mysterious Mount Wellington. Above it the sky is spectacular; dark blue with big smears of red, surrounded by silver-lined clouds.

Thank you God for the painter you have employed for tonight.

The questioning letters about our wellbeing in that faraway place called Australia and the underlining suspicion about the truth of our information kept coming from Yano's family, mainly from my mother-in-law.

'Yano, I think we should bring your Mami out here so she can see for herself that you are all right.'

'How can you be that stupid? Where would she get the money for the plane ticket do you think?'

'We will have to buy her the ticket then.'

'Do you have any idea how much a ticket would cost? We have no money to buy lampshades and you want to pay for a plane ticket? From Europe?'

Bit by bit, letter by letter, Yano realised that his mother was getting older. We both agreed she should not worry herself about the wellbeing of her son, it was only money anyway and we were doing all right now that he was employed by the government. What we can't afford to buy this year, we will buy the next. The government job was good and secure employment. 'Okay then,' Yano agreed.

I wrote the letter, Yano dictated.

Dear Anyuka. It would be great if you could spend Christmas with us this year in Tasmania. Yena and I would love to have you for, say, three months. We will cover the cost of your air ticket and the insurance …

More letters crossed the ocean. No, she doesn't think she would like to travel that far. And what would she do in Australia anyway? Well, she could see for herself that Yano and the family were okay, that he had a good job, that we have a nice house and how the children have grown. Tasmania is a very beautiful island, there is a lot to see here, we wrote back. After many persuasive letters she agreed. Could we please send an official 'invitation letter' signed by us in the presence of a Justice of the Peace, for the Czechoslovakian authorities?

Okay, Anyuka was coming. No new furniture, lampshades or carpet. Only a mattress will do, which will be spread under the window of our bedroom and made into a bed for Ishtvan. His bedroom will become Anyuka's room for the time she will be with us. We bought the plane tickets.

Yano started to look forward to his mother's visit. He was proud of his achievements and would show her how he had done up the garden and the yard, the wall unit he had made, which held all our books sent over by Pinki. She would be able to see for herself the way he dressed every morning in a clean shirt, jacket and tie to go to work and witness him driving his car. He wanted to show her the beauty of his new home, drive her up to Launceston and maybe, maybe a boat trip? For weeks he was planning the itinerary.

'What do you think Yena? She should like that, she worked hard all her life, never had a chance to enjoy herself. We'll give her a time to remember, introduce her to our friends, then she can put her mind and heart at rest.'

Amid all this Bruce told Yano about an auction of secondhand government cars. Yano should tender for one, Bruce thought. All the cars were in really good nick, most only a couple of years old, well looked after.

Yano tendered and shortly after the auction he drove home the new light aqua-coloured Kingswood sedan, while Bruce drove the old Vauxhall. What a car! What a beauty! Not a scratch anywhere inside or out. We circled around it a few times, inspecting the exterior to the smallest detail, then piled in for a short drive around the suburb. What a difference from our old car! Now we had two cars to show off to Anyuka.

Yano borrowed a movie camera to film the arrival of his mother for the rest of the family and as a memento of her visit to Australia.

CHAPTER NINE

The Clouds of Discontent

A warm November afternoon in 1973. My mother-in-law is taking the steps from the TAA plane in Hobart airport carefully, as she descends the steep stairs. One arm circled around a large crystal vase, in the other an overnight bag, she continues to move slowly on the cemented tarmac a little confused, covering the distance between the plane and the airport, looking for the familiar sight of her children. The almost silver hair is cut unskilfully short and is stuck to her skull. The coat she is wearing is the same she was wearing when we left Košice. To me she has barely changed, only she somehow looks more fragile. I feel sorry for her being so obviously lost between the hurrying crowd until she spots our small group with our hands lifted high, waving excitedly.

Then, after five years, the tired woman, with a relieved smile, gives her first hugs to her son and grandchildren.

The Kingswood arrives at Rokeby.

'… and this is our second car, and this is our new house, and this is … The house is not quite furnished yet but we have already the most important things for us to be comfortable, and this is our garden and this is Zsofia. What do you think Anyuka?'

'Very nice, very nice,' she keeps repeating.

'Look, I made roast pork, your favourite. We will have dinner in a short while.'

'No, no thank you, really, I would like to lie down. I feel very tired.'

❦❦❦

She slept the first night, half of the second day and the following day. In between sleeps she moved inside the house lethargically while she sorted out the presents.

'This vase is for you, Yenni, from Zita. And this is from Svetya.' She handed over a long, handwoven runner with a familiar peasant design. '... and, this is a cushion cover and a throwover for the table.' All very beautiful. What a thoughtful friend Svetya was.

'And what would Svetya like in return?'

'She wants you to send her some wigs. Two or three wigs.'

'What sort of wigs, what colour or style?'

'Svetya said that you would know what she likes.'

During his seven days' leave from work Yano waited for his mother to recover from her travel and begin to enjoy herself. It did not happen. It took only five days before Anyuka started showing signs of boredom and disinterest. Fiona and Bruce came to visit and, with their typical kindness, brought a small welcoming present for Anyuka. We tried to make conversation, translating as best we could.

'I would like to go to bed now. I can't understand a word you are saying.' She got up and left us sitting around the dining table.

Yano took her to his office on the eleventh floor on Murray Street, which overlooked the Derwent River and the shore. She was impressed, but: 'Can we go home now?'

'Be patient. We have to make an effort, she will come right eventually,' I said, when Yano, sitting at the table with his face buried in his hands, reported about their day.

'Perhaps. But in the meantime what can we talk about? She is not interested in anything. I think she is ready to go back home.

She thought that she would pop over to Australia, check us out and go back to tell her neighbours how well her son was,' Yano thought disappointedly. 'And all that for $2500.'

The distance between Yano and his mother grew even wider. Curiously, she became more attached to me.

Once again I found myself sandwiched between those two, defending my mother-in-law, while her son complained that it was my idea to bring her to Australia, and what for?

Yano organised a picnic to Mount Field National Park with another Czech family. 'She will be able to talk to them,' he said.

On that morning Anyuka moped around the house. 'No, no, I am happy to stay at home. I have seen what I wanted.'

Yano was angry.

'I don't like your mother all that much Yena, but I would take ten of her rather than one of mine. I am going to fetch Mami and will go to the picnic anyway. If Anyuka wants to stay at home, it's okay with me, she can stay at home alone.' He picked up the Esky prepared in the laundry, slammed the door, started up the car and left for the picnic with Mami and the Czech family to the national park.

'Anyuka! Tasmania is beautiful, there is much more we would like to show you,' I tried again. Would she like to see the sea? No. Not really. So what is she interested in? A-a-a-ah, well as she said, she has seen what she wanted to. She is only a simple woman; she likes washing up, ironing and things like that.

'Do you like cooking? That would help me while I am at work.'

She thought for a while. Sometimes she doesn't mind it but no, no cooking, only washing up. Gone are the plans of a boat trip and everything else.

The children did not take to Anyuka either. They were polite but never chatty or affectionate. Yano's holidays finished, he went back to work frustrated and I went back to work too.

'Leave me alone in the house, I will be all right,' she said, and spent her days in bed. This wasn't right. We decided to drive Anyuka to Mami every morning. The first days, while they talked about the experiences of the last few years, it was good but, 'What can I give her to eat?' Mami complained. 'She is a diabetic but doesn't know what she can eat.' As soon as we got home, Anyuka went off to bed.

'Are you all right?'

'I am, I am, but you know there is nobody to talk to here. Yano is not interested in talking to me and you are busy around the kitchen and the children. It's best if I get out of your way.' So, what would she like to eat? Well perhaps some ham or things like that. I bought ham. It was left to dry out in the fridge. Anyuka was losing weight.

I remembered Yano's sister Zita's remark back in Košice: 'You know,' she said, 'our Mami is like a good chicken soup without the salt and pepper, like something is missing but you can't figure out what.'

After the traditional Christmas celebrations we decided to hold New Year's Eve at our place for a few reasons. We had Anyuka, who wasn't interested in going anywhere, and the relationship between Mami and Chopi had deteriorated further. Those two barely talked to each other. Honza and Yanka, who had become frequent visitors since we moved to Rokeby, were also invited. This way there was no problem with the language; we all spoke Czechoslovakian.

The dining table in our kitchen is made up and decorated, the stove is covered in pots of traditional food and the fridge is full of cold meat, juices and wine. The Kingswood is back, with Mami, Chopi and Roman, from Stainforth Court.

Mami, wearing a dressing gown over her nightie, pale and sad faced, steps out of the car.

'I had to call the doctor this afternoon. I feel sick,' she sobs. 'All this because of that, that bastard Hans.' She squeezes her hand into a tight fist. 'That bastard has destroyed my life. And my idiotic daughter doesn't love me any more; she prefers him.' Mami's tears are flowing freely onto the concrete drive. She doesn't care that Anyuka, Honza and Yanka are witnessing her outburst. This is the first time that Honza and Yanka have heard about the problem in our family but obviously my mother-in-law was well informed about the situation through her visits to Mami.

Chopi stands next to her with an expressionless face.

'Mami, you are a great actress. The doctor told you it's only nerves. You are destroying my life too.' Turning on her heels, she walks into the house, straight to Zsuzsi's bedroom, where I find her lying on the bed sobbing loudly.

'Hans invited me with Roman to celebrate the New Year at his place. As soon as I told Mami about it she had one of her nervous fits, almost fainted, lay in bed and demanded the doctor. I can't stand it any longer, Yenni. Something terrible will happen. I can't live like this.'

'But Chopi …' I start up.

'What? Tell me Yena, what can I do?'

I have no answer, so I stay with her until her tears stop flowing.

Eventually we all sit around the table. Deep inside we are all blaming someone or something, silently accusing Hans, ourselves or each other. None of us have a clean conscience.

Even though we all try to pretend, lifting the glasses high for the Happy New Year of 1974, it doesn't start up well. Our family is torn apart and the worst part is just coming; we feel it in the air.

⁂

Hobart has just finished building its Wrest Point Casino, the first one in Australia.

It's a Saturday afternoon. Feri and his wife call in, both dressed in evening outfits in the middle of the afternoon. Would we like to go and see the casino from inside? They say it looks spectacular. The prescribed dress is a jacket and a tie for men and an after-five dress for women.

Yano isn't sure but, 'All right. If you want to go Yena, we'll go.'

Mami is staying with us over the weekend; she wants to see this new spectacle too.

'Anyuka?' Yano turns towards her.

'I don't mind to go.'

We all disperse into different corners of the house to get ready.

'Anyuka, could you please give me one of Svetya's wigs?' I had already made the purchases and Anuka has packed them, ready for her return. She pulls them out of her suitcase. I try on all three.

'Which one do you think?'

'Perhaps that copper-coloured one with the short, straight page style will look good.' She thinks.

I try it on again. What a difference! With my dark, curly hair tucked under the wig the woman who stares at me from the mirror looks sophisticated, quite sexy. *Perhaps too sexy in this dark-brown ankle-length dress,* I think, enjoying the change in my appearance. With the hair moving around my face at every step, I sail into the loungeroom and stop to pose with a smile on my face.

The words of conversation trail away and a dead silence follows. As if they have seen an apparition they all stare at me, mainly Yano. His friendly expression is replaced by a dark disapproving stare and the angry unkind words are blurted out, barking, thrown towards me.

'What the hell have you done to yourself? You look like a whore! I am not going anywhere with you looking like this. Take off that masquerade and wipe that smile from your face!'

There is not much happiness around us lately. A little fun would have gone a long way.

Yano can't see this and in his usual manner he yells and abuses.

I cry for an hour while everyone in the loungeroom tries to calm Yano down. In the end we all go to the casino, the wig is tucked back into Anyuka's suitcase. I pile my hair up and apply a load of makeup to cover my swollen eyes.

The only thing I remember from that first visit to the casino is the chandelier in the foyer.

My mother-in-law departed. The last days were spent shopping for presents. During those shopping trips in the city somehow she did not seem to be all that tired. 'Zita would like this,' she pointed to this and that for her daughter. Her bags were filled with presents for the family, including the three wigs and other things for Svetya.

She told me that now, since she had seen the way we were living, she would die in peace. By her observation we were living in a very beautiful and prosperous city.

In my mind the fact that she felt that way balanced out the $2500 and the problems we had with her. To be fair to her, she wasn't a healthy woman.

I was impatiently waiting for Svetya's letter. Did she like the wigs? Did they fit her? Will she wear them? Which one suited her the best? What did her friends think? Her letter never came.

'How is Svetya? Is she still living at the same address? Did she like my presents?' I wrote to my mother-in-law.

She had not seen Svetya for a long time, but yes, she still lives at the same address.

Now and then I received a card from Svetya, never mentioning any of my presents. Each of those cards was answered with my long reporting letters.

Svetya, if you don't stop answering my letters with impersonal postcards, I will stop writing to you. Surely you can find time for an occasional letter …

Another card arrived.

Many regards to you and your family. We are all healthy.

Yours Svetya

I did not answer that one and we lost touch.

I was a productive and passionate letter writer and expected everyone to be the same. Svetya wasn't the only person I kept in touch with. My next-door neighbour's daughter in Košice had escaped and left for Canada at the same time we left for Australia. Eva was a young girl trying to find her place in Canada, her new home, and we regularly exchanged letters. Even though our experiences were different from each other, in many ways they were curiously similar.

Dear Yenny

I moved into Montreal and I love it here. What do you think of me in the photo? Do you like the way I wear my hair now? I met a man; he is a German Canadian and is very handsome. I am thinking of moving in with him, but please don't tell my mami. I don't think she will understand …

When Svetya's letters stopped and the closeness between me and Chopi was badly bruised it was so good that I had Eva to write to.

Not long after their return from Europe, Hedineni became sick. A heart problem, the doctor thought, and prescribed a medicine. It didn't do much good. Hedineni battled on but was still unwell. The doctor suggested some tests, and after a few days' hospitalisation the results were shattering. Something was wrong with her glands. Perhaps chemotherapy would help, or perhaps radiation. Nothing helped. Hedineni died after a few months, with Yanibachi day and night at her side.

Since we had lived in Tasmania, Yanibachi, Hedineni and Nana had become our extended family. The successes, the achievements and problems were felt and shared equally. The years 1973 and 1974 were hard for all of us. The sadness and sorrow kept turning up frequently in different shapes and forms and for various reasons. Nana, besides being Hedineni's daughter, was also her friend. She was shattered by her mother's death and stopped talking to her father, blaming him for not looking into Hedineni's sickness more seriously and earlier. Yanibachi spent his lonely days and nights at Mami's and on the weekends with us. True to his upright principles he tried to be brave, but we knew there was nothing we could do to ease his pain.

The news from Europe was not much better. Opapa was getting older. After Omama's death the spark had gone out of his life, his letters were sad and full of longing. *Could Mami arrange a visit to Košice? He is not going to live much longer. Could they meet for one last time?*

… there is also a problem with the house. I can't look after it any longer, it's too big. Etaneni is looking after me, she has moved in now.

Tibor and Olina want to move in too. Perhaps it is a good idea. If I stay here on my own, the government will put some lodgers in and I don't want to share my last days with strangers. It is hard on my own …

Mami was relieved to hear that Etaneni, Opapa's sister, who had lived in our house, only across the corridor, in a one-room flat, had moved in with Opapa and took care of him. Tibor was her son and Olina was his third wife.

Marta, I have some money saved up, which I am sending over to you via Yolan, who is going to America again. Perhaps you can buy yourself an air ticket for that money and come over.

Yolan was Omama's younger sister. The idea was to take the Czechoslovak korunas to America, change it into Australian dollars and send it over to Mami.

The money eventually arrived but, rightly or wrongly, was much less than what Mami expected. Another reason for bad blood, lamentations and complaints.

'I knew this would happen, as soon as Opapa told me about Yolan. You could never trust that woman. I bet she did not even take the money out of Czechoslovakia but spent it before she left for America, then exchanged some of her wages as a kitchen hand into Australian dollars and sent it over.' Mami complained day after day.

The irony of the situation was blindingly clear. Opapa, living in a poor socialist country, was sending money to Mami, who was living in the prosperous west, so she can afford to buy an airline ticket. From Opapa's point of view the thousands of Czechoslovak korunas, savings of many years, was a small fortune back there and would provide a comfortable living for a couple of years, but it certainly wasn't enough for a return ticket from Australia to Europe.

Mami was a resourceful lady and always found a way out of a tight spot. She had some watches and some family jewellery. Even though her English wasn't very good, without telling us about it or asking for any assistance with the finances, she managed to do business with a jeweller and sell much of the family jewellery in Switzerland. And she kept quiet about it. At least this was the story she told me after many years. I would have never thought of that solution, but Mami did. With that money she had enough dollars for her airline ticket.

When she applied for the Czechoslovak visa it was refused, with a letter from the Czechoslovakian Embassy. Even though an Australian citizen, they couldn't guarantee her safety because she hadn't lost her Czechoslovak citizenship, the letter said. As soon as she stepped into the country she would be jailed for her illegal escape, as the court had ordered in 1971.

How could she visit her native country? How could she meet up with her father? Perhaps she should try the Hungarian Embassy? She rang the Hungarian Vice-Consul. Sorry, she can't get a visa, because Hungary has a deal with the government of Czechoslovakia about handing over dissidents. But wait a second! When was she born? In 1910 Košice was still in the Austrian–Hungarian monarchy. It was many years before the creation of the First Czechoslovak Republic. Hungarian citizenship was her birthright. Mami got her Hungarian citizenship and with it a visa. She could visit Hungary and meet Opapa in Miskolc, in the city one hour by train over the border from Košice.

In her desire to be loved by her two daughters, whatever it would take, Mami started losing the very thing she wanted most.

The good old days filled with laughter now were full of arguments, discussions and tears as Chopi tried to reason. Mami persisted, as I knew she would, and to the end she drew us all apart and into desperation.

Chopi left Baker's Milk and started working at the technical college, in the Department of Chemistry, where she was in charge of the laboratory. With her position came the responsibility for a number of chemicals that were held in the cellar under the building. It was a huge task to put the small and large bottles, boxes, containers and Petri dishes into some kind of order. On my first visit to her new workplace

I found her in the cellar and found out that she spent many evenings after her ordinary working time there, shifting things around, marking them, putting them into alphabetical order. I offered to help.

For some weeks, whenever I could, I spent hours with her, catching the last bus to Rokeby. Those evenings brought us closer again for a short while. Down there in the dim light of the unprotected globes, inhaling the familiar musty smell of the earth, we shifted the bottles and boxes and talked. Chopi confided in me about her relationship with Hans. She was happy with him, even stopped smoking from one day to the other, because Hans did not like her smoking.

'Mami, listen. Chopi is really happy with him. Leave them alone. This is not going to end well. I have a terrible feeling,' I confronted Mami.

'How can I leave it alone when Chopi is hurling into disaster? No caring mother would allow it. That vagabond, he alienated my daughter from me.'

Hans came up with some more advice for Chopi. Why couldn't Chopi stand up for herself and tell her mother to back off? Mami was doing more harm than good by bringing Roman up like a toy kid. And the food Roman was fed was no good either. He should not be on European food, but on good Australian tucker.

Poor Chopi. She had to make up her mind and choose between the two people she cared about most. She chose Hans. Mami had to go. They could not live together any more.

Mami, in her last effort to hold on, demanded my opinion. Even though I agreed with Chopi regarding her relationship, I strongly opposed Hans's interference and advice about Mami's way of bringing up Roman. Seeing Mami basically on the street without a home, I finally took Mami's side.

That was it then. The end of the caring and loving relationship between Chopi and me. Mami, who all our life taught us about helping and looking after each other no matter what, with the sweep of her hand and her strong will destroyed that bond. I did not speak with Chopi for years. There was nothing that would fill the emptiness that was left by Chopi's absence. Nothing. It hurt terribly.

The week when Mami was to fly for her first visit to Europe she was forced to move out of Stainforth Court, her and Chopi's lovely home, which they were so proud of and created with so much love, hard work and skill. Her silver, books, the new Queen Anne bedroom furniture and other things that Chopi did not want because they reminded her of Mami were all stored at Yanibachi's, at Yanka and Honza's house, who took pity on her, and in our house. After all that effort she had put into the trip to Europe, she left for her first visit to Hungary with a heavy heart, not knowing where her home would be on her return.

It's a cool summer morning in 1974. Yano and I and the children are at the airport to see Mami off. Chopi is there too; the estrangement hasn't taken full effect yet. She stands there with eyebrows pulled up high, her mouth tightly shut, not a sign of sympathy. My tears in my throat are choking me as we kiss goodbye and I watch that brokenhearted woman walking across the tarmac towards the stairs, departing on this much-anticipated trip. My heart aches for Mami, thinking about the self-inflicted irony of her life; her desperate unhappiness and the dream-come-true trip. That morning I cry for hours. I cry out all my tears that are meant for Mami. After that there are no more tears left.

The Hungarian dinner-dances kept happening. Zsuzsi and myself needed new outfits. I missed Mami's sewing skills while she was away in Europe.

I had watched Mami sew since my childhood. *Perhaps I could make some dresses myself?* Zsuzsi also was gifted with her little hands and was enthusiastic about it. Why not? There was no shortage of material; the Silk and Textile parcels, some still unwrapped, lay at the bottom of my wardrobe. All we needed was a sewing machine.

I talked to Yano so long about this very urgent need, until I talked him into getting his very first hire-purchase loan. Empowered by his

'Okay, okay, do what you want but make sure you don't spend much money' agreement, I went to Myer to buy the sewing machine.

They have a Singer! I think, relieved. I know the brand. Mami had one of those in Košice in the small room next to the kitchen.

'Excuse me, I would like to purchase that sewing machine.' I point to the Singer displayed on the shelf between other machines. 'No, not that one, the one next to it. That's the one. Thank you.'

No worries. Have I had a loan with Myer before? No. Never. Do I have a loan with anyone, to prove that I can pay this loan back? No. No loans whatsoever. I lift my head high with pride.

'My husband doesn't believe in loans. Everything we bought so far was for cash.'

'Sorry, no loans, no sewing machine.'

'But I am employed with a wage, my husband is a public servant, isn't that enough proof? I could bring a certificate from our employers telling about our wages,' I argue, with my English getting worse with each leap of my blood pressure.

'Sorry. You need a guarantor.'

Once again I realise that we do not belong, we are still outside the system by our ignorance of it. So, if you have a loan, you could have another one, but if you have never had a loan, you can't get one. How do you get your very first loan, if you don't happen to have anyone to guarantee you? I am trying to sort it out in my mind and completely forget about our land loan, which by then was paid for and would have been a good reference. Piri! She works just close by.

'Piri, can you be my guarantor?' Does Piri have a loan, any loan? Of course she has a loan; everyone has at least one. It's not about the loan but about the ability to pay it back.

'C'mon, I'll sign the guarantee.'

I am in the system. Now I can have as many loans as I want.

I brought the sewing machine home, set it on the dining table, cut out the patterns and ripped open the Silk and Textile parcels. 'This material is nice. What you think Zsuzsikam? The blue will suit you.'

Zsuzsi and I slaved over our first dresses after work for three nights and the result was great. The dresses were wearable. Zsuzsi and I became our own seamstresses for many years to come.

After Mami's moving out, Chopi was trying to balance the care of Roman and the job she was doing. Sorry, Hans said, he couldn't help; it would be the best if Chopi found herself a live-in housekeeper or something. As a matter of fact he knows a reliable German woman.

'It's all because of your mother,' he told me on the phone. 'If she had really loved her daughter she wouldn't have moved out. She deserted Chopi when she needed her the most. Now she is holidaying in Hungary, while her daughter is battling on her own.' He thought it would be best if Chopi stopped working and took care of Roman. Hans did not like the people Chopi was working with anyway. They knew him and talked to her about his past. But his past was past, all finished, so there was nothing to talk about, Hans thought.

My blood pressure shot up sky high. 'Mami did not desert Chopi!' I could barely control my temper. 'Mami was thrown out on your advice!' I yelled into the receiver.

'You and your mother! You're both the same.' With that he hung up and we stopped talking to each other altogether.

Chopi battled for a while longer with unreliable live-in housekeepers and nannies, but eventually gave up her job and became partly dependent on Hans.

She cut all ties with us, with Yanibachi and all our friends. For the lack of Mami's and my opinion she developed a one-sided view of the situation, trusted Hans and completely took over his ideas. When Mami returned she prohibited her from seeing her little boy Roman. This broke Mami's heart. Chopi also stopped talking to Roman in Hungarian and, as it goes with languages, he soon forgot his mother tongue, the only language he could communicate in with his grandmother.

Mami arrived back from Hungary and settled into our house. Zsuzsi was allocated the day-and-night couch in the loungeroom. She was happy; there she couldn't hear Yano snoring at night. From then on, after nine thirty the television and the lights went off in that room and the door leading to the kitchen was closed. Yano did not mind; he liked to go to bed early. If Mami and I wanted to talk we could do it in the dining corner in the kitchen, but only quietly, because Zsuzsi was trying to sleep.

There, Mami, a little happier than when she left, in whispered conversation told me about her meeting with Opapa and the week they spent together. She had also met up with other friends from Košice who knew about her visit in Miskolc. Her long-time friend Mancineni came too. As a matter of fact, the ballet ensemble of Košice's National Theatre was in Miskolc performing *Sleeping Beauty* and yes, she met them in a coffee house. They all remembered her. 'Look, here are the photos.' I looked through the snapshots: Mami and Mancineni, Mami getting off the tram, Mami in her red jacket and off-white hat, looking like she was out of a magazine. Then a photo of an old, old man, my Opapa, with a toothless smile, sitting next to Mami, holding her hand.

Yano wasn't happy with Mami sharing our lives in our home. Just when he thought we had finally got rid of her by moving from the Darcy Street house, here she was again, living with us. So, Mami applied to the Housing Department for a unit. In the meantime she was mainly with us, some weekends she spent at Fiona and Bruce's and some weekends with Yanibachi.

Many weeks and months went by.

'When is your mother going to move out Yena?' Yano confronted me.

'I don't know Yano. When she gets her unit, I suppose.'

'I don't want her living with us any more; it's like an invasion.

Wherever I turn in the house I bump into her. I don't feel at home here with her around.'

'I can't throw her out Yano, where would she go?'

The plaster walls in the Housing Department houses were not soundproof. Mami overheard the conversation.

'So this is what has become of me?' Mami cried. 'My own daughters don't want me. Why did you talk me into coming to Australia, Yenni? Why?'

My conscience stirred. I loved Mami; she had done a lot for me and for all of us in the past. Even now she was doing her best to be useful by cooking a meal or just being there for the children when they came home from school. Yano felt uncomfortable. He had to be on his best behaviour. It was difficult to cover up the many arguments we always had between us.

'What does Yano do when I am not around? Why am I such a problem? I am trying so hard.' Mami couldn't understand and cried. I felt so guilty, so sorry for her, yet I also wanted us to be on our own. This was hard.

But I knew why she or anyone else living with us was a problem for Yano. Besides the arguments, which he had to hold back from, on his return from work he liked to strip down to his jocks, hang his jacket on one armchair, his shirt on the other and the trousers on yet another chair.

'Yano, put your things into the wardrobe, please. We have nowhere to sit.'

'They need airing,' he told me, leaving everything as it was, and there was not a chair in the loungeroom that could be used. Then he stretched out on the couch and we all had to congregate around the dining table in the kitchen.

Mami had had enough. One day she decided to move in with Yanibachi. He was lonely, she said; he needed a woman's hand to look after him. It was a good move and for a while it suited both of them. Yano and I could continue our bickering and disagreements uninterrupted.

With Mami gone Zsuzsi moved back to her bedroom, which was next to ours. But she had already experienced the nights in the loungeroom without hearing Yano snoring. He had regularly gone to bed earlier than I did. Zsuzsi waited out the time when I went to bed and night after night I would meet her in the passage, walking with sleepy eyes squinting in the light of the lamp, dragging her doona and pillow to the loungeroom, where we found her every morning.

It was always about the balance. The balance between my two worlds. At various times the two worlds were represented by different issues and subjects. Right then it was about balancing my private world, which was my workplace, the people in it and the fulfilment of my inner ambitions, and my world on the other side of the scale, my family life, its relationships and my marriage. The only time, for a short time, when the scales were almost balanced was after our arrival in Australia. Even though then we had no possessions to speak about, we worked hard and long hours and we knew it to be temporary. Then the family concentrated on the important everyday issue of living and enjoyed the achievements of each member as we basked in the warmth and goodwill of our new friends.

As soon as our immediate financial problems were sorted out and we stopped focusing on our survival, things changed back to where I knew all along they inevitably would be. When my private desires were fulfilled, my family life was down in the dumps, and vice versa.

In the year of 1974 my private life was fulfilling. I was wanted and respected at work and was achieving the standard I was striving for. But my family life! Because of my bad conscience about not being able to help Mami, I had constant arguments with Yano, but also with Mami, who I blamed for breaking us up with Chopi. I missed Chopi terribly and couldn't forgive myself for taking sides. But most of all I blamed Hans for many, many years and, even though the differences perhaps did not exist, I felt them, deep in my heart.

CHAPTER TEN

Responsibilities and Respect

Mary, fresh from London, started working in the canteen as an assistant cook, after a brief experience filling my old position in the yoghurt factory. She lived up the road from Baker's Milk with her husband and two children. 'Did you say children?' one would ask, watching this sexy-looking petite blond with large brown eyes, ready for a laugh any time.

After Chopi left the laboratory, Mary applied for her position. Mary's application succeeded and she started working with us in the lab. I was to teach her to become a competent laboratory assistant.

Mary was great fun, admired by men, many of whom would make it their business to bring a test or two to the lab in return for having a short chat with her. She liked those short chats, her mind all over the place, never focusing, running in and out of the laboratory for this and that.

'So, where are you going now?' I caught her, one foot already out of the door.

'To my car, I have forgotten ...' Her big brown eyes looked at me in surprise.

'Mary listen, you can't do a hundred things all at once. You are leaving everything halfway, not knowing where to continue to finish it. Try to concentrate only on one thing, whatever it is. Only one thing. Think of what you're doing. Once you finish that one, put it in a small imaginary box and in your mind place it on a shelf, where you can find it next time you need it. You understand?'

'I do Jenny, I do, honestly.' A revelation. It was the biggest *a-a-a-ha* in the whole of Mary's working life. 'So you want me to put my mind into boxes?'

'Yes, kind of.'

Despite her naive appearance she was a tough girl.

When an injustice was done to her she would exclaim, 'He is not going to get away with it!' and assure me in her strong accent (was it Cockney?) 'I haven't been living in the East End of London for nothing. I know exactly how to deal with those sorts.'

This was the first time I had heard of the East End of London. From then on I knew that there must also be a West End and figured that there was a real difference between people living at each of those ends.

Otto was ill and had to be hospitalised. Who is going to run the lab? The factory manager thought to ask Michael from the Launceston laboratory to help out. No need. I know exactly what to do, I assured him. I was doing it all anyway, while Otto was ailing.

'Okay then. We will try,' he nodded.

I took over the running of the laboratory. The bigger the responsibility, the more I enjoyed it. *I can do it,* I thought encouragingly, and competed with myself.

By then the tipping bay was history and the screeching rollers on the conveyer belt just rusting relics of the old era. The milk was transported in large tankers. Suddenly it was up to me to organise the routes and the timetable of the tankers, arriving and leaving, carrying the milk from all parts of southern Tasmania into the factory. I was in charge of the forecast – a pick-up schedule for the tanker drivers as well as for the factory foreman, who had to prepare the necessary silos to store thousands of litres of incoming fresh milk. I was living through one of the most satisfying periods of my working life. The fantastic part was that the management, including Mr Baker and the factory manager, trusted my judgement and let me do my job, knowing that I would do my very best.

Besides the organisation of the tankers, I became responsible for the quality of the milk. It meant that the milk couldn't be unloaded from the tanker before I tested it. The first tanker arrived from its early-morning run sometimes at four o'clock. During the weekdays it was the factory manager who did the tests, but on the weekends I had to be there before the factory could start up.

Saturday morning, half past four. A taxi pulls up in front of our gate in Rokeby. I tiptoe quietly out of the dark house, pulling the door closed behind me gently. Taking the steps through our front garden I feel the cool, dark morning and gladly curl up in the warm taxi. With the car riding fast on the deserted roads I watch the green letters on the dashboard, listening to quiet background music, smelling the scent of the 'wildflowers' air freshener, which must have been sprayed just before I opened the car door to disguise the smell of the tobacco.

In the laboratory the fluorescent lights flicker before they flood the room with their bright light but I have no time to waste. I can see my image in the white lab coat mirroring on the block-out film of the laboratory windows, as I hurriedly walk alongside the benches, turning on the water baths and other testing machinery. I hear the hum of the factory and the dying engine of the arriving tanker.

A short knock on the lab door and Peter, the foreman, appears carrying two small bottles of milk. 'G'morning Jenny. Alex has just arrived. This is from his tanker, the other is from Geoff. The pumps are ready to pump it into Silo Number 2, if the milk is all right.'

I test the milk and Peter is mooching around the desk, looking into the forecast.

'The milk is all right, Peter.'

Saturday's milk production in the factory is ready to start.

Otto was sick for a long time, needing rehabilitation, and after his recovery he took a couple of months off to visit his native country. I was in my element. Was it my responsible attitude? I am not sure but I was free to organise my working time, as long as I was there when I was needed. It did not mean shorter working hours but it meant that I could delegate some duties to Mary and could take a few hours off when I needed them. I was in control of my life. The feeling of insecurity that came with being a new Australian ceased to exist, evaporated. I felt that, regardless of my nationality, I had proved my integrity.

The days, weeks and months came and went, the camaraderie between Mary and I strengthened, and my children grew.

Ishtvan was sixteen, going on seventeen, and during the school holidays he was allowed to work as a helper around the factory, sometimes even in the lab. To his absolute delight he received wages and also had his first taste of work discipline. This brought Ishtvan and I closer to each other in those years when teenage youngsters usually turn away from their parents in pursuit of independence; we knew the same people, laughed about the same things and loved the same canteen food. The following year Zsuzsi started helping in the lab during her school holidays. It solved my problem: *What are the children doing while I am at work?*

The scales were still tilted in favour of my workplace. At home it was different. Yano and I still had our daily, sometimes hourly, disagreements, some of which were followed by days of not talking to each other.

Honza and Yanka were regular visitors, especially at the weekends, when Yano and Honza would empty glasses in the dining corner of the kitchen while Yanka and I, feeling locked out of the conversation, would sit in the loungeroom, wishing that those two would hurry up and empty that last bottle, so they could go home.

Other things were happening too. Yanibachi found himself a lady friend. She was unmarried, lived in the same block of units as Yanibachi, and they were both members of the body corporate. Yanibachi often talked about her with great respect.

Life is unpredictable. Yanibachi's friend Margaret worked in the office at Baker's Milk, the same lady who presented me with the amber-coloured vase in the first days of my working there. This friendship was good for Yanibachi and Margaret but not too good for Mami. She once again was made to realise that there was no need to fill Yanibachi's lonely evenings any longer and that she had no home to go to.

'We will have Mami living with us until she gets her Housing Department unit,' Honza and Yana announced unexpectedly.

They lived in a three-bedroom Housing Department house, had only one child, were at work most of the time and one of the bedrooms wasn't furnished anyway, they reasoned. Mami always liked Honza and Yanka. She gladly moved in with her Queen Anne furniture and promptly started sewing up doilies and a curtain for her new temporary home.

My bad conscience was given a rest for a little while. I knew Mami was comfortable in her new environment and especially liked the constant company of those two goodhearted young people. Yanka was happy too; whenever they needed it Mami was there to babysit.

The Hungarian Club flourished, though it still did not have clubrooms, and with it our involvement with the club. We maintained our friendship with Pauline, George and their friends, by then also our friends. Through the dance practice sessions Ishtvan, George Junior and Stephen found that they were interested in the same things; namely, girls and surfing.

Yano was well liked by the club members and frequently helped with various tasks in organisation or with transport. His talent in drawing, painting and decoration was well appreciated; when he was approached to paint the street images of Budapest from postcards onto large wall-sized plaster sheets. 'Why not?' he said confidently. Yano became enthusiastic about this difficult task and set out to realise it with great vigour.

Our bedroom became his studio. 'Yena, give me a hand with the bed and bedside tables will you?' The double bed was pulled away from the wall into the middle of the room. Then the five over-sized plaster sheets were carried from the truck through the narrow passage one by one – 'Caref-u-u-l-l round the corner!' – and propped up against the back wall. 'Don't hover around me Yena, don't you have anything to do in the kitchen?'

Yano set out to create. He moved between the bed and the wall as a true artist, holding the relevant postcard in his hand, squinting in the glare of the ceiling light, transferring the images of streets, bridges and castles, using the tools of an artist, mixing and matching the textas with chalks and watercolours as needed, drawing the exact images, bringing the Danube, the churches and the hills of Budapest right into our bedroom. I could but admire his talent and perseverance. When one picture was finished a clean plaster sheet appeared from behind to be painted with another image.

❦❦❦

Sunday morning. Yano and I are still in bed. The phone rings. There is not much space between the wardrobe against the wall and the bed in the middle of the room. I clear the bed sideways. It's mostly me answering the phone calls. 'It will be your mother,' Yano would say. But this phone call is too early, the morning light is trying to break through our lacy curtains, making the outlines of the furniture just visible. I don't like those early-morning phone calls; they usually herald bad news.

'Hello?'

'Yenni? This is Zita. I am phoning to tell you that Anyuka has died.'

'What happened Zita?'

'She has been unwell for a few weeks and was in the hospital.'

'Would you like to tell me what happened?'

'Not really. It's a long story. We are all pretty upset.'

'Would you like to talk to Yano?'

'No, you tell him Yenni.'

'I will Zita; thank you for phoning.'

I hang up the receiver and think, *What would be the best way to tell this to Yano? He is still in bed thinking that I am talking to Mami.*

Through the corridor into the bedroom, I realise that there is no easy way.

'Yano? Are you awake? We just had a phone call from Zita.'

'What about?'

'Anyuka died in the hospital yesterday. She had been sick lately. Zita did not tell me any more; they are all quite upset.'

While I am telling this to Yano I stroke his forehead. He places my hand onto the doona.

'It's all right Yena, we haven't been very close to each other. I knew when she was here that she would not live much longer. I am glad that we brought her out so she could see how we live. Could you leave me alone for a while?'

Anyuka died of complications from her diabetes, two years after her visit to Australia. She was seventy-one.

Many weeks later, when all five pictures were done, a member of the club pulled up with a truck. They carried the plaster sheets out through the passage – 'Caref-u-u-l-l round the corner!' – loaded them up on the back of the truck with great care, covered them with bedsheets and transported them to the Polish Hall, where all our meetings and social events were held. They were used at every Hungarian evening as decoration around the walls and on the stage. I finally could vacuum out the bedroom properly and push our beds back to the wall. Everything was back to normal again, thank goodness.

After that Yano became some kind of a celebrity. Combining his talent with his good looks, humour and willingness to drink with the boys, he certainly was a popular figure, not only among men but also women.

There it was again, my old friend jealousy. Was it jealousy? Or, as I kept telling myself, did I simply not like Yano making a fool of me?

I felt that way especially about a particular woman with shiny black hair reaching almost to her backside, and with sparkling dark eyes targeting Yano.

'Why don't you keep him in the fridge, if you worry so much about him?' she told me smiling, and threw her head back, sweeping the mass of shiny hair behind her ears, after my remark to leave him alone.

Perhaps it was like that. Perhaps I felt insecure in my marriage, perhaps I had other hang-ups, but certainly Yano did not help to restore my self-confidence. Every time I talked about those feelings, Yano laughed it off saying, 'You are mad Yena, leave me alone with those idiotic ideas.' All I wanted was reassurance, his arms around me, loving me.

❧❧❧

It's warm, summer, and it is Saturday evening. The sun glows orange through our corner dining-room window. There's a knock at the back door.

'Come in,' I call out

The door opens and they walk in. They have come to visit. He in light sandy-coloured trousers and she in a low-cut summer dress, suntanned well-shaped legs, feet in slip-on sandals. I have a front-seat view of those legs and painted toenails, because when they step into our kitchen I am on all fours scrubbing the kitchen floor after returning from work in the lab. Resignedly I sweep the sweat off my face with the top of my hand and let the old tea-towel drop into the bucket of soapy water.

Yano has a great time conversing, exchanging jokes and glances, while I am in the kitchen making sandwiches and cups of coffee.

Finally they leave and I can finish wiping up the kitchen floor. By than I have had enough. I object about Yano's behaviour and he laughs as always and calls me names. I try to reason.

'But Yano, look at me. I work like a horse and all I want is a little consideration, a little kindness. I want to feel like your wife.'

'You are my wife. What do you want from me?'

How can I make him understand that I would have liked to look like that woman with polished toenails. I would have liked to sail in on the arm of my husband, who would courteously open the door for me. I know, I know it couldn't have been done because I was wiping the floor, but a kind word, a gesture of recognition from him would have gone a long way to improving my self-confidence.

Yano sits in the armchair with a cigarette between his fingers, sweeping the air with his arm, dismissing my misery.

Without a word, the way I am, in the dress that I only wear at home, old slip-on sandals, hair uncombed, sweaty face, I walk out through the back door, letting it shut with a bang, and keep walking.

When I reach the main road I turn left, stamp, fume, boil, bubble, right to the very top of Rokeby Hill, huffing and puffing from my uphill walk. *Should I go home or what? No way!* I keep walking.

The sun is setting and the Lord decides to engage an extra-skilled artist to paint the evening sky with huge smears of red and pink. When the canvas disappears behind Mount Wellington all is dark and I can see the light of the Shoreline Hotel at the end of the long road where I carefully step alongside the ditch that hems it, trying to keep out of the traffic by walking on the opposite side. Cars with their headlights shining into my face swish by, but I don't care. After thirty minutes' walk my temper simmers down, my steps become gentler and I reach the footpath. *Okay, so what am I going to do now?*

I walk on, in my mind arguing with Yano with effective and descriptive words that couldn't ever be repeated when facing him because I can never remember the right words when we argue.

If he wants to leave me, fine. If he wants to find a more attractive woman, okay. The only thing I can't stand, even though it might be jealousy, is to watch Yano showing adoration and special interest to this woman, or any woman, who I know has a crush on him. My vanity hurts. I don't know how to behave in these circumstances. I am not smart enough to turn the situation against him. I feel a fool and I am not going to be part of it.

I pour my heart out onto the asphalt path with every step I take, marching along Howrah Road to Bellerive, turning at the Yacht Club towards the bridge, walking on. Who knows how long I have been walking? An hour and a half, two hours? It's dark but I don't feel tired, plenty of energy for some more thrashing out with Yano, plenty of energy for many more steps. Rosny College. *So, where am I going on this balmy Saturday evening? Perhaps I should catch a bus to the city or something.* I stick my hand inside my pocket. In the depth of it I find some money. Without a second thought I catch the bus to the city. What now? The casino! That's it. From Franklin Square I catch another bus to the casino and I walk into this world of smiling, laughing and talking well-dressed people.

The chandeliers flood the entrance hall and me, with their lights exposing the smallest detail, my outfit and the drops of sweat on my forehead. In times when only men in jackets and ties are allowed to enter the sanctuary of gambling I am standing there in my summer dress, old slip-on sandals, with toes black from the dust of the road, no makeup, no hairdo. Suddenly I feel dead tired. My body sinks in the large armchair in the foyer. I could not care less, close my eyes and fall asleep as the crowd comes and goes around me.

When I open my eyes I check the time. It's half past nine. The scene in the casino hasn't changed. The people are still laughing, talking, coming and going. *What am I doing here?* Time to go home. Outside the revolving door I call a taxi, haggle the price down to the few dollars I have in the pocket of my dress, sit at the back of the taxi and after half an hour arrive at the dark house with the front door unlocked. I suppose Yano expected me back. I tiptoe through the house and think, *They are all asleep, they didn't miss me.* I have never left home at night before on my own and even though I didn't tell Yano where I was going, or when I will come back, he wasn't worried. So, who have I punished after all?

Dear Marta

I have decided to sell the house. It's far too big for me and it needs maintenance. The two brothers who rented out the front part now want to buy the whole house. We have signed an agreement that they will let me live my days out in my part, together with Etaneni ...

wrote Opapa. He said that when he gets the money for the house, he will find a way to send some over to Australia for Mami.

I barely listened to Mami's summary. In my mind the house, Košice and all what was before was in a very distant past, no relevance to me, to our present. I had so many more things to be concerned about, so many things to sort out.

Another letter followed. The contract for the sale of the house had gone through but for some reason the money was not forthcoming, Opapa wrote. He was suspicious. And the new owners wanted him out of the house. Where would he go at his age?

That was odd. I started to listen to Mami when she was reading out Opapa's letters. He said that his nephew Tibor and his wife Olina were very good to him. They had moved in and begun a court process to reverse the sale of the house on the basis of a broken contract.

Soon after Tibor wrote:

Dear Marta

Olina and I are living now with Opapa in the house. We are taking good care of him. As the house is no good to you in Australia could you please send us a letter in which you would state that you are giving up your part of the inheritance to my benefit.

'Mami this is not right. The house belongs to you after Opapa's death. It's not a piece of cake that will go rotten. The house will be there for you whenever you are able to return and claim it.'

'I know, I know, but what can I do? Tibor and Olina are so good and they are looking after Opapa.'

'Mami, Olina knows exactly what she is doing. After all, they are living in the house for nothing. Don't send them the letter. You never know what will happen in the future.'

For a while the frequency of letters crossing the ocean slowed down.

Ishtvan was seventeen, spoke English with no accent, was attending Rosny Matriculation College and had a girlfriend. He was a freedom-loving, independent and spirited young man. When Yano took out the scissors to tidy Ishtvan's hair he threatened to leave home if his father dared to cut his hair short. He talked for a while about sharing a flat with his friends, and he would have done so but none of his friends wanted to move in with him because, I was told, he was too tidy.

Ishtvan had inherited his father's artistic talent and was a coeditor of the school magazine. About five of them, students of the college, were very enthusiastic about the magazine and other things that were the main reason for a few early mornings finding me in the loungeroom, waiting to hear Ishtvan's steps on the drive alongside the kitchen windows and then for the back door to open. *Ph-h-hew! Thank God he is all right,* I would think with relief, and trot off to bed for a few hours' sleep.

Mutual interests, similar temperaments and our friendship with their parents created a natural camaraderie between Ishtvan, George Junior and Stephen that, as the time passed, became more permanent. It did not take long before on the weekends the boys would turn up with their girlfriends to take over our loungeroom, consuming large amounts of coffee and salted peanuts. I became Mrs M, Yano Mr M, and Mami became 'Ishtvan's granny'. Because we had no other room to be in, we all shared the loungeroom and the television programs and, at the end of the day, the big pots of food I cooked up for this great group of youngsters and us. To me they all became family and my concerns reached out to each.

Some weekends the boys went surfing, leaving at four in the morning to chase the waves, piling into George Junior's yellow Datsun. Luckily I did not know enough about that sport to be worried. Later on in the morning the girls would arrive at various times to wait out the return of the boys. The Eastern Shore had more beaches around it than the west and our home was a convenient place to meet. More coffees and salted peanuts for the girls, sometimes a cake I had just taken out of the oven. 'Hm-m-m. Very nice Mrs M. Can I help you with anything at all?' one or the other would ask. 'Yeah, here …' I would take them up on their offer.

We talked, the age differences disappeared and we all learned a great deal from each other. The teenage kids kept Yano and I 'with it'. We learned about their ideas, self-image and their music.

'Is this what you call music?' I would confront them.

'Just listen to the words Mrs M,' they advised.

In return they learned about my family values, cooking and stories from the old country, including the exciting tale of our illegal escape. 'You should write a book about it,' some of them suggested.

Inevitably the parties started. The fifteenth, the sixteenth, the eighteenth. They were shared between us and Pauline and some other lucky parents.

At this point my neighbour Marlene, living across the street, made herself known to all the teenagers who congregated at our place when Yano and I slipped out of the house to let the youngsters enjoy themselves. 'Ishtvan, make sure you are not too noisy, you understand?' Yano would lecture, wagging his finger in front of his nose, before departing.

Marlene was a no-nonsense woman of my age, who herself had brought up five children.

'Ishtvan! Turn down that music at once, the whole street can hear you, and back to the house! All of you! It's past nine o'clock!' She stood in the middle of the road, slender, hands on her hips, her voice strong, and they all obeyed.

On our return at ten or eleven at night we checked out all the rooms, bathroom and toilet and made sure that the ones who wanted to departed safely. The rest found their comfort around the loungeroom, on the couch, in armchairs and beanbags or just stretched out on the carpet. On those Sunday mornings I would tiptoe quietly out of our bedroom, step carefully between the sleeping bodies to the kitchen and start preparing the breakfast.

Zsuzsi in her 'mature age' of fifteen also had a boyfriend.

It seemed not too long ago when on our wanderings around the shops in the city I decided to have a meal in a restaurant, just for the two of us. 'Mamuka, do you think there will be a boy who will ask me out? And if he does, what will I do then?' Now Geoff, the boyfriend, frequented our house on the weekends and, with the rest of the group, walked through the paddock to the beach, with our Zsofia leading the pack.

In a way it was good. Yano and I had not much privacy and we were too busy to have arguments.

Activities for the Hungarian Club also kept us in full swing. The dancing group practised at least once a week. Some skilled mothers, including Mami, started sewing fourteen authentic Hungarian costumes, one for each dancer. Piri flew up to Melbourne with the calf measurements and shoe sizes of the girls to order the knee-high *rancos csizsma* – red boots. Latzi practised his violin and Andrash refreshed the tunes of the Hungarian dances on his accordion.

Each season of the year in Hobart was distinctly beautiful, with the autumn being the most colourful. In autumn the crisp nights were dawning into temperate days, the suburbs displaying roses in thousands of colours in their second bloom, and a golden carpet of leaves surrounded the European trees. The hills hemming the horizon folded into each other, dark blue, as they contrasted with the vivid blue of the sea and the sky. Autumn heralded the end of the fertile season; it was harvest time.

In Europe Hungary was known for it's good wine. In the autumn in Hungarian villages the workers picked the grapes for days and at the end they celebrated the good harvest. By tradition it was at the village harvest festivals that the village girls had a chance to show off by dancing and to comb with sparkling eyes the circle of men, flirting and teasing them. The hard work was finished for a year; this was fun time. The whole village took part in the harvest celebrations, a kaleidoscope of social classes – the dignitaries, the vineyard owners, the workers and the Gypsies – they all celebrated together.

The Hungarian Club was organising a Grand Grape Festival in Hobart. It was going to be big; entertainment, a live band and a dinner-dance. The city council representatives, the state Minister for Immigration, the local MP and some other politicians were invited to thank them for their support of the club.

'We need a village Gypsy,' a Gypsy fortune teller who would tell fortunes for a small donation to raise funds for the club. What a grand idea! Yenni, you would make a good Gypsy. Yeah? Okay then.

Up to the first floor at the Cat and Fiddle Arcade to the costume hire. I want a Gypsy outfit with a sexy wide skirt, a crisp, white, off-shoulder blouse and a tight black bodice. They have just the outfit. Bare feet, large earrings, lots of bangles around my wrists and ankles and a small money pouch fastened to a garter around my right thigh under the skirt. A cup of strong instant coffee and some cottonbuds to smear the cool liquid over my legs and exposed parts of my body, and there I am, an instant Gypsy.

The event is advertised in the local newspapers for weeks with great success. On Saturday night the Polish Hall is full. The lights are lowered and the long procession, true to the Hungarian village tradition, starts up from the entrance hall, led by the village judge, followed by the village drummer and other dignitaries. The Hungarian dancers, fourteen great-looking young girls in colourful costumes with wide just-above-the-knee white silk skirts propped up by starched petticoats, knee-high red leather boots, velvet bodices decorated with golden yarn worn over white, deep-cut blouses with big puffed sleeves, hemmed with lace and a headdress made of velvet with long ribbons of red, white and green flowing over their shoulders. At the end of the procession is the village Gypsy and the Gypsy violinist. The hall explodes. The band plays, the girls dance. The sounds of the fast Hungarian *csárdás*, our national dance, stir up passion; the food is good and the wine flows.

There are people who know me in my 'real life', but many don't. The ones who don't know me, think that I am a Gypsy and believe that whatever I tell them will come true. I realise this and am extra careful with what I say, keeping to the usual innocent predictions of travel, small money wins and perhaps a romance.

There is a table, two politicians and their wives who are regulars at our dances and some others. One of the politicians is the state Immigration Minister and the other I know from the television. I also know that he is the MP who helped Yano get his job in the public service.

Wandering around their table, I stand in front of the MP, lift my skirt a little so the corner of the money pouch is visible and offer to tell him his fortune. He is willing. I look at his palm and can't think of one thing I could tell him.

'You are in a position to help people,' I start up slowly. 'You are very goodhearted and have helped quite a few people already. For that you will be blessed.' I look deep into his eyes. 'You are also admired by many ladies,' I throw in for good measure. His eyes are shining; he obviously agrees with me. I tell him some more lies, and at the end lift my skirt higher still, so he can spot the little money bag hanging from my garter. He lowers a note into it and his wife puts a note in as well. So, I wander around some more tables and tell some more lies. 'You are going to travel a long distance in the near future,' I say to a lady who assures me that she is horrified of travelling.

This particular lady in a couple of years time will see me at Hobart airport and will fly through the crowd with open arms to embrace me. 'You were right. I am going to Europe. I am actually flying to Europe in a few minutes' time.' The only thing I can do is to wish her a happy journey.

Back to the harvest festival. At the end of the evening I empty the money pouch on the large table in the Polish Hall kitchen. There, among many large notes I spot a white slip of paper.

Could you please ring this number … at your convenience? I would like you to tell me my fortune. Sincerely.

Her name – the wife of the MP. I wonder if she wants to know about her husband's admirers? Who knows? I never contact her.

'Bruce rang me at work. There is a block of land near his house for sale, he thinks it would be a good buy, a bargain,' Yano informed me. 'If you want to we can go and see it after dinner.'

We still had the block at Springfield.

'So what are we going to do with that?'

'We will sell it,' Yano said.

We sat in the Kingswood, drove to Howrah and turned up Wenthworth Street. The street coiled up and down, up and down, following the contours of the hills on which the suburb was crawling up. Number nine. This was the block Bruce was talking about. Our eyes absorbed the magical view above the houses, bushes and treetops down below, where the darkening horizon eastward was making a definitive line between the water and the sky. In the light-blue twilight the city lights and the casino, as if sitting in the lap of Mount Wellington, was embraced by the long arms of descending hills, the whole image mirrored in the Derwent River as far as where it united with the sea.

What a location! Almost a double block of land and all for only $5000. Bruce was right; it was a bargain. From that day on I knew that our Rokeby house was only a temporary home, that shortly we were going to build the most beautiful home, at this most beautiful location.

Even though I had a driver's licence that was recognised by the

Tasmanian Transport Commission and the Tasmanian Police, Yano didn't recognise me as a driver. He was probably right. I had only limited hours of driving years ago and even that was on the 'wrong side of the road'. But I would have liked to learn to drive the Australian way, on the left side. Yano was agreeable; okay he will teach me how to drive.

So, under Yano's supervision he sometimes sat with me at the wheel.

It was hell. He yelled and gesticulated and worried that I was going to kill him, adding after a while 'and yourself'. I was nervous and when a car, any car, attempted to overtake I drove off the road and stopped to let it go past. Yano yelled some more and each time I drove he promised me that he would never sit in the same car when I was behind the wheel. Never.

But he did. Not because I was getting better, but because when we went out he liked to have a drink. In fact, he liked to have quite a few drinks. So I drove us home. And because Yano was tipsy, he was cheerful and did not yell, and I drove better and got us safely home.

I could never drive our *new* Kingswood though. 'It's a big car, much harder to drive,' Yano assured me, and when we headed to a party or Hungarian evening we would take the Vauxhall. During the day the Vauxhall sat in the drive while Yano took the Kingswood to work.

This hard year of 1974, with it's mixed bag of events, perhaps a few good ones but mostly bad, was coming to the end. The Christmas celebrations were held in our home as usual and for the very first time in my life Chopi and Roman were not there to share it with us. There were two new friends though, to whom we had introduced our traditions, Ishtvan's girlfriend and Zsuzsi's boyfriend.

Because of those two I realised that celebrating our Christmas on the Christmas Eve was an advantage. The girlfriends and boyfriends could easily participate in our Christmas dinners without it clashing with their traditional Christmas days.

Even though in my heart I knew Mami ached for Chopi and

Roman, we got carried away with the mood of Christmas as we sang our traditional carols, ate our feast and sorted out the presents. The two young Australians, as under a spell, watched, embracing the spirit of our celebrations.

Christmas day in our tradition was a family day. The dishes were washed up after last night's meal, the ceiling-high Christmas tree in the corner shining with *salonky*, decorations and tinsel, and the electric candles giving a warm glow to the room, this was the Christmas I knew.

It was a tradition at Pauline and George's to have a few close friends for a Christmas drink on Christmas night. We were close friends and were invited, all of us, including Mami.

It will be the old Vauxhall, I think to myself. There is just enough room on the back seat for Ishtvan, Zsuzsi and Mami.

Through Howrah, Bellerive, over the bridge and the city, to South Hobart. Pauline and George's house is on top of a steep street. When we reach the bottom of their street the Vauxhall conks out. Damn! Yano tries to revive the engine a few times but it's dead.

'Let's walk up,' he suggests and we crawl out of the car, climbing up in single file to George's red-brick double-storey house. The climb is terrible but the view is good, the windows look out over South Hobart.

We laugh, eat and drink, except me. I have a duty to perform, if, if, if the car starts up. Yano hopes that it will. But it doesn't. Yano looks under the bonnet. 'Give me that torch.' George is looking under the bonnet and George Junior is looking under the bonnet. In the single ray of the torch there is nothing to see, all looks normal. We order a taxi home and leave the Vauxhall at the bottom of the street.

Boxing Day. Early afternoon Mami and I are sitting in the Kingswood and are driven by Yano to South Hobart to pick up the Vauxhall. George comes down to the bottom of the street and once again with Yano tries to revive the engine. But it is a stubborn old car, not a sign of life in the motor.

'It will have to be an RACT job,' George reckons. 'Come upstairs, have a coffee, I'll phone them.' Yano, Mami and I climb up that hill to the house. Pauline gets busy with coffees and the leftover cakes. After a while the RACT arrives and starts up the car. Easy. I couldn't care less what was wrong with it, as long as it goes.

'This is what we will do,' Yano says decisively, and I am getting strict instructions as to how to drive the Vauxhall home, all by myself. I will drive in front, followed by the Kingswood driven by Yano. Mami will be in the back seat of the Kingswood. I am looking forward to this independent drive. I know the way home anyway from many previous night drives.

Faultlessly starting up the engine, I am up front, Yano follows, and Pauline and George wave us off. The transistor radio on the passenger seat floods the interior of the car with music. Now and then I glance into the rear-vision mirror. For a while I can see the Kingswood following, then the lights in front of the GPO turn amber, I just sneak through before it changes to red and then I can't see the Kingswood any more. I feel in absolute control of the situation, the car runs smoothly, the radio plays my favourite tune, *Hey Jude.* I sing along loudly and am contented.

In front of our gate I turn off the transistor, open the low gate and drive onto the driveway. There. I am happy with my performance.

Ten minutes later the Kingswood arrives, Yano jumps out of it, his face white. He is raging. He walks into the house leaving the door open and yells.

'Where the hell did you get to? You idiot, you. How fast did you drive? I couldn't catch up with you.'

'I kept to the speed limit. Honestly,' I defend myself. 'Why couldn't you catch up with me? It was you who disappeared, not me,' I argue.

'I knew it. Every time I do anything with you, or your mother, it turns out no good.'

'With me?' Mami pipes up. Up till now she was quietly witnessing the scene.

So what's happened? Mami found a Huntsman on the back seat, started screaming just past the GPO, Yano had to pull out of the traffic to the side of the road and chase that bloody spider out of the car. It all took time and the Vauxhall with me disappeared round the corner.

'It's not my fault, nothing to do with my driving,' I press the point. Yano is inconsolable. I am not a driver; I am a maniac who will kill the whole family if *he* let's me. This is the last time I touch the car. He has had enough.

True to his word, shortly after this episode Yano presented the Vauxhall to Ishtvan, who was on his L-plate and learning to drive.

Ishtvan got his licence. His mate, a panel beater, painted the front panel and doors of the Vauxhall with red flames, and the police stopped and checked Ishtvan every time he left our driveway.

Yano believed that if Ishtvan drives he will not drink. The Vauxhall was getting old and a little ridiculous so he bought Ishtvan a secondhand Torana from a friend. Ishtvan sold the old Vauxhall at the service station for a full tank of petrol for the Torana. And I was still not driving.

CHAPTER ELEVEN

Our Lives Change Forever

Mornings that are followed by tragic and big events usually start up the same way as mornings of not much importance. The sun comes up on the horizon and the clouds move across the sky. People have showers, get dressed and plan their day, and probably the next one after, not knowing that this sunrise was the last in their lives.

Even though it's summer, the weather has been drizzly for days. The evening of 5 January 1975, a Sunday evening, will be the last in the lives of at least ten people, but they don't know about it just yet.

❧ ❧ ❧

It's something past nine in the evening. Yano and I are in the dining part of our kitchen with Honza and Yanka, nibbling at Christmas leftovers. Their four-year-old son sleeps tucked in numerous blankets with a soft pillow under his head at the back of their station wagon, parked outside our window. Yanka has left the car radio on for him to fall asleep with.

Ishtvan, Zsuzsi, George Junior and Stephen are watching television in the loungeroom. George and Pauline are holidaying on the mainland and while they are there I feed the boys in the evenings.

George Junior is already employed and will be going to work tomorrow morning. He gets up from the armchair, stretches out his long body and says goodnight.

'I'd better be going home to catch up on my sleep. Thanks for the dinner Mrs M.' He smiles, walks out, jumps into his yellow Datsun and pulls out of the drive.

Yanka frequently ducks out of the kitchen to check up on her little son.

'Something has happened on the bridge,' she reports on her return from one of her visits.

I click on the transistor radio that is sitting on the windowsill, now that the Vauxhall has been sold.

Gasping words: 'God, this is it. My God, she's gone. The bridge is gone.'

'It must be a dramatisation, some kind of a play,' I say, reassuring us all. It doesn't sound like a report, more like learned bits and pieces of disbelief thrown into the microphone.

Just to make sure that everything is normal I stick my head through the door to the loungeroom. The television is carrying on with the Sunday-night movie.

'Must be a play,' I say again and turn the radio off to continue our conversation.

Around midnight, with the last bottle of wine empty, Honza and Yanka depart. Stephen is staying with us overnight. When the sounds of 'God Save the Queen' die away the television is turned off. Ishtvan and Zsuzsi go to their rooms. Stephen sleeps in the loungeroom. I quietly pull the kitchen door closed. The full ashtrays are emptied into the bin outside, the table is wiped and, while I am tidying the kitchen, I click on the transistor again.

The play about the bridge is still on. I tune into the words and listen to broken sentences in which the big gaps are filled with sighs and heavy breathing.

… we hit at twenty-five past nine. Actually I am the mud pilot and

the captain didn't want me on the bridge until half past nine. When we hit I thought: My God, this is it. She didn't go quick, she went halfway and then stopped. I thought her bows were on a mudbank. But we had ten thousand tons of ore in her and it was just a matter of settling. Most of us got in the lifeboat, but that went too, so all the boys went in the water. I think we have lost a few …

A different voice informs us:

This interview was conducted with Able Seaman Ronald King, married … who was on the bridge of the ship when it struck the pylon.

In utter disbelief Yano and I realise that the voices on the radio are not part of a play. They are voices of real people who have just lived through a disaster.

With hands in our laps we sit out some more interviews and listen to more broken sentences. What do they mean by the bridge has gone? Our bridge? The only connection between the Eastern Shore and the city? How could a bridge of such beauty and strength collapse? What happened? An eyewitness watching the horrific scene from the windows of his sunroom is interviewed.

I heard a great bang – it was more like an earthquake – I looked up, saw the lights off and the top of the bridge coming down. Then a few cars followed. They just seemed to topple over …

After a few hours listening Yano and I make head and tail of all those disconnected and shaken words uttered by survivors.

The 10-ton bulk carrier Lake Illawarra, sailing to Risdon from Port Pirie, hit the Tasman Bridge. There were forty-two crew members on board. The ship sank in about ten minutes and our bridge was cut in half.

We don't sleep much that night. Oh my God. Did young George get to the other side before the bridge was hit? Oh God, did he? Hurriedly I dial his number on the wall phone. The number is dead. I dial the information service. 'There is no phone connection between the Eastern Shore and the city,' they tell me.

How are we going to get to work? There is no point in taking the car.

In the morning the bus I usually take turns up on time and Yano and I get on, not knowing where it will go. It takes us to Bellerive.

The queue from behind the Clarence Hotel, with people three and four abreast, creeps from the waterfront past Bellerive Shopping Village, turning at the Howrah roundabout, and continues to coil up Howrah Road. I would never have believed how many people live on the Eastern Shore. Our busload, including Yano and me, are the last ones in the line until another bus arrives.

In the morning drizzle, with noses eagerly stuck into the newspaper, we near the waterfront step by step and read the stories of last night's survivors: those who were fished out of the water, those who managed to stop their cars before reaching the gap, those lucky ones who, in overtaking the car ahead of them, saw in their rear-vision mirror the very car they overtook disappear in the gap. We read about the heroes of the night, the Salvation Army, the police, the youngsters from Lindisfarne Rowing Club. They were all on the scene, they all did their very best. Without them the death toll would have been much higher.

Four small ferries are providing a free service carrying thousands of us across the river from the eastern to the western side, then they turn back for another load. Crossing the Derwent River on the *Matthew Brady* we see the unbelievable. A huge gap, forty-three metres wide, which had once been two spans of the Tasman Bridge has been neatly cleft at the edge of the supporting pier, no jagged edges, only a straight line. Peering over the end of the western section are the ghostly images of a Holden station wagon and a Monaro, their front wheels a little overlapping the gap, with their headlights still turned on, staring into a twenty-seven-metre plunge into the dark waters of the Derwent River. Just there, below, is the large tanker, the cars and the people who on that morning got out of their beds, had showers and planned their day and the next one after, not knowing. Now they are all embedded in the mud and the waters of the river close above them as if pretending that nothing has happened.

On the choppy waters of the wide river in the grey morning the passengers, tightly packed, look up at the gap and huddle closer still, shivering with horror. *What were the last thoughts of those who couldn't turn back? Did they know?*

We find out that about four cars plunged into the water and about ten people died (this number eventually increased). *The Mercury* carries a 'Worry List' of people who could have been near or on the bridge when it collapsed and the local police open an information line. Thank God George isn't on the list. After many tries I get him at work. He is safe, already home when the bridge went.

No one believes what has happened, hoping that at any moment they will wake up from this terrible dream. Not our bridge! Not the bridge opened with such pomp and ceremony only ten years ago.

Pauline phones from Melbourne. 'All is well Pauline, the boys are all right.' I hear her relief on the phone.

'It's terrible. We will cut short our holidays. We'll be home tomorrow,' she says.

❦❦❦

The private ferry companies got organised fast, establishing a twenty-four-hour shuttle run, and the government provided parking on both sides of the river on the large public expanses.

The two cars were removed from the rim of the bridge by the Public Works Department, with the help of the owners. Ishtvan knew the man who owned the Holden. He was the father of his schoolmate, a girl at Rosny College. Only a week ago Ishtvan attended her birthday party. She was in that car on Sunday night and crawled out of it while it was hanging over the gap by the skin of its teeth. True and less authentic stories about heroic people circulated between the commuters and filled the twenty minutes bobbing on the water with gasps of disbelief. Really? Oh my God! I can't believe it!

The bus services changed to a shuttle service carrying people to and from the waterfront on both sides of the river. Emergency transport was set up and the names of the dead were released. A team of nine army men began work to salvage equipment from the *Lake Illawarra*. An additional eighteen navy divers assisted the Hobart police divers in finding victims. Thirty-one survivors of the crew of the *Lake Illawarra* flew out of Hobart.

In the next few days the government departments started to argue about the reasons for the collapse of the bridge and about the cost of repairs. The operators of the ferry services were upset by fare issues. The immediate danger was over and all things slipped back into the usual routine of bureaucracy.

For the next three years the population of the Eastern Shore commuted by bus and ferries and the travelling time to and from work quadrupled for everyone. Sales of properties on the west bank of the river doubled and the local papers carried pages of requests for house exchanges from the Eastern Shore to the west.

The banks, supermarkets and large department stores realised they would be severely affected by the fact that people had stopped strolling and shopping, instead queuing up to catch the ferries. With the wisdom of corporate minds they started buying up empty houses on the Eastern Shore, demolishing them and building new shopping centres and office space.

Services on what used to be termed 'the other side of the river' doubled and before long Eastern Shore residents had access to all conveniences without the need to travel to the city. This severely affected businesses in the city.

Book sales soared as people travelling for hours in buses and ferries lapped up the paperbacks. Men and women who used to drive in cars now walked to and from work and were talking to each other. New friendships were made. Husbands and wives had less time to spend together and were exposed to regular social interaction with other husbands and wives.

People started dressing in the latest fashion and cared more about their appearance. The sale of beer in the bars on the private ferries surged as people, using the public transport, relaxed after work.

I have met my destiny.

The year of 1975 marked the beginning of the most important years of my life. Years of maturing and understanding, losing and gaining, the years of my initiation. In those years I became the person I am now.

One of the government efforts to ease the early-morning rush on the ferries was to vary working hours for public departments at all levels. Flexitime gained momentum and helped to spread out the mass of people boarding the ferries. Yano started work at nine in the morning and I had to be at work by eight.

With a few crossings already behind me on private ferries of various sizes, but mainly small ones, I made peace with the newspaper article that informed us in large letters: 'A clairvoyant's prediction for another disaster in Hobart'. This clairvoyant had a vision of a *small* ferry, loaded with people, sinking to the bottom of the Derwent River and in his head heard the cries and saw the dead. I was just a human and resigned to the fact that it could happen. At every crossing I eagerly searched for the facial expressions of the ferry staff and was greatly relieved when a new, *large* ferry arrived to help carry the population from one side to the other. The freshly painted, blue and white *Lady Wakehurst*, which could carry 800 people, had been borrowed from Sydney. Now I felt safe and made sure that I was on board the *Lady Wakehurst* at seven every morning when it pulled out of Bellerive terminal.

For this peace of mind I had to buy an alarm clock, which echoed in the house at five thirty and made me scramble to the bathroom, while the rest of the family tried to shut the noise out of their ears and go back to sleep for another hour and a half.

Showered, dressed and with makeup at least partially done – I only had time to apply my makeup to one eye – I would stick my sunglasses on my nose and begin my day. I wore them rain or shine to shield against the curiosity of the bored public. Sometimes I found a seat on the bus; sometimes it was full when it arrived at our stop. Hanging onto the handrail or the seat in front of me I was weighed down by my heavy shoulder bag in which I carried everything I considered necessary for all possible events. A sewing kit, spare undies, a cardigan and jumper and a light blouse in case it's hot, a makeup box, manicure set, some cotton wool, some creams and an umbrella. It was like an overnight bag. Just in case.

People were pushed against the sides of the bus, sitting in bulky coats, parkas and jumpers with their noses in newspapers or paperbacks. At each stop the repeated murmur of g'mornings echoed through the narrow interior with the fogged-up windows.

The buses, lined up in dozens, constantly spilled out hundreds and thousands of passengers, all of whom were targeting the ferry terminal. Given the circumstances, the weather and the time of the morning, it was a civilised descent into the bowels of the ferry. The regular commuters considered the spaces they occupied at the very first boarding as their own and wriggled into them deeper to guard against some ignorant stranger daring to take them.

Passing the gap in the bridge we were all repeatedly reminded of the tragedy of those who were still below, near the pylon, down there in their muddy graves.

Carried out of the ferry by the mass, I walked across the street and around the corner, straight into the vestibule of the Hydro-Electric Commission, found my usual secluded space, removed my sunglasses and applied my makeup to the other eye. Now I was ready to face the day without the sunglasses. Just when I finished, the bus to Lenah Valley arrived.

Out of the bus window I observed the fast-flowing stream of brown, black, blond and grey heads, walking in the same direction; in the mornings up Elizabeth Street, in the afternoons down to the waterfront.

It's afternoon. I am part of the procession flowing towards the ferry terminal. The sounds of hurried steps following the footpath slightly downhill are all around me. Who is going to get there before the rest?

Who is going to be cut off by the skipper and will have to wait an extra twenty minutes for the next ferry?

In front of me a young woman tiptoes down the sloped street. In her arm, lifted almost up to her shoulder, is a small, wrapped-up bundle of a newborn baby bobbing its head from side to side with each step. Over her shoulder I can see the reddish, expressionless little face. The young man walking next to her is carrying a suitcase. *Just out of the maternity hospital,* I think to myself.

I walk on behind them but my eyes don't see around me. Instead a picture forms in my imagination; in it the young woman is crossing the road. She slips, losing her balance, and falls on the hard concrete of the waterfront; the baby lays spread out on its blanket, motionless.

The image disappears and the young woman is still walking in front of me. *Should I run up to her and tell her to be careful, to stop walking so fast?*

I have no time to finish my thoughts. My vision comes true. The young woman is stretched out on the concrete. I run forward. The young man is helping the woman. The baby cries. *Thank God.* The blanket has absorbed the fall.

How could I have known? How could I have seen it in my mind, exactly the way it happened before it happened?

The afternoon queues started past the Marine Board Building and snaked through the whole expanse of the waterfront. Stepping from one leg to the other, once in the queue there is plenty of time to observe, gossip or exchange a meaningful glance with that good-looking stranger, progressing to the spot where the skipper counted the passengers and, reaching the desired number, would hang the rope across the wooden plank, cutting off friends or husbands and wives from each other.

'See ya on the other side.'

February. At five in the afternoon the sun is still hot and there is nowhere to hide. At this time of day Mount Wellington starts changing its light-blue day cloak to that of a dark charcoal, as the sun slowly falls. I stand surrounded by people on the sun-drenched concrete of the waterfront, satisfied with my appearance in the light-yellow costume and knowing that I will be making small steps to reach the skipper for at least an hour and a half.

In front of me another person – tall and dark, perhaps handsome, I can't be sure, I see him only from the back – is making steps in the same direction, progressing slowly towards one of the ferries. Bored with doing nothing, I take in all the details of the person in front of me, his outfit, his movements. He is carrying a neatly closed tradesman's bag. The dark, wavy and well-cut hair is greying at the sides and is a little longer at the back, covering his clean shirt. The long legs are tucked into tight dark-blue jeans and his feet into a pair of black leather street shoes polished to a high shine. Italian. *Only Italian men wear shiny black shoes with a pair of jeans,* I think, sure of my assumption.

'Thirty-three, thirty-four, thirty-five.' The skipper of the *James McCabe* counts out. The tall, dark man crosses the small bridge and the skipper hangs up the rope in front of me.

I am intrigued. He looks okay from the back. The ferry swallows the man and I don't see anyone even vaguely resembling him for days.

After many mornings travelling on the ferry, combing the crowd with my gaze, I spot a man with his back against the wall, facing me. *Is it him?* Blue eyes, dark eyebrows, straight nose. The regular features, the way he caries his head, with unsuspecting eyes over the heads of people observing the scenery, he looks exceptionally handsome to me.

'Mary, Is there such a thing as love at first sight? If yes, I am in love,' I announced that morning walking into the lab.

Mary laughed in reply.

Over the next few weeks of standing next to him, morning after morning, following him off the ferry, I tried to work out which bus he was catching to work and in the afternoons made sure that I was at the same spot at a certain time. I was sure he would have noticed me by now. But no. It seemed I was just one more head in the crowd.

Why was I doing it? It wasn't as premeditated as it sounds, more by instinct, but basically to fill in the time, just a little private game. There was nothing in it, only the curiosity, *Will he notice me?* As soon as I sat in the home-bound bus the man didn't cross my mind. My life went on with late-evening food preparation, time shared with the family, visits from friends and pleasant moments, smaller and larger arguments with Yano.

Throughout my life it had always been the same. If I strived towards something nothing would happen for a long time; it felt like wasted energy. Then one day, suddenly, without me making any effort, the very thing I wished for would manifest. *Be careful of what you wish for.*

Off my bus I head to my usual queuing spot and stop to cross the road at the traffic light, which has turned red. A man stops next to me. That man, tall, dark and handsome, and after a quick glance in his direction I realise who he is.

'Hello.' His voice is soft, deep and very English.

The light turns green; I smile at him and keep by his side until we both board the ferry.

A very shallow conversation takes place while we cross the river. Would I like a lift once on the other side? His Austin is parked near the ferry terminal. No thank you, I need to do some shopping. Okay he will drive me there. Thank you very much.

'By the way what is your name? My name is Brian.'

'Yenni, but they call me Jenny in Australia.'

'Nice name. What nationality are you?'

'Australian of course,' I smile. 'But I am a native Hungarian.'

'From Budapest?' He faces me.

I am impressed. I have not met many people who know that Hungary and Budapest go together.

'You seem to be very familiar. Did we meet somewhere in the

past?'

I should look familiar after standing next to you every morning, I think.

'No, I don't think so. Where would we have met?'

'A-a-a-ah. I don't know. In the theatre or some other place; perhaps we know the same people?'

'No, I don't think so. The only place we go is the Polish Hall, to Hungarian evenings.'

He has been to the Polish Hall but not lately.

From that day on we crossed the river together every morning and every afternoon and sometimes walked off the ferry together to the bus stops, catching two different buses. In spurts of twenty minutes we talked about our lives. So what did he do? Was he married? Any children, dogs or cats? Does he like going out dancing, like to the Polish Hall for instance? Brian was throwing the same questions at me. What about me? Am I married; do I have children?

In the course of intense interrogation I found out that he worked as a welder for a company assembling garages. He came from England in 1967, or was it 1966? Actually he was not English but Welsh and proud of it. Yes, he was married with three children. Right now he worked very hard on his marriage – there were problems – but he was sure it would come right.

'No time for dancing.' He gave me a short, shy smile.

The summer spills into early autumn and the gardens change to orange and mauve as the chrysanthemums come into full bloom. The flower shops carry pots of white, pink and magenta cyclamens, the daylight saving has gone back to winter mode, the mornings get cooler and darker. I buy myself a white lambswool coat for $99, and Brian and I continue our interrogations.

Does he like reading? I have some really good books. Yes, he likes reading.

What else does he like? He likes to draw and hopes to learn more about sculpting.

'I like drawing too!' I exclaim, happy that we have something in common.

What else do I like, he asks. I like crisp, white and clean bedsheets and pillowcases. I like tidy homes with large kitchens and the smell of food on my arrival. I like classical music, reading, dancing and I absolutely adore Ray Charles. Hah! He too likes all these things.

'I love your eyes Jenny. You have lovely eyes.'

Am I surprised? Don't I know that he likes me? Of course I do. How else would we want to keep each other company day after day?

I smile to cover up my embarrassment and tell him how busy we are with the Hungarian dancing group. We will be catching the ferry later this evening back to the city, taking our daughter for her dancing practice.

'By the way. There will be a Hungarian Club dinner-dance in the Bavarian Tavern this Saturday. Anyone can come. Would you like to come and see the dancers?'

Depends. But he might come.

Off the ferry, onto the bus: 'See you tomorrow morning.' A look, a smile. 'See you.'

⚜ ⚜ ⚜

It was not unusual to see men in dark suits with ties and ladies in long evening gowns boarding the evening ferries on Fridays and Saturdays. A gap in the bridge here, a gap there, and people lived their lives the best they could. We did the same.

When Mark, Yano's colleague, invited us to his wedding I tiptoed in my high-heel sandals and long evening dress to the ferry, from there across the streets of Hobart to the church to attend the ceremony, back to the ferry, which was hired by the groom for the whole wedding party, then across the river to the reception. This was the first Australian wedding we had been to. I loved the bride, the groom, the flowergirls, the dresses, the colours, the laughs and the speeches. What a wedding!

❦❦❦

Saturday night at the Bavarian Tavern. As usual there is a meeting before the dinner. The food is excellent, more Austrian but with a Hungarian flavour. The owners are Hungarian, the same people who used to run the Tasman Hotel in Launceston when I stayed there to do my exams.

'Is everything okay?' the owner, Mr Foster, goes around, asking.

George, Pauline and Mami share the table with us.

'Was the food all right?' He reaches our table.

'Wonderful,' Yano and George say in unison. 'Pull up a chair, have a glass of wine with us.'

He accepts. They talk. By the way, did George and Yano know that the only Hungarian restaurant in Hobart, the one next to St David's Cathedral, is for sale? No, they did not know that. It would be a pity if someone buys it and turns it into something else. That is the only restaurant with true Hungarian food. Mr Foster keeps talking. If he wasn't committed to this one, he would be very tempted to buy it.

'Why don't you two buy it?' He turns to Yano and George with a cheeky smile.

'Ah! But wait! We might just consider it,' Yano laughs and fills Mr Foster's glass. George laughs too.

The violin and the accordion play; the girls dance. The hours of practice are paying off, they are getting very good in their dance routine and look so pretty in the colourful national costumes. Pauline and I, standing in the doorway between the dance floor and the restaurant, are bursting with pride and clap our palms red.

Back at the table. 'Would you like to dance Yenni?' George lifts his tall body and walks me to the other room where the floor is already full of couples. Passing a full-size mirror I catch my image. Even though red is not my favourite colour, this long and tight silky red dress suits me and compliments my skin. Yano thought it was too revealing with my back bare halfway down and with a big décolletage on the front.

He wondered if I should wear a blouse under it. *How ridiculous. It's still very respectable,* I think to myself. *I am not a nun.*

From the corner of my eye I spot Brian. His shoulder against the doorframe, a glass in his hand, he is smiling at me. *Oh my God, what do I do now?* He looks gorgeous. The grey jacket he wears with an open-neck shirt suits him. He is so relaxed. *Oh my God. Hurry up, finish this number,* I think, looking towards the orchestra.

George walks me back to the table.

'Excuse me for a moment,' I say, assuming they all think I am going to the ladies, and I walk out of the restaurant. He is still there. Just when I reach him the music starts up again.

'Would you like to dance?'

Brian can't stay long, only this one dance; has to catch the next ferry, but came because he promised. It's all over too soon. 'It looks a good evening. See you on Monday morning.'

❦❦❦

On Monday morning we were boarding the ferry when Brian said quietly, 'I did not sleep much last night. Problems at home.'

When off the ferry he found my hand and we walked to the city holding each other's hands.

'Actually, I also have some problems in my marriage,' I said walking on. 'I've had them for years. My husband and I are two different kinds of people; we see things in different ways.'

'I love my wife. I still hope that things will work out all right,' he told me. 'But I will hold your hand when you need it.'

A thought crossed my mind. He was honest, but did I want to be the second woman? I had to think about that one. For now it was okay though.

The twenty-minute ferry rides continued.

He was enrolling in an adult-education class about 'how to think logically'. Would I like to join him?

'I don't think I could be taught but all right. It sounds interesting.'

Yano did not object. 'How are you going to get there and back?'

'I'll catch the ferry and the bus. The course finishes at nine.'

Okay then. I enrolled.

'I had lunch with Latzi and George,' Yano told me one evening. 'Latzi thinks it's a good idea to buy the Hungarian restaurant. What do you think?'

'Would you give up your job then?'

No, of course not. It would be a partnership between the three of them. Latzi said he would run the restaurant during the day and play the violin for entertainment and George and Yano would work in the evenings. George could be the barman. Has George told Pauline about his plans? Yes, he has, but Pauline doesn't like it, she has had enough of him working at nights. Anyway, George thinks he could talk her into it.

'What about us then?' I asked. 'How would it work, I don't know anything about running a restaurant and I am not a very good cook anyway.'

'Don't be stupid. You don't have to do anything, perhaps sometimes help out. Michael, the owner of the restaurant will teach me how to cook.'

What did I think? I thought it would be good for Yano to find something he enjoys doing instead of lying on the couch after work and on the weekends. And perhaps, if I could help, we would have something in common and it would bring us closer together.

In the meantime, once a week, on Wednesday nights, when I got home from work I would make sure that everyone was fed, then change and catch the bus to the ferry terminal.

The course was interesting, but it did not leave me with a lasting impression. What really mattered was that I could spend those evenings with Brian. The short walks in Franklin Square while waiting for the next ferry contained more confessions on both sides.

He was trying to figure out why his wife wanted to leave him; he was trying to turn things around but it did not seem to make any difference. It looks as though he would have to move out of the house for a while, just to be on his own and think things over. He might move in with his aunt and uncle, who had an empty flat attached to their house. They lived not too far from the ferry terminal. *Thank God for that,* I thought. *He will continue to travel on the ferry.*

The course finished and for now Yano did not talk about the Hungarian restaurant all that often.

The ties between Yano and Honza, which Honza did not recognise as a friendship, continued. We regularly visited Honza and Yanka and saw Mami at least once a week. Surprise, surprise, Mami was saving up for another trip to Europe.

'Come and have a look at this jacket,' Mami called me into her room.

'Did you make it Mami? It looks like from the shop. You are very good.'

'You telling me? I worked really hard on this one.' She smiled confidently.

Mami was sewing up a new wardrobe for herself, getting ready for three months of summer in Budapest.

'Tibor and Olina keep writing that we have to talk over the ownership of the house. They will be coming to Budapest while I am there.'

'Mami, just make sure you don't give the house away to those two. Olina has been after that house for years,' I warned Mami, even though I wasn't all that interested. I felt that there was a plot behind all those letters full of pretended concern.

The ferry rides went on as usual.

'How are things at home Brian?' I enquired. 'When are you going to move out?' He had already done so, on the weekend, but only for a couple of days. He will see how it works out.

The government realised that repairing the bridge would take a long time, years. In the meantime there was a need for an alternative. They started the alternative solution by replacing the one-lane road around the coastline of the river, with a well-constructed road built for high-density traffic. The government was trying hard.

An army pontoon bridge was constructed to connect Glenorchy to Risdon. On both sides huge carparks were established, with attendants who slotted each arriving car into parking lines and supervised the one-lane traffic over the pontoon bridge in fifteen-car lots. At any given time, day and night, the carparks were completely filled with cars, trucks, utes and station wagons waiting their turn to cross. In my memory I can still hear the drum-like sound of the wheels as they crawled over the pontoon bridge at a maximum speed of twenty kilometres per hour. It took hours to wait out our turn.

'Would you like to meet me tomorrow, say at eleven in the morning? I have a day off.' Brian surprises me.

'Tomorrow? I am working. But wait, I might be able to take an afternoon off. How about twelve o'clock?'

To get to the western side he will drive his car around the Tea Tree Road and will pick me up in front of Baker's Milk.

Sitting in his Austin I become aware of the clean, soapy smell inside it. Back to the Eastern Shore. He drives us to Brighton, then the Tea Tree Road to Seven Mile Beach and parks the car almost on the sand. Tasmania is renowned for long and lonely beaches. That beach is seven miles long and there is not a soul in sight. Holding hands we stand not far from the car. The waters of Frederick Henry Bay, with the light-blue hills hemming the bay on the far horizon, mirror the dark sky with a spectrum of grey shades. The autumn sea breeze is coming in, carrying the salty air.

'Cold?' He puts his arm around my shoulders.

'Not too bad.' I smile, looking up at him, holding his blue eyes with my stare.

The inevitable happens. Brian bends above my face and his lips touch mine.

How is it that whenever I am near him it feels like a homecoming? As if I am in the right place, as if I belong there, with him.

❦❦❦

The next afternoon he waited for me in front of the GPO.

'How come you are meeting me here instead of at the ferry terminal?' I asked.

'Come with me,' he said and started mounting the stairs of the GPO. Reaching the platform, his back against the pillar, knee lifted to support the tradesman's bag, he undid its lock.

'Here. This is for you.' From the depth of the bag he pulled out the most beautiful bunch of flowers.

When was the right time to be honest about your feelings and tell your husband that you loved someone else? When would you know for sure that you wanted to share your life with someone else?

To kiss a man in the magic of a moment is not an adultery, I told myself.

But this is more than a magic moment, my other side argued with me.

Should I tell Yano? What should I tell him? Did I really want to leave him? Was it just because this man was so wonderfully attentive, gentle and unassuming, so thoughtful, that he made me feel wanted and loved like I had never felt before, even though he kept saying that he was still trying to work on his marriage?

Those gestures, that emotional response, was exactly what I always wanted and never really got from Yano. I continued arguing inside myself.

Was it possible that I loved two men, and both of them for the wrong reason? Seeing Yano I thought of the things we had achieved together. Such a long time, almost a lifetime. I truly couldn't imagine my life without him.

When I was with Brian, though, I was *me*. Relaxed, happy, giving and taking, in the right place with the right person.

It was Brian's destiny, not his decision, that his marriage was breaking up and I was there to help him through. He needed me and I loved him. But what would happen if he succeeded and put his marriage together?

As through my whole life, once again I found myself between two different worlds.

Six months went by, a hard six months of soul searching and lonely tears on my part; a hard and heart-wrenching six months for Brian. He had to leave his family; his wife did not want him around. He moved out and rented a hotel room to live in.

What was he going to do? He didn't know. And what about me? Would I like to share my life with him? He knew that he loved me, we could be happy together.

Once off the ferry he went to his hotel, I caught the bus. The heat in the bus and the darkness gave me the comfortable privacy to think things out.

So, what would happen if I left Yano? Perhaps Yano wouldn't mind. We had so many arguments. Perhaps he would be relieved. But what would my life be with Brian?

My thoughts were so intense, so focused in my honest desire to make the right decision and not to hurt anybody, at least not too much.

Have I dozed off or was it a vision? The picture is quite clear to this day:

A large, very green and lush paddock. I am sitting at the foot of a huge leafy tree turned to one side, with my legs bent under. My romantic-looking, frilly white dress is spread around me. One hand rests partly on the grass, where it feels the cool moistness of it, and partly on the brim of a straw hat. I am smiling. On the horizon, just behind the low and long wooden fence, are the people. Many people. It looks like a large gathering, perhaps horseracing. They are far away but I know that I can reach them any time if I wanted to. But, not now. Brian is crossing the paddock, walking towards me with a huge smile. I feel so light, so happy.

The bus was shaking, climbing Howrah hill. I opened my eyes. The happy feeling was replaced by heavy thoughts. We were over the halfway point to Rokeby.

I wonder what my life will turn out to be with Yano, I think.

Then there is another vision:

Everything is grey. We are in the driveway of our Rokeby house. Yano is in the overworn jumper that he always wears at home and is crouching, placing large stone pavers next to each other. He is paving the drive. I am crouching too, perhaps paving, I am not sure, but Yano is turned with his back towards me and I feel alone.

The vision disappeared. I decided to talk to Yano and be honest with him.

❦❦❦

It is a Friday in the second half of October 1975. When Yano comes home from work I ask him to the loungeroom. With Ishtvan and Zsuzsi sitting around, I tell them all about my intentions. I want to leave. I have met a man I think I could be happy with. It is not working out between Yano and I; it hasn't been working out for years.

They are all stunned. In the descending evening an uneasy quiet lies across the room. We all are trying to put our thoughts together.

'I knew something was wrong,' Yano says quietly as to himself. 'You have been behaving so strangely.'

I try again. 'Perhaps it will be better for both of us. Perhaps you will be happier without me. We have so many arguments.' My words float around us unconvincingly.

Yano is sitting still in the armchair opposite me and keeps repeating, 'What am I to do? What am I to do?' Each of his words feels like the slash of a whip. 'I have no one to talk to. Back in Košice at least I had close friends, good friends who listened, who understood. But here?'

'I will stay with you, Dad,' Ishtvan says. Then, turning towards me, as an explanation he adds, 'Dad will have no one to be with.'

I can but admire the integrity of this teenage boy, who most of the time is on a war footing with his father.

'I will move in with Geoff,' my little girl decides with the wisdom of her sixteen years. She can't choose between Yano and I so she will live with her very first-ever boyfriend.

'Perhaps if I will go back to Czechoslovakia; perhaps they will let me off the jail sentence if I tell them what has happened.'

'Don't be silly Yano.' I am horrified, realising how very dependent and lonely he is. Lonely for his old friends.

'… and just now when George, Latzi and I have decided to buy the restaurant.' He follows his own thoughts.

My decision is shaken as I look around me at Ishtvan, Zsuzsi, Yano, and the destruction I would leave behind. And, as once before, eight years earlier, I can't do it. I can't break up my family and force my children to take a path in their lives that would be totally alien to everything they had seen or heard from us. There is no way I can force their lives into a direction that they never intended to take.

Yano's face turns pale. In his distress suddenly he gets up, walks fast through the room and the passage. I hear him entering the bathroom. Ishtvan and Zsuzsi are right behind him. Zsuzsi comes back.

'Mami, Dad is sick in the bathroom. Please tell him you love him. Please, Mami. Tell him you are not going to leave. This is all he needs to know, that you love him and that you will stay. Please.'

Neither Ishtvan or Zsuzsi think of themselves. They are both concerned for their father, who needs their concern the most.

Twenty years of marriage, intense years of love, passion and anger, hard work and achievements, leaving our country together and settling in a new one with the hope of a better life for all of us. Now I am going to tear it all apart. The children are not old enough yet, not ready to leave their home. In their young lives they have already lost people they loved. My life is not only about me; it is also about the people I belong to and gave life to.

Yano is back, sitting in the same armchair as before. His hair shows the traces of his wet fingers through it.

'Yano, listen. I will not leave, I will stay with you. I love you.'

He looks at me intensely, searching. 'Can I believe you? Can you promise that you will not see that man ever again?'

I am thinking. *It was not a flirty affair. Brian is a person of integrity. I can't turn my back on him as if our relationship, for whatever it was, has had no meaning. I love him.*

'I have to tell him in person why I will stop seeing him, Yano. I have to explain why I am staying with my family. On Monday I will catch the ferry and talk to him. He is a fair man and deserves my honesty.'

It was Monday morning. I met Brian in the terminal with puffed-up eyes.

'What's happened?' He was concerned.

'I told my husband that I wanted to leave him. I told him that I wanted to live with you, but …' my voice trailed away. 'I couldn't go through with it Brian. I can't do it.' I broke down crying.

'We will not catch the ferry.' His car was parked nearby; he will drive me to work.

'It will take hours,' I said resignedly.

It doesn't matter to him. Does it matter to me?

'No, not really. They will understand.'

The driving took an hour and a half. An hour and a half of my intense crying. I was so sorry. So sorry for Brian and me, so sorry for Yano and the children.

He understood my decision. I should be worrying about myself and my family; he will be all right. Honest. But I loved him, how was I going to be without seeing him? He loved me too. It will be hard, but life will go on. More tears from me, more tears from Brian.

I looked terrible by the time I arrived at work.

'What's wrong?' The factory manager looked at me searchingly.

'I had an argument at home,' I lied to him, but told the truth to Mary. She knew everything.

Chopi, you should be here now. I need your friendship, your understanding, so much, I thought.

Later the phone rang. It was Brian.

'Are you all right Jenny?' he wanted to know. 'I will be catching a different ferry home tonight, all right?'

'Yes.' I said.

I worked for the rest of the day with my sunglasses on.

CHAPTER TWELVE

The Hungarian Restaurant

When the intensity of feelings had simmered down and I was able to be rational, I made a conscious effort not to think about Brian or about the future. I decided to live a day at a time with people I loved and cared about, including Yano, because I did honestly care about him. But no matter how I tried I could not shake off the deep sadness inside me. It was always there when I worked, when I talked, when I smiled, when I watched a movie, read a book or heard a song. The melancholic sadness was in every cell of my body and the tears were just below the surface.

Following that horrible weekend Yano started travelling to work with me on the ferry and then meeting me after work at the ferry terminal. Just how much damage I had done to him by telling him about my intentions became instantly apparent. It was much more than I ever thought possible. Yano physically held my hand during the ferry rides, reassuring himself that I was there with him. For weeks he would phone daily at work before I left, asking, 'But you will be there for sure, won't you?' He told me that he was afraid I would leave, that perhaps one day I would not be there waiting for him.

'I don't know what's happened to me but I have fallen in love with you again,' he confessed.

Too late Yanichku, too late, my heart whispered. All I could do for now was to keep to my promise, be caring and loyal.

In November Ishtvan matriculated, finishing his study at Rosny College. As he had done in his school holidays, he started working at Baker's Milk.

'What are you going to do after the school holidays?' Yano wanted to know.

Ishtvan did not know. He would have liked to find a job to make some money. He could do with a new car. Perhaps he would continue working at Baker's Milk.

'As an unqualified labourer?' Yano was outraged. 'Is this why I work my butt off?'

'Dad I want to be happy. I want a new car, I want to go around with my friends and perhaps travel a little. This is all I want.'

'Listen you, you …' Yano didn't finish what he was going to say. 'What about your future? What about your family, if anyone would have you? What about that? Ha?'

'A-a-ah! The future. I want to be happy now; this is what I am trying to do. This is what every young person is trying to do. It's only people like you who prevent us from doing it. You are so old-fashioned.'

'Happy? H-a-p-p-y? What do you know about happiness? Do you think that money will give you happiness? Schooling is not only for learning. It gives you self-confidence, a platform to build your life on, it puts you into a certain social structure. What do you know about being happy? You idiot, you.'

The arguments went on day after day.

'Ishtvan, you are going to get some kind of schooling behind you and that's it!' Yano decisively finished every argument.

'You can't make me,' said Ishtvan, outraged.

'Yes, I can, while I am paying your bills, petrol, food and board.

Yes, I can!'

This was getting out of hand. Both strong willed, neither of them would budge, just to prove they were right.

'One of the reasons we left Czechoslovakia was that Dad and I were concerned about you and Zsuzsi not being able to study at university, because of our involvement with the Dubcek era,' I remarked one evening when only Ishtvan and I were in the loungeroom. 'We came to Australia because of the freedom in this country. Perhaps a little too much freedom. We hoped that you both would have a good life. To get it, you have to have some kind of skill. You might lose all your possessions, your car, even family members, but you will never lose your knowledge. That is your foundation for a good life.'

Ishtvan considered our conversation. Yano soon told me that Ishtvan had agreed to study at the technical college. Not at the university, as it would take too long, but he did not mind the technical college. It wasn't quite what Yano and I were hoping for but, all right, at least he would become a draughtsman.

In December the city was dressed in its Christmas gown. Garlands, reindeer and stars were hung across the streets in the main business centre, as they were every year. The windows of the largest department store, Myer, were framed in a white mist, with moving dolls dressed in shawls and beanies carrying candles and bells, and the artificial snow fell above the wintry countryside. They made me homesick for the white Christmases of my childhood. *I wonder why they don't decorate the windows with beach scenes? That would be more appropriate in Australia,* I thought.

Christmas in my mind was always a symbol of togetherness, warmth, happiness and family. What would Brian do? He had no one to belong to. To picture him in his basic hotel room was painful.

I phoned his work. 'May I talk to Brian, please?'

'No worries. B-r-i-a-n! Phone for you!' echoed in the workshop.

'Hello?' His soft voice sent shivers down my spine.

'I have a Christmas present for you Brian. Could we meet somewhere?'

For a while the receiver went quiet.

'Are you sure?'

'Yes. Could you take an afternoon off work some time this week?'

We decided that it would be best if I drop the present at his hotel; it wasn't too far from my bus stop. I bought his present – a white cardigan, which I knew he wanted – and I walked up to the Clarence Hotel foyer, down a few steps to the lower ground, where the rented rooms were, and knocked on his door.

❦❦❦

The door opens. Oh my God! I see his pain, his suffering, in a thin, almost skin-and-bone body.

'Oh, my love.' We fall into each other's arms and stay there for an eternity.

'You have lost so much weight. Are you all right?' I hold his face in my palms, trying to wipe away his tears and mine.

'I am all right now. After we broke up I cried non-stop for two days. I cried for you, for my family, for my home. But I am getting better; actually I think I have put some weight on.' He smiles. 'Look what I have for you.'

He unwraps the double LP album. A dusty-pink cover, on it an image of a woman with outstretched arms. Her fingertips are touching the title of the LP, *The Shadow of Your Smile*, by Edward Woodward.

'One morning driving to work I heard a song on the radio, 'The first time ever I saw your face'. It reminded me of you. From then on I looked for that single but could only get it on an album. I hope you like Edward Woodward.'

'I love Edward Woodward.'

Our meeting is short. I have to get home before Yano arrives.

'Look after yourself my love.' We part once again, promising not to see each other, ever.

Dear God, I think to myself while travelling in the bus, *help me to put all my memories about Brian in a box and that box on the top shelf where no one will see it. Help me close the lid on those memories so tight that not one will escape, so when I am strong enough to look at them they will all be there for me.*

It was hard to get through the Christmas season that year. The Christmas carols, family dinner, presents, good wishes, kisses and cuddles all magnified my emotions and made me swallow my tears for Chopi and Roman, and for Brian, all the time. The best remedy was the working days; no time to indulge in private emotions, only focusing on the task at hand. Even though Yano was attentive, the lingering sadness stayed with me over the whole holiday.

On Christmas night we were at Pauline and George's as usual. George, giving me his welcoming hug, smiled at me.

'We are so pleased that you and Yano worked out your problems.'

I returned his smile and said nothing. *How did he know?* I thought. Yano must have talked to him. It proved to me that Yano and George were closer than Yano thought to begin with. I was relieved that he had a friend to talk to.

With the Christmas over, one holiday was gone and one more to go. We welcomed the New Year of 1976 at the house of the young couple whose wedding we attended the year before. They had just moved into their new home in Kingston.

At midnight, holding hands in a circle, the beautiful sounds of 'Auld Lang Syne' brought tears to my eyes. *Where is he now? What is he doing? Happy New Year my love. I hope you find your happiness this year.* I stopped short of finishing my thoughts. *What kind of happiness? Perhaps a woman? He needs a partner in his life.*

Happy New Year 1976 everyone! The young couple went around hugging us, filling up the glasses.

With our glasses full, Yano and I wandered outside into the garden. 'What an absolutely perfect summer night.' In the warm darkness the stars hung above us like Chinese lanterns. Yano wrapped his arms around me.

'Happy New Year Chitri. Perhaps I did not show it often but I really love you.' I tilted my head onto his shoulder. The sadness thoroughly absorbed me. *O Yano, this is all I wanted right through our marriage,* I thought.

Mami was sewing her new wardrobe for the Hungarian trip with intense excitement. Did I see this one? What do I think? Would the colour suit her? She had a different outfit to show me at every visit.

Some of the reasons that made her want to go to Hungary were more pleasant than others.

'I keep getting letters from Tibor. You know that he wants to meet me in Budapest to discuss the house?' I nodded in agreement. 'He is still asking me to give up my inheritance in his favour and has promised to look after the house and Opapa. He thinks that I will never be able to claim the house, considering my police record and my illegal escape.'

'Mami think about it. Don't give him anything in writing. My God, I don't have to tell you this. You were a legal representative of a company before you came to Australia; you know exactly how it goes. Don't let them fool you into anything.'

'I know, I know.'

Amid her preparations a letter from the Housing Department informed her that she had been allocated a one-bedroom unit in Glenorchy.

'This is going to be a good year, I can feel it in my bones,' Mami exclaimed. 'It started up better already than the last one. By the way Yenni, you knew that Yano told me about you wanting to leave. Did you know?'

'No, actually I didn't know.' I was surprised.

'Well he asked me to talk to you and make you see, what you were about to do to your family.'

'Then why didn't you talk to me, Mami?'

'A-a-ah, you know, before I put my thoughts together it was all settled between you two. Thank God for that. Come here Yenni, I am so glad that you came to your senses.' She hugged me and pressed a kiss on my cheek. Before she completely released me from her embrace she held me at arm's lengths and, looking intensely into my eyes, said, 'I know, I can see that you are not happy, Yenni.'

'I am Mami, honest. It's all over. Everything is right now.'

'I know, I know,' Mami said nodding her head.

I did not want to worry Mami; she has had enough sadness with Chopi, so I never told her about the whole drama, but Yano had no problem confiding in her. Of all people it had to be Mami he asked for help, Mami, who he never stopped belittling and having arguments with.

'I have the keys, Yenni. Let's go and see the unit,' Mami breathed excitedly into the receiver one morning.

Her unit was one of four terrace units in Continental Road. Everything was perfect. The bus stop was near, the view was of Mount Wellington, it was newly built, clean and bright, and the bedroom large enough for Mami's Queen Anne combination wardrobe. Mami walked in and out of rooms, opening the cupboards, inspecting the built-in wardrobe and the pantry. And she had a small garden in front of her windows, just big enough for her to potter about.

'Do you like it Yenni? I am so happy. Finally I have my own place. After so many bitter years. Finally …' Her eyes misted up with tears. I cuddled her. Poor Mami. I just hoped she would be happy there.

Regarding her plans, they were simple and practical. Nothing was going to stop her going to Europe. She will move into the new unit as soon as possible, even if it meant many return trips on the ferry.

'You and Yano will help me won't you? I have already asked Honza and Yanka for their help.'

Then she will pack her newly made skirts and coats and catch the Qantas flight to Budapest, where she will stay at her cousin's for three months.

The instructions kept coming. By the way Yenni, I talked to that Hungarian cabinet-maker. He took the measurements for the bookshelves. See that he does a good job; make sure. I want the shelves to sit on the breakfast bar, facing the loungeroom, not over there, she pointed, but here, you understand? I will leave you the keys. And make sure that you keep an eye on the unit at least once a week. Remember Yenni.'

'Okay, okay I will Mami.'

By coincidence Brian's and my birthday were only two days apart. It had been two months since I'd seen or heard from him. *It's not a sin to wish someone a happy birthday; it's not adultery,* I bargained with myself.

❦❦❦

'Could I talk to Brian, please?' I phone his work again.

'Jenny?' He is surprised.

We decide to meet. He will bring his car around and wait for me after lunch in front of Baker's Milk.

He looks so good. No sign of that skin-and-bone man. He also seems more self-confident.

So, what is he doing with himself? Not all that much; he goes to the gym and has joined a club, Parents without Partners. There are lots of people in the same predicament as he is; they talk to each other, organise picnics and parties. It's good. He has new friends. They are going to give him a birthday party this year.

'And what about you?'

Me? Always the same, not much change. You know, home, work, the Hungarian dances, some Hungarian evenings. A-a-a-ah. I almost forgot. We are buying the Hungarian restaurant – Matra – in partnership with another Hungarian man. You know the restaurant next to St David's Cathedral? That one. Matra is the name of the Hungarian mountain range. There was a third man to the partnership but his wife disagreed with them being in business, so it's only Latzi, his wife, Yano and me. We will take over by the end of the month.

'That's nice.'

By the time we discuss it, we have arrived at the Shot Tower in Taroona.

'Have you been here before?' he asks.

'No. I did not even know about this tower.'

The sixty-five-metre Shot Tower, the largest of it's type in the Southern Hemisphere, had been standing since 1870, surrounded by hills clad in gum and wattle trees, in the suburb of Taroona. I had been living in Hobart for eight years and had not even heard of it's existence. My life has been absorbed by work, ferry and bus catching and the family.

'Why do they call it the Shot Tower?'

'It was constructed to make shots by pouring the lead from the top of the tower through colanders with different-sized holes and letting them fall into a tub of water at the bottom. By the time the shots reached the water they were perfectly round. Would you like to climb the stairs to the top? There is a platform with a 360-degree view.' Brian is already ushering me through the old wooden door.

There are 291 steep steps inside the narrow tower, going round and round until we reach the door, which has to be pushed against the gusty wind.

The city, the broken bridge, the mouth of the river with small, toy-like ferries pedalling there and back, the whole Eastern Shore, South Arm and Bruny Island is laid out all around us. There is no one about, only the two of us high up from the green patch of grass and the little cars parked at the foot of the tower. The sky feels just a stretch of a hand away.

Brian rests against the wall of the tower.

'Come here Jenny.' He pulls me close. 'I want you to know that I love you very much and you will stay in my heart forever.'

'You will too Brian.' I burst out crying uncontrollably. After so many months of crying inside me I can finally let it out. I can tell him how much it hurts, that I do understand that we can't go on like this. We both agree, that we can't hold each other back from living our own lives, that this should be the last meeting between us, that we should look towards the future and try our best to be happy, that it was wonderful for us to meet and get to know each other but it has no future.

There on top of the Shot Tower, with Hobart spread out in a beautiful display of greens and blues, Brian and I hold each other close and cry our hearts out.

We promise that we will not phone or seek out one another, ever.

'Still, if something very important happens in your life Jenny, here is the phone number of my aunt. Just in case. They are not likely to move, even if I do.'

On the way down I can barely see the stairs through my tears. As we sit in the car I stick my sunglasses on and Brian drives me to the ferry terminal.

'For the last time, goodbye my love.'

I catch the ferry. Now Brian and I are free to live our lives the way we want to, the way we can.

That evening on Yano's return from work I press the usual welcoming kiss on his cheek. I feel more in control of my destiny and ironically more balanced.

Deep inside, tearlessly I cry for days, nights, weeks, for years, but my conscience is clear.

Soon the bank loans were finalised, the contract was signed and we became restaurant owners, partners with Latzi and his wife. After signing over the business the old owner lingered around for weeks, making sure that we had at least a basic knowledge about what to do. Basic knowledge was the right word to describe the combined wisdom between the four of us. The most we had was a large dose of enthusiasm and optimism. The rest will come, Yano thought cheerfully. Fancy a draughtsman, a social worker-cum-laboratory analyst, a builder and a housewife trying to run an upmarket restaurant. I wasn't even enthusiastic. Having a restaurant wasn't something I ever contemplated being part of.

Latzi's wife was the same woman with long black hair and dark eyes I used to be so jealous of. But that was last year, in fact light-years away, since then much has changed. I have learned about myself and about Yano through the heartaches. By the time we had taken over the business there was nothing left from those fruitless emotions. I had no reason to be jealous, I knew exactly how Yano felt and curiously it was more of a burden to me. I did not want to leave Yano, but … but … if someone … if he fell madly in love with someone, that would be a different matter. Then it would be his choice, then he wouldn't be hurting and I couldn't be blamed.

'How does one get a divorce?' I questioned Mary in the lab. 'Every second person I know is divorced, how do they do it?'

'Do you want to get a divorce?' asked Mary.

'No, not really, but I just wonder what you have to do to get one.'

'Perhaps, for some, even less than what you have done would be enough for a divorce.'

I did not really want a divorce any more. In my mind it was all settled. Yano had recovered from his shock, the children had forgotten, or had they? And Brian was out of my life.

Yano was eager to learn everything about the business. This was his independent project, without my influence and nagging. After work he would cross the park in Franklin Square with one hand in the pocket of his trousers, whistling through the narrow walkway alongside the administrative building of the cathedral, straight into Matra restaurant. The warm kitchen held a stainless-steel table, a large bain-marie and a commercial gas stove. Here, under the patronage of the old owner, he learned how to clean the eye fillets, how to cut the meat and how to prepare the dishes on the menu.

Yano loved the cooking, the atmosphere in the restaurant and the glory of being in charge. Before long he thought of himself as a chef, and started behaving like one. As soon as the last dish was served and taken out to the restaurant, he untied his apron, washed his hands, walked to the bar for a glass of wine and sat down at the staff table lighting a cigarette. This was the end of his shift.

The kitchen assistant, a lady who worked during the lunchtimes as well as in the evenings had everything ready for Yano. The onions were chopped, the mushrooms cleaned, the bain-marie filled with potatoes, rice and sauces. Yano, with the seriousness of a conductor, tasted all the dishes, instructed to add this and that if needed and was ready for the à-la-carte orders. He cooked well, the food was tasty and the compliments flowed from young and attractive waitresses through the serving hatch. The restaurant boomed.

Yano did not want me near the stove; it was his place, his glory. 'There is room only for one boss,' he reasoned. I was washing up.

This didn't worry me, but the dark-haired, fiery-eyed wife of our partner made me absolutely and furiously angry. Occasionally she worked during lunch hours as a waitress, but most times she did not work. In the evenings she turned up regularly at nine or ten o'clock, after all the hard work had been done. The first thing she would do after stepping into the restaurant was to walk to the dimmer switch, dimming the lights. 'This is more intimate, more romantic,' sending a smile towards Yano sitting with a glass of wine and a cigarette at the staff table.

Through the serving hatch she would call into the kitchen.

'Hello Yenni. Is there anything left in the bain-marie? Would you like to transfer it into this dish?' Leaving her dish on the serving bench, with a sweep of her hand she would throw her hair back and sit next to Yano. I was left furious, washing up between the towers of dirty plates. *It's only temporary; I am not going to do it for long. I don't want this restaurant.* It was in my anger that I decided quietly for myself. *I could do more than washing up. A coffee house perhaps, but never a restaurant!*

I wiped my hands and calmed myself down by lighting a cigarette.

Most times we crossed the river with the last ferry at quarter to one in the morning, dead tired, my head resting on Yano's shoulder, and caught the ferry again at seven in the morning back to the city. In the first months Yano and I worked every weekday evening and Saturdays. The only free days were Sundays.

When our lunchtime cook left for another job, things came to a head. Latzi, who was still working as a builder, did his lunchtime slot looking after the bar from noon to two o'clock. He would also come most evenings, dressed in Hungarian costume, to play his violin and look after the bar. The three of us worked hard.

But we couldn't do without the lunchtime cook. Yanka! She was looking for a job. Would she like to be a cook and perhaps do the washing up in the evenings? There was no question in our minds about her capability to learn the menu.

Yanka and Honza needed the money and she didn't mind working broken shifts. After lunch she would go home and come back for the evening. This was a turning point in my routine. I could catch the ferry home on my own from my daytime work. After being forced into the straightjacket of going from work to work, the feeling of independence was overwhelming. For twenty minutes I could sit on the upper deck of the ferry with the salty breeze in my hair and with closed eyes listen to the music from the amplifiers: 'My eyes adore you …'

Even though during the weekends and sometimes for group bookings I had to help out in the evenings, it was a large improvement that contributed to a much more settled homelife.

Everything that happened to Mami affected me. Her happiness was directly linked with my peace of mind and, in a way, with my clean conscience.

Mami returned from Hungary transformed, loving her new unit and the improvements made by the Hungarian cabinet-maker.

I took a deep breath. *Thank goodness there are no complaints.*

'How was it Mami?' Did she meet Opapa? No, she couldn't meet up with Opapa, he was too sick to travel; the veil of sadness covered her eyes. But she has met Tibor and Olina. So, what was the outcome about the house? No outcome, they couldn't agree on anything but Mami gave her power of attorney to Tibor so he can see to the affairs of the house and act on her behalf.

'Oh my God Mami! You just gave the house to Tibor.'

Ah! What could she do, with her living in Tasmania and the house being in Košice?

The family from Prague also came to visit in Budapest; Opapa's sisters and Milan and his wife. *My tall, blond, blue-eyed second cousin, the love of my teenage years,* I thought, and intensely listened to Mami's recall.

'Milan could barely wait to see the photos of you Yenni and then he couldn't take his eyes of them. He wanted to know everything about you,' she reported.

I hadn't seen Milan for twenty years.

'I can tell,' she smiled, 'Milan still has you in his heart. Here are some photos of him.'

Still good looking, I summed him up.

Mami left the biggest news to the last. She has met a man, a handsome engineer who wants to marry her, providing she lived with him in Hungary.

'Why don't you? Do you love him Mami?'

Well, she wouldn't go as far as loving him, but she was very fond of him. Yes. And she was certain that he loved her.

'Why don't you go back to Hungary then and live there? It would be the easiest thing for you to do, with the language, family and friends. You know? You could even draw on the Australian pension. You would have no financial problems, that's for sure.'

'How can you even suggest such a thing? My home is where you are. Do you think I could leave you all here? Besides, I love Tasmania. If he really loves me, he could come and live in Tasmania.' Mami was quite outraged about my suggestion.

In the following months many letters were written on both sides of the ocean. It wasn't that easy for him to pack up his well-paid job just a few years before his retirement. What would he live on in Tasmania? Besides, he was supporting his son, a university student for another two years. Mami stood her ground and so did he. In the meantime he showered her with parcels of Hungarian books and expensive figurines from Herend Porcelain. This relationship going nowhere did give a spark and meaning to Mami's life though. She stopped being *only* a grandmother and mother with a broken heart. She became a woman who was cared for by *that handsome man*; someone was in love with her.

She enrolled in English classes and created her group of friends, inviting them for afternoon teas into her cultured and beautiful unit, her castle, with all the paintings, silver and figurines she had brought with her from her native country.

This was only one part in the complexity of Mami's life, the shiny and good part. Regardless of the positive, she had never lived down the humiliation of being rejected by her daughter and being prohibited to care for Roman. It left her bitterly disappointed and helpless. Mami never missed out on a chance to remind us that 'that bastard, that vagabond destroyed my life when he took my daughter away from me', with her tears readily filling her eyes.

She started working on how to keep in touch with Roman. With her resourceful intelligence she found out about Roman's school, what time he started and finished and which way he went home.

The rest was easy. Mami turned up at Roman's school in the afternoons, on the dot when the bell rang, carrying packets of chocolates, biscuits, fruit and you name it. Through Hans's deliberate effort and Chopi's belief that English would be easier for Roman if he forgot about the Hungarian language, in a short few months Roman could no longer speak his mother tongue. Did Mami have an agenda in attending the English classes? Perhaps there were more reasons for her learning but the fact was that Mami had learned enough English to have a basic conversation with Roman. There was a special bond between those two, which no one could ever destroy. Roman and Mami never lost touch with each other, not then and not later.

When Chopi found out about Mami's visits she forbade her to feed Roman with sweets. Another dramatic phone conversation took place between mother and daughter. As soon as Mami finished her phone argument with Chopi she dialled my phone number and cried into the receiver asking over and over, 'What can I do Yenni, what can I do?'

Mami persisted with her visits though and the next phone call from Chopi she said, 'Okay I will take him only fruit. But you can't stop me from seeing my grandson!' and she hung up. After that there was no debate about her visits.

And there was more tragic news for Mami and me before that miserable year finished. Opapa died on 12 August 1976 at eighty-four years old.

I loved the lab, the people I was working with and my job, I enjoyed the activities and friendships of the Hungarian dancing group, but those activities were only superficial. They did not balance out the deep emotional problems with Mami, the hole that was created by Chopi's absence from my life and the constant effort to reinstate and keep my marriage happy. I was looking for something that would give me a feeling of satisfaction, something I could immerse myself in.

In the spring, when the swallows returned and the sun lingered longer in the sky, I felt an urge to get closer to nature, to make and see things grow. The garden, the veggie patch and fruit trees had been part of my young years. Just watching, listening and growing up in a household where the food was supplied largely from the garden and dictated by the seasons, I had learned a lot about gardening and preserving. Perhaps this desire was part of my coming to terms with all that was inside me and outside my control.

Yano fenced off a large patch in the backyard and I enthusiastically started establishing my garden of homegrown vegetables. During the weekends and some afternoons, bared to a bikini and with Zsofia at my heels, I planted, weeded and in the end harvested strawberries, carrots, radishes and other vegies, and my heart healed.

Wonderfully satisfied with my effort I kept watering and watching the lush harvest, wondering about the miracles of nature … *and it all grew out of seeds!*

On the home front the youngsters kept congregating at our place during the weekends and I kept cooking up for them big pots of Hungarian food and cakes. Girlfriends were left behind and new ones came. Some girlfriends got attached to Yano and I and visited even after breaking up with the boys. The birthday parties progressed through all the eighteenth-birthday celebrations, and the oldest of the group, George Junior, reached his twenty-first.

Even though in the mid-1970s the Hungarian dancing group and the Polish dancers were exceptionally popular in Hobart and were often invited to perform at various venues, Ishtvan, Stephen and George Junior lost interest, finding the discos more inviting. But the girls still diligently practised.

An invitation arrived at the Hungarian Club in Hobart to take part in the third Australian–Hungarian get-together, in Adelaide. Four dancers were selected, among them Zsuzsi.

They returned with an invitation to the Fourth Hungarian Cultural Convention, to be held in Melbourne in January 1979. Three years to practise. The Melbourne festival was going to be a big one.

Still, some dancers left the group. New ones joined: Australian girls with their family trees reaching back to the first settlers; others were Australian girls with roots in Europe. It made no difference; they all enjoyed the lively dances and the spirit of belonging. The group grew back to fourteen. Zsuzsi's friend Kerry came to practices as an observer for a while until someone suggested that, since she was there, she might as well start dancing. And, even though her knowledge about Hungary was limited to my cooking and some wall decorations in our dining area, she wore the knee-high red boots and the Hungarian costume with pride and poise, and performed the intricate dance steps with the fever of the Hungarian temperament.

The mothers kept sewing, washing, starching the lacy petticoats and ironing the costumes, except Kerry's costume, which was cut and sewn in it's entirety by her father, an Australian gentleman who worked as an engineer when he wasn't making his daughter's Hungarian outfit. And it turned out to be beautiful, just like any other, no difference at all.

Pauline was very involved, taking part in every dance practice, as I knew she would. I came to believe that she, even though a born Australian, was the most passionate Hungarian between the whole lot of us. Her loungeroom was filled with embroidery, pictures, vases and ashtrays all decorated with Hungarian motifs. Every time I walked into her place it felt like home.

The dance group couldn't exist without the devotion of the parents, including Mami, who acted as head seamstress. Besides taxiing the girls to dance practices, the parents supplied the club with platters of food for dinner parties and washed up hundreds of plates, cups and glasses in the kitchen of the Polish Hall well into the early morning hours. There was no end to fundraising, with fashion parades and even a visit from the Hungarian Vice-Consul from Canberra to take part in a grape-harvest festival, where Zsuzsi was voted Grape Harvest Queen. Hobart's Hungarian Club became a well-known and vibrant part of the multicultural community.

Some members were not happy though. 'It's not a Hungarian dancing group,' the puritans were saying. 'Just look at them. Most girls can't utter a word of Hungarian.' 'Is this what we Hungarians were fighting for in 1956?' 'They should be taught to speak Hungarian. Let's have Hungarian language lessons on Sunday mornings,' they suggested.

The problem started when the parents realised that the main musician and the dancing teacher also felt that way. The girls said, 'No way will we spend our Sundays learning Hungarian. What for?' And most parents supported them. The discord was felt right through.

There was a meeting of dancers and parents with the teacher and the main musician. They couldn't agree. The teacher and the musician stormed out and took with them the audiotapes. So what are we going to do now? The parents, including me, looked at each other.

'We want to dance, we want to take part in the Melbourne festival,' the girls voted unanimously.

'What about the music though?'

'I have a copy of the tapes,' Pauline said. 'But what about the teacher?'

'I know!' Shirley, one of the dancers, also danced in a ballet group led by a well-known ballet master. 'I will ask Misha. He should know the Hungarian dances; he is from that part of the world.'

Misha was an extroverted, good-looking, middle-aged ballet master who had learned his skills in the Bolshoi Theatre in Russia and lived in Hobart with his hairdresser partner from Amsterdam. How much more controversial can you get in a small town like Hobart in the 1970s? A gay couple living together, both ex-Europeans with huge accents and the well-dressed Misha with a flowing shawl around his shoulders making sure that his entrance was noticed: 'Hello darlings.' But everybody loved Misha.

He agreed to teach the group. But only if the club or the parents, or he did not care who, would make sure that the discipline was going to be tops, that whatever he said went and that someone would take him to the sessions and bring him back home, since he did not drive.

'Okay, okay, we agree, we agree!'

This was when I got involved properly. Pauline and sometimes Yano were the drivers but I was there next to Pauline, Saturday afternoon after Saturday afternoon, sorting out the audiotapes, watching the girls.

The music was changed and the Brahms Hungarian dances filled the gymnasium of the Sacred Heart School in New Town. The dancers adopted the new choreography, with compliments of Misha; they danced to the new music and performed like angels. They became more professional and the group improved out of sight.

CHAPTER THIRTEEN

I Have to Rethink My Idea about Tasmanian Farmers

'Milan is dead.' Mami sat in the armchair with teary eyes. 'I knew there would be bad news from home. For a week now night after night I was dreaming about muddy plains and masses of people walking through it up to their knees.'

'Milan? My God, he was only forty-five or forty-eight! What happened?'

'Heart attack. They found him last weekend in their shack on the floor, stone cold.'

'How could it be Mami? You just met him in Budapest. He looked healthy and so good in the photos.'

'You see? And now he is dead.'

The man who taught me to love architecture, the city of Prague and Schubert's *Unfinished Symphony* is no more. A chapter in my youth has closed for good. I had hoped to meet Milan some time in the future perhaps ... somewhere, just for old times' sake. A sunny afternoon, the promenade alongside the river Vltava in Prague, two young people walking, holding hands. My memories colour orange in the bright sunshine.

That was the last time Milan and I were together, many, many years ago. Since then he had finished university, become an architect, married and had a family. And now he's gone.

Was it in 1966 or 1967 in Košice?

Mami phones. 'Milan is here. He would love to see you,' she says. 'If you want to meet him you should hurry up, because he has to catch the evening flight back to Prague.'

Yano isn't home yet, I can't leave the children alone.

Finally! Yano walks into the passage. I throw my mackintosh on and kiss Yano on his cheek. 'I will explain when I get home, I am going to Omama's.' I dash down the stairs, out to the street, run to the bus stop, no sign of the bus, keep running towards Omama's house for twenty minutes. Once there I stop for a moment, breathing heavily, then up the few steps to the entrance door and I ring the bell.

'He's just left, couldn't wait any longer. He would have missed the plane Yenni,' Mami says.

We celebrated New Year's Eve and the incoming year of 1977 in the Matra restaurant with the children and some of our friends. Yano was cooking throughout the evening and I was washing up, but by the time the large hand on the clock overlapped the small one at twelve we were all in the restaurant hugging, kissing. 'Happy New Year Chitri.' '... and to you Yanichku.'

Shortly after I walked into the toilet, tilted my head against the cool tiled wall and closed my eyes. *Happy New Year to you my love.*

'This is Rosie and Peter.' Yano introduced me to a couple sitting at the table in the Matra restaurant. 'Peter and I are working together.'

This was another longlasting friendship in the bud. Rosie was a high-school teacher of French and German and Peter, an Englishman, was a draughtsman.

Rosie was anxious to get home for a dip in the sea. 'It's a hot day isn't it? We have friends coming over next Sunday. Would you like to come?'

We went. Lauderdale, where they lived, was only ten minutes' drive from Rokeby.

Rosie and Peter's children were grown up but Anna, their labrador, was counted as a family member. She was the *flowergirl* at their wedding a year ago.

'Look at her, isn't she pretty?' Rosie pointed to the framed wedding photo, Anna positioned between Rosie and Peter with a rose wreath around her ears and with a pink, silk throwover on her back.

'Meet Barb and Clarie, and this is John and Jean.'

Nice-to-meet-yous, handshakes and a kiss on my hand from John. *A-a-a-ah! That's different,* I thought.

All of them are farmers from up north, from Deloraine, Rosie explained.

Farmers? Barbara, an attractive blond, her fingernails immaculately painted with pearl-pink nailpolish, Clarie with a cravat inside his open shirt. 'Farmers?'

The sort of farmers I knew in my native country were in the village where we stayed prior to World War II and then, much later, those from the United Farms to whom I had been allocating old-aged pensions at the Social Security Department. The other sort were the Tasmanian dairy farmers, who carried their milk to Baker's Milk on trucks. They wore wellingtons and on introduction pumped my hand with firm, coarse handshakes.

❦ ❦ ❦

'What are wellingtons?' I ask my friend Roy when I first hear the expression.

'Gumboots. You know, the ones you wore when you were a little kid.'

'I did not wear gumboots,' I protest.

'What did you wear then?'

'In summer I ran barefoot, but otherwise I wore shoes.'

'No wellingtons.' Roy clicks his tongue and shakes his head. 'Did you have a teddy bear?' He is mocking me.

'No, I had no teddy bear.'

'You poor deprived child. No wellingtons, no teddy bear,' he laughs.

❦❦❦

None of the farmers I had met in the past looked as refined as these ones.

What kind of farmers were they? Dairy farmers. And John and Jean? Well, John is a pig farmer. A pig farmer?

How come then that he kissed my hand? That's done only in sophisticated European circles. I pondered and in the course of the evening tried to find out more about our new acquaintances.

'You don't seem to believe that we are farmers,' Barbara threw the challenge my way.

With half-good English I painted them my picture of a farmer. They all laughed.

'The best way to see it for yourselves is to come up with Rosie and Peter next time.'

'Thank you for the invitation, we will.'

In the height of summer, sitting in the back seat of Peter's yellow Renault, Yano and I took off for a three-hour drive to Deloraine, to spend the weekend at Barb and Clarie's farm.

The stopover for a cold one in Ross was just right, after a hot hour and a half. Yano and Peter were elbowing the counter in the twilight of the cool pub while Rosie and I went for a walk. 'What a quaint little town.' We walked to the banks of the Ross River, observing from the large grassy patch the historic sandstone bridge built by the convicts in the nineteenth century and the beautiful church up on the slight hill to our left. Just an hour and half out of Hobart, and I had never heard of this place. How many more surprises does this small island have?

The sun came down from the middle of the sky, looking straight through Peter's windscreen as we turned left at Perth for another hour's drive on the North West Highway.

The country we were driving through was much greener than down south, farming country. The Western Tiers with their blue peaks in the background, the shorn lambs congregating in the shade of a gum tree and the cows with bowed heads, carrying their heavy udders, slowly, lazily grazing. *The image of peace,* I thought indulgently again, as I did every time I was driven through the countryside; and I am part of it.

After eight years living in Australia there were still many new, and to me unusual, things to learn. It took me weeks to recover from the shocks of that weekend. A farm? The things I saw and the life I experienced in those couple of days were at the top of my list of luxuries.

❦❦❦

Barb and Clarie's property, Hill Crest, is at Exton, just past Deloraine, and their spacious home is full of antique furniture. 'Go to the sunroom, help yourselves to drinks.' Sitting in an easychair it takes me a while to realise that there is a stream running alongside the wall … *and what was that?* A live frog living in the stream, which is surrounded by lush indoor plants. Through the large windows I look out to the grassy lawn with the swimming pool. 'See the caravan? That's for you and Yano.' Barbara points towards the caravan sitting in the shade of gum trees.

The sun is still hot, the pool water is *oh so nice* and the glasses are miraculously filling up with wine every time they are emptied. John, the pig farmer, is in and out of the pool, calling in for a glass of wine at regular intervals.

'Ready for dinner?' The rest of the farmers from the area, about sixteen of them, are starting to arrive. We are all seated around the huge dining table. As well as being farmers they also work as reporters, teachers and the like, well travelled, well educated and well informed. The conversation around the table is about European history. *Gosh! I better brush up on it for next time,* I think, and quietly listen to what they have to say.

'It's not always like this,' Barb assures me. 'We do work really hard most of the time. Like milking at five in the morning in gumboots,' she adds with a smile.

Sure, I see the cows in the distance but only with a great deal of imagination can I see our new friends running around in gumboots.

The next day we visit John's pig farm. Clean as a laboratory. 'Pigs are not dirty animals,' John explains. 'It's the pig farmers who are dirty and lazy when they don't keep their farms clean.'

Then we are invited to his home. John gallantly offers his arm to help me up the stairs and opens the door. The first thing I spot is an open grand piano.

At night we are treated to a spa evening.

I have to rethink my idea about Tasmanian farmers.

❦❦❦

The harvest in my garden was picked. Zsofia, our bottlebrush dog, and I had spent many afternoons together, she stretched out leisurely, me crouching, picking or weeding. Sometimes we walked to the shop, Zsofia leading the way with the bushy long tail wagging from side to side to the beat of her steps.

'Zsofia is very sick,' Yano said one morning as I was sitting next to him in the bus travelling towards the ferry terminal.

'What's wrong with her? Perhaps we should take her to the vet?'

'I don't think he could help her.'

All day at work I thought about Zsofia. Even though she was already fourteen, perhaps Yano was wrong, perhaps by the time I get home she would be okay.

Zsofia had died that morning. Yano had found her in the garden curled up peacefully. Knowing how much I cared for her, Yano had no heart to tell me; he wanted to prepare me for the bad news. I was grateful for Yano's kindness.

After Zsofia we never had another dog.

Ishtvan had no steady girlfriend and, because of that, he was going to parties. Zsuzsi had no boyfriend and, because of that, she did not go to parties. Instead she knitted. Sitting in the loungeroom watching TV or listening to music, she knitted up hundreds and thousands of stitches, a whole bedspread for her single bed, with the thinnest knitting yarn and thinnest needles you can imagine.

Saturday 13 August 1977, another Saturday, another party for Ishtvan.

'You want to come, Zsuzsi?' he asked.

'Not really, no thank you.' She kept knitting.

'C'mon Zsuzsi, why don't you go and enjoy yourself?'

'Yes,' Ishtvan said 'C'mon.'

After some more nagging she went.

On Sunday morning a young man knocked on the laundry door.

'Come in!' I called out and he came into the kitchen.

Tall, in shorts, no top, barefoot, his light-brown hair hanging over his face and his shoulders. 'G'day,' he said cheerfully. The white VW with the surfboard tied to its roof was parked in the drive behind our Kingswood.

'This is John,' said Zsuzsi.

This John guy wasn't exactly what we had in mind for Zsuzsi as a boyfriend, but if he behaves he will be all right. She will surely mature and eventually find herself someone more suitable, Yano and I contemplated.

After two weeks going together, one day on my return from work I found John, barefoot and as usual no top, only shorts, sitting on a chair in the middle of our kitchen. Zsuzsi was busy with a pair of scissors, cutting his hair.

How fond and trusting you would have to be of your girlfriend to let her cut your hair, which you had carefully grown and cultivated to the length that suited the image of a uni student? With his hair out of his face, finally I could see his blue eyes and his friendly features.

Life went on.

John became a regular visitor, mostly sitting the evenings out in the loungeroom conversing with us or watching TV. When nine o'clock came he bade us goodnight and jumped into his VW. The ignition regularly refused to start and our little Zsuzsi regularly pushed that small German sewing machine in front of the house, until it rolled down the slightly sloping street and the motor started rumbling.

Because John was always there, he was introduced to our customs, Christmas celebrations, our food, friends and our language, and he became a regular spectator at the Hungarian dancing group practices. Everybody loved John.

Mami, who spent the weekends with us catching the bus to Rokeby, also loved John.

'Yenni, how long did it take you to get over that man?' She surprised me with her question.

I thought for a while. 'I don't know Mami, I am not sure that I got over him.'

'You know Yenni I admire you; you are a very strong person.'

Thanks Mami, it might look like it but inside I don't feel that way at all, I thought to myself.

In October 1977 the bridge was reopened, almost three years after the disaster. During that time the Eastern Shore had grown into a satellite city with all commercial conveniences and shopping possibilities. Because of the circumstances that had been forced on all the residents by the collapse of the bridge, at the end of those years we all were different people to the ones we had been in 1975.

My relationship with Yano settled back to where it had been to begin with. Intense, full of arguments and making up, loving, hating, purposeful in our goals and achievements.

When the spring of 1978 came I planted a new veggie garden, but Zsofia wasn't there with me any more. Mami travelled to Hungary one more time, her third and last trip. The tragedy was that, even though she was only an hour's train ride away, she was never allowed to enter the city of her birth.

When she returned from the trip, for a short while it looked like her man in Hungary was close to a decision to come and live in Tasmania.

One day Mami informed me that she had found a small lump on her breast. The doctor thought it was cancerous. They did the mastectomy. The operation was a great success, the doctor assured her, no radiotherapy, no chemotherapy needed. Mami was convinced till she died, some twelve years later, that she never had a cancer. They took off her breast just to be sure. The doctor thought that it did not matter to an old woman like her, she was sure of it. After that operation Mami never talked about her man coming to Tasmania. She kept in touch with him through correspondence though.

The year kept rolling towards the end and the preparations for the Fourth Hungarian Cultural Convention in Melbourne were almost concluded.

In the meantime Yanka, our lunchtime cook at the Matra, became pregnant. 'We will have to look for another cook after our return from Melbourne,' Latzi and Yano agreed, and packed their bags.

It would be the first time, almost ten years after our arrival from Europe, that Yano and I would venture out of Tasmania. By October everything was organised, the plane tickets and motel accommodation paid for and my list of things to take completed. Surprise, surprise, John was coming too. He would travel on the Trans Bass Strait Ferry with his new secondhand van. The expenses of that trip will take all his savings so he will sleep in his van, possibly in the carpark of our motel. Ishtvan will stay home under the watchful eye of Marlene, the neighbour across the street, who has assured us that she will be strictly supervising his parties.

Melbourne, 30 December 1978. I am overwhelmed. Melbourne reminds me of Vienna, with its tall stone buildings, large shop windows, trams and buses and the constant mill of well-dressed people. Even though I love Hobart, to me it's bliss to soak up the big-town atmosphere. I long to walk between those tall buildings, to look into the shop windows, to observe and mingle with the people. I tell anybody who would listen about my desire and they say, 'So, why don't you?'

After a lengthy explanation from Pauline as to which tram to catch and how to get to the centre of the city from our motel, I find myself in front of Flinders Street Station. Besides wanting to walk through the city I want to buy a wide leather belt. It's a mission. I walk from shop to shop; many sell similar belts but there is such a huge price difference. While having a cup of coffee in a side café I realise how much I miss the big-city life. I am dead tired. *I will buy the belt in Hobart, it's much easier there,* I think, and return to our motel with the money in my purse and many new impressions.

In the following days there were more visits to the city centre. Swanston Street, Little Bourke Street, Collins Street. Pauline moved in the grid of Melbourne city as if she had been born there.

'I need to sit down somewhere and see that the tickets and the change are right. It's twelve o'clock, who wants a Chinese lunch?' Pauline looked around us, four women, with the tickets and the money crumpled in her closed fist, after we had bought theatre tickets for the musical *Annie*.

I found it odd that the Chinese restaurant owner stood outside his establishment waiting, shaking hands with each of the arriving guests, including us. But the food was good. The first Chinese meal I had ever had.

Besides the visit to the city the whole group of parents did a lot of moving about in relation to the girls' impending performance: visits to halls, dancing rehearsals, getting on and off trams, meetings and the New Year's Eve celebration organised by the Melbourne Hungarian community.

A feeling of absolute exhaustion spread inside me. The double shifts at Matra and the lack of sleep during the Christmas season had left its mark. With a spinning head and a queasy stomach I stretched out on the grass of the park and closed my eyes for a second or two.

It's afternoon. In the motel Yano and I lie on top of our bedsheets for a little rest. When I wake up Yano isn't on his side of the bed.

All the rooms in the motel open to a continuous balcony. Pauline and George's room is next to ours.

'Where is Yano?' I question George.

'Don't be alarmed Yenni, everything is all right.' With the intention of calming me down, he creates a hollow feeling in my stomach. *What's wrong?* I think, and the panic sets in.

'Yano had to go to the hospital.' George sends my fear and my heart up to my throat, where it starts beating with a frequency never experienced before, the light-headedness from early this afternoon returns. I have to hold on to the handrail of the balcony.

'Why?'

George notices my drained face.

'It's okay. Yano asked me to tell you that his ears were blocked, he couldn't hear and thought to get them syringed. The hospital is just down the road; he will be back soon.'

I look up at George suspiciously.

'Believe me, it's the truth. Look, here he comes.'

Down below the balcony I see Yano measuring the yard with long strides, smiling up at us. I take a deep breath and I feel the blood returning to my face.

The Hungarian House provided cheap meals for the ones who wanted it.

Pauline, George, Latzi, Yano and I went to check out what the Melbourne Hungarians were eating.

'Hm, hm, very nice. Who is the cook?'

'That lady at the serving hatch, see? She is a good cook. Her name is Marishka.'

Marishka was in her early forties with a largish frame, short dark hair and a cigarette hanging out of her mouth.

'Where is that bastard?' we heard her calling through the hatch.

Who was she talking about? We speculated among ourselves. Most likely her husband. He should have been here helping her, but he was a lazy man, liked his drink, unreliable, so poor Marishka was battling it out on her own.

Before I knew it, Marishka was sitting next to me at our table.

'Have a glass of wine with us and here, have a cigarette,' Yano offered.

So how was she doing in Melbourne? Latzi and Yano interrogated. How? No good. She had four children, a bloody man who was good only for effing and drinking and after twenty years in Australia they were still only renting a flat, no car, no money and she was working for shit.

Well, by the looks of it there was nothing holding her in Melbourne, Latzi concluded. Marishka nodded, lit another cigarette and had a sip of wine. Would she like to move down to Hobart? Would she like to work as a lunchtime cook for a well-known Hungarian restaurant? The pay was good, at least better than here. Latzi had a house she and her family could rent, at least until she found her feet, and her husband could work for Latzi during the mornings as a builder's labourer.

Marishka had to think about it. Even if she said yes, she had no money to cover their travel and moving expenses.

'We will pay for it,' Yano and Latzi said in unison.

Okay, then she would consider it.

Her husband arrived. Not a bad-looking man, with large dreamy eyes, he sat himself next to his wife and bore her disapproving and fiery stares. The whole story was retold for his benefit.

'Have a glass of wine and a cigarette,' Latzi offered.

They all decided there and then, Marishka and her family would move to Hobart in a month's time.

The Hungarian Cultural Convention was a triumph of organisation and variety. There were sport events, evening dinner-dances, picnics, expeditions and exhibitions. The closing concert in the Sidney Myer Music Bowl, with performances by Hungarian dancing groups from all over Australia, was to be the culmination and the conclusion of the week.

Inside the dressing room, below the large podium of the Myer Music Bowl, Pauline and I nervously busy ourselves around the girls, tying their bows, straightening their headpieces. There are groups of dancers everywhere. Each dancing group has a different costume. The beautiful hand-embroideries, representing the motifs of particular provinces in Hungary, look exquisite. Hungarian and English are spoken simultaneously. The words and the laughter mingle with the smell of deodorant and hairspray. From above, the final tunes from the group performing before our girls seep through and are drowned by clapping and cheering. Our girls are lined up on the stairs, on each step a pair of knee-high red boots, slowly progressing up to the podium.

Quick. With the camera in my hand I run down the stairs and out to the seats, positioning myself in the first row. This opportunity can't be missed. This is a one-off. The girls look beautiful. Fourteen of them, Hungarians and Australians hand in hand, all united, take their positions confidently with a smile. Finally. The first chord of Brahms' Hungarian Dance Number Five fills the air above the audience, reaching far, far back behind the wooden seats to those on the elevated grassy hill.

In the sudden silence the music takes over as the girls start dancing. All the nervousness goes; they are as good as we knew they would be, the smiles on their faces are there to stay. Now it's only the rhythm, the familiar sounds and the routine they know so well. The audience erupts and the clapping mingles with the last tunes of the music. The sun is setting and, as it does, covers us with warm rays. It is unforgettable.

Marishka moved to Hobart with her husband and four children and started cooking in the Matra. She truly was a great cook. I loved her stuffed cabbage leaves; they tasted the same as the ones my Omama used to make.

So how long has she been living in Australia? O-o-oh! She came with a whole bunch of Hungarians in 1957, a year after the Hungarian uprising.

'But you know Yenni, my life was a heap of shit straight from the beginning.'

I observed her face. An intelligent face with dark eyes, almost pretty, and she had a great smile; her eyes lit up when she smiled. With an empty restaurant after lunch she helped herself to a glass of wine from the bar, pulled up a chair, lit a cigarette and looked into space.

Her parents' house was flattened by a bomb only days before the end of World War II. The whole family died; she survived only because she happened to be at the bottom of the garden when the bomb fell. The villagers looked after her. When she was fourteen she worked as a builder's labourer, dressed in boy's clothes. He wouldn't have employed her if he had known she was a girl. She also drank and smoked like the boys did. She married at sixteen and had a child. The marriage did not work out, they parted and she found herself a job in the underground mines. Mines? What did she do there? Well, she was a truck driver. It was good though, she laughed. They paid well and her child was looked after by her mother-in-law in the village close by while Marishka worked. Then came the Hungarian uprising.

In October 1956 the students went on strike in Budapest, the Russians disagreed and moved in with tanks and heavy artillery and with this act occupied the country. Everyone in Hungary fought the occupation. Marishka worked in Tatabanya. You know? Tatabanya, where they mine the brown coal? The New Revolutionary Government made a covenant with all the miners in Hungary: if they keep working, help the industry and everything else in the country, the government will see to it that no harm would come to the miners. The miners agreed under the condition that by the end of the month the government would get rid of the Russians, push them back, out of Hungary. Marishka and the miners worked day and night to supply the coal for electricity. The government couldn't hold back the Russian tanks and the miners in the whole country went out on strike. No more deals with the government! No production, no industry, no electricity! The foreman told them, there and then while they were still underground, that the whole lot of them should walk to the border, cross into Austria and leave Hungary behind.

Marishka and her miner mates started walking. They walked for two days, crouching under bushes during the day and making headway at night until they got to Austria. They did not even realise that they were there until someone in the village started talking to them in German. It was at the beginning; the borders were not guarded so much just yet. So what happened with your child? She thought she would be able to return to Hungary and see to him. But she couldn't and had never seen him since. It was better that way. At least he had a home. And in Vienna, in the emigration camp, she met her husband, that no-good-for-anything effing man.

'I told you I had a shit of a life,' she said, lighting another cigarette, her other hand fiddling with the lacy tablecloth. 'But it's not bad here in Hobart.'

At Baker's Milk things were changing. Some tasks that had been performed for years by us were delegated to different departments outside the lab. A young, ambitious man started working in the lab and, even though no one put it into words, his sight was clearly set at management. The atmosphere had changed.

Shortly after, there were celebrations in the office; we were all invited. Mr Baker had retired and the company was sold to a mainland firm. Mr Baker would remain as an adviser on the board of directors though, at least for a while, they assured us. From one day to the other everything changed. No longer were we allowed to decide on any immediate issue without approval from head office, which was in Melbourne. The going got tough.

'What do you think Mary?'

'Blow this,' she said after a few weeks. 'Gregg asked me to do some promotional demonstrations for Baker's Milk products in supermarkets. That way I could please myself and work independently. I'm off.'

She went on part time. I was stuck in the lab with the company man who thought he knew it all much better than Otto, the factory manager, or myself. When the enthusiasm and motivation went, we all started to work for a wage, and everything we loved and cared for not long ago became only a job.

Perhaps I could work for the Department of Social Security, I thought. I had many years of experience, knew how to liaise with government departments, how to advocate on behalf of clients and how to deal with them. I could also speak a few useful languages and my English wasn't all that bad.

I phoned to make an appointment to see the director of the Social Security Department. I was told that I couldn't talk to the director but could talk to his secretary; she will see to whatever issue I have to discuss.

I used to work in government departments; I knew the drill. All government departments functioned the same way, whether it was in Czechoslovakia or Australia, they were all bureaucratic and impersonal establishments. The level of interest lay with the employee. If you were lucky you could get one who was interested in your problem. I wasn't lucky.

I walk into a warm, pleasantly furnished office. The whole impression is blue. Blue walls, blue window blinds, the pictures on the wall with a blue overtone, the chairs are covered with blue upholstery. *It has a calming effect,* I think to myself, but I am far from calm. The secretary is wearing a dark-blue suit. She sits behind the only desk, which is in a prominent position, in the middle of the room. Her hair, close to her skull, is tightly pulled behind her ears and tied with a long georgette scarf at the back of her neck. That is blue also.

'Hello.' I smile.

'Hello.' She doesn't.

I tell her about my desire to work in the Social Security Department. Could she please tell me how to go about it? This is where my work expertise lies, and I mention the languages I speak.

She looks at me with disinterest, acknowledges my language skills and says that I am too old to start working in the public-service sector.

'Old? I am only forty-two,' I object, looking at the skinny creature in her mid-fifties.

She tells me that they like to employ girls of sixteen, seventeen.

But surely the Department of Social Security requires a more mature approach, people with life experience, the ones with the compassion of years behind them.

No good, sorry, and she dismisses me.

Apart from my dissatisfaction at Baker's Milk, 1979 started up with the promise of a good year.

Immediately after our return from Melbourne the dancing girls started losing interest in giving up their Saturdays for dancing practice. There was no goal or motivation to continue; besides, one had a boyfriend, another had moved away from Hobart and others just did not want to dance any more. Zsuzsi felt the same. This was it then. The beautiful costumes were covered with plastic wrap and hung up in wardrobes.

Good news from Yanibachi. After some time keeping a friendship with Margaret they had decided to get married. The reception was at Matra. The whole family was present, except Chopi. We all enjoyed the atmosphere of friendliness and hoped for their good future. They planned a honeymoon in Europe later on that year, for the European summer. Yanibachi wanted to introduce his new bride to the family in

Hungary and wanted to show her Spain, the country he talked to her so much about. They would be leaving on a large cruise ship. It was going to be a lifetime experience for Margaret with a good-looking and caring man at her side. She had never been married or outside Australia. The only black patch in their blue sky of happiness was Nana's reaction. Nana had idolised her mother and couldn't forgive her father for replacing her.

Zsuzsi and John also made a decision about their relationship. They would get engaged in August, the exact week of their meeting at that party a year ago. Our family met John's family; everything was going according to plan. John still had a year to study at the university, preparing to be a teacher of biology, and Zsuzsi finalised her studies at Rosny College.

At the end of the 1970s unemployment, to us an unknown phenomenon, was raging. It was unthinkable to Yano and I that our children couldn't be employed, that in our new country they would not be allowed to develop their chosen skills and achieve the prosperity we were hoping for them, the very consideration that had played a part in our decision to emigrate to Australia.

'I often thought whether leaving Czechoslovakia was the right thing to do. Though the wages were not overly good, at least they would have had a job there,' Yano questioned himself. 'Even the socialist countries considered a job to be the right of their citizens.'

During the long hours washing up in the Matra I promised myself to never, ever get involved with another restaurant business. Never a restaurant. Too much work, too many worries and too much competition. But a coffee house would be different. A small, elegant Viennese coffee house with exclusive cakes, perhaps some open sandwiches, that's all. A place where people could meet each other in a cultural environment, read the papers, have a decent cup of coffee without the milkshaker rattling of the hollow-sounding and cold coffee shops. There wasn't anything like that in the city.

In the mornings, waiting at the bus stop in front of the Charles

Davies store in Elizabeth Street, I stared across the road at the couple of grey, two-storey narrow houses with the broken windows, obviously unoccupied for years. One of them had belonged to a tailor; that was all I could make out of the washed-out old sign on the building. Instead of those grey unkempt structures there should be the Viennese coffee house of my dreams. I could almost smell the coffee. What a great location! In the middle of the city. One morning I found the old houses surrounded by a tall new wooden fence made out of butter-coloured planks. I supposed the dilapidated houses were a danger to the people walking by.

On the upper level of the Cat and Fiddle Arcade is a chocolate shop where I treat myself to a Belgian chocolate bar sometimes. A 'for sale' sign is positioned at the side of the door.

'Are you selling the shop?' The owner remembers me. Yes. She is selling because she is moving to the mainland. And how much is she asking for it? Eleven thousand and the stock. Thank you very much I say and walk through Murray Street, down towards the waterfront, then through the entrance of the twelve-storey public service office building and catch the lift to the eleventh floor.

'Yanichku, there is a chocolate shop for sale in the Cat and Fiddle. It would be perfect for me and Zsuzsi. We will not need to worry about her being unemployed. They want only $11,000 for it. What do you think?'

What does he think? He thinks that I am crazy. Where would he get $11,000? Even if he could somehow, somewhere, get the $11,000 what about the rest? And what's wrong with Baker's Milk?

Yes, Yano is right. It's too much money. But gosh, it would be perfect for Zsuzsi and me. Perhaps there are other businesses in the city for sale, at a cheaper price, that could be turned into, I don't know, maybe a chocolate and coffee shop or something like that.

Without telling Yano about it, on my afternoons off I visited some real-estate agents in the city area. The idea of a shop that Zsuzsi and I could run together was so very appealing that I held to it as a dog to a bone.

Zsuzsi hadn't changed much since she was a little girl. The same hairstyle, the same posture, the same large blue eyes with lots of mischief and energy, no makeup. It wasn't hard for me to recall her decisive answer many years ago.

'… and what would you like to do when you grow up?'

'I will be a shopkeeper in a lolly shop,' standing as tall as she could, she answered with the certainty of the six-year-old. So in a funny way it would be close to the fulfilment of her childhood dream.

Some real-estate agents listened as I pursued my mission to find a suitable shop, but the outcomes were the same. 'Sorry. We have no shop of that kind for sale on the list. Why don't you see the agent across the street, they might have something.'

❦❦❦

I climb up the narrow staircase hemmed with a shiny but old wooden balustrade. This agent is the last one on my list. *If he has nothing, I will give up the idea of the shop for me and Zsuzsi for a while. But not for good,* I assure myself.

'Just a second,' the secretary says, and ushers me to a waiting room. Shortly a young man appears. He listens. I impress even myself with the smallest details of my coffee house. So far I had not told anyone about it and as I talk the picture grows into this fantastic establishment and it gets more glamorous by the minute.

I would like it to be an upmarket place, I say, with lacy tablecloths and regency-striped wallpaper, you know? I would like to provide my customers with the daily newspapers and magazines and would like perhaps a display of Hungarian embroideries and good-quality porcelain, which people could browse while they are drinking their Viennese coffee. The goods will be for sale of course. And certainly the cakes and the food will be authentically Viennese.

The agent is interested. It is good that I came to see him, he says, because they have already started building a shopping arcade and the plan is that there would be a food outlet inside. They have a Greek businessman interested, who wants a fish and chip shop there, but the agent likes my idea better. So where are they building this arcade? 'Do you know Hobart?' he asks and I assure him that I do, reasonably well. The arcade is going to be on Elizabeth Street, opposite the Charles Davies store. Is he serious? Yes, he is. They had demolished the old houses and had already started building; they are hoping to open the arcade some time in the middle of the year. Next week he will have the floorplans and the number of shops inside the arcade; if I like I could call in and see it for myself, perhaps even choose the most suitable shop.

'Yano, Yano, listen. I have found a place where we can have our coffee house.' I throw my arms around Yano's neck and explain to the smallest detail.

How come suddenly I talk about nothing else but this coffee house? Yano questions me. He has no money to throw out the window, I don't know the first thing about business, I am a lousy cook; so what am I talking about?

'I have had enough of Baker's Milk, Yano,' I say, and explain again that everything has changed there. And think of Zsuzsi; she could have a job with me. I know exactly how to run a coffee house, trust me, honestly. We could borrow the money and pay it back as we go. I keep hammering it in. Borrow? B-o-r-r-o-w? He is not going to borrow a cent. He has managed to get by without a loan for ten years and we have been all right. He is not going to start borrowing now. But he has borrowed for the Matra. That's different.

Step by step, argument by argument, I made him come and see the floorplans. Something happened at that meeting. Yano seemed to like the set-up, even the idea of the coffee house, when my description, my plans, which Yano never wanted to hear from me, were repeated to him by the agent. And the fit-out will be up to us, the young estate agent explained. There would be no pressure from the landlord; all we had to finance was the plumbing. The costs and rental will be discussed in a couple of months' time at the meeting of tenants with the National Mutual, our landlord-to-be. In the meantime we should decide for sure.

I knew then that Yano would agree. I knew it, I knew it! I could see it in his shiny eyes. And this was still only the beginning of 1979.

CHAPTER FOURTEEN

The Best Viennese Coffee House in Town

I was planning the best and most upmarket coffee house in Tasmania, perhaps in Australia. Yano and I found ourselves deep in discussion about this new business. The problem was that Yano did not want to borrow money.

'How about a partner?' he suggested.

H-m-m-m! I wasn't going to share my ideas with anyone, not until I absolutely had to.

'Who do you have in mind?'

'One of Latzi's mates, a good, reliable guy. You know Yozshi?'

Yes, I knew Yozshi, but he was a builder. A feeling of definite refusal completely absorbed me. *What would he know about running an upmarket coffee house?* But, if this was the only way to have the coffee house, let's have a partner, whoever it might be.

'Yes, that would be good. Yozshi could be very helpful also with the fitting out.' Yano and I reached one of our rare agreements; he would talk to Yozshi.

Besides the new business, we had other problems. Matra restaurant had not been doing very well. Latzi was in the middle of a nasty divorce, in and out of courtrooms, and he would perhaps have to pay his wife out. He barely had time to put in an appearance during lunches, let alone to run a restaurant. The staff was patched up the best that could be managed, but without supervision the business started on a downward slide. Latzi wanted to sell. Yano thought of selling too but there were no takers.

But Yozshi was interested in the partnership. As a builder he had some money saved up and he liked the idea of the coffee house.

I kept planning my coffee house in minute detail and, as the days went on, I hated my job at Baker's Milk more and more. Yano and I agreed that I should resign.

After a farewell party *up in the office*, I departed from Baker's Milk in March with a set of six Bohemian-crystal wine glasses, a crystal ashtray and a cheque for $3000 as my superannuation payout.

Now it was full speed towards the new venture, starting a coffee house from nothing, with big ideas but without any real experience.

We attended a meeting with National Mutual. The rentals for the shops were outrageously high, the most expensive in the city, all modelled on the rentals in Melbourne. The tenants objected. True, true, the representative nodded his head but, consider this, it was the most exclusive location in the city; besides, if we didn't want it, there was plenty of interest in the premises, no worries. Here is the contract. You will need a lawyer to check it out and, if any of you have any problems or objections, we can discuss them at the next meeting.

So, how much would it cost to employ a lawyer? Perhaps $80 or $100 per hour. *No way,* I thought. At home I placed the sixty-page document on the dining table, made myself a cup of coffee, lit a cigarette and opened my dictionary. Word by word I read the whole legal document and made notes.

'What do they mean by square metres? Are the public toilets included and charged for as 'prime real estate? What about that dark corner? It can't possibly be used as part of the interior because it is too narrow. They can't possibly charge the same price per square metre as they do for the rest. How about the kitchen installation, extra plumbing for the dishwasher, for the coffee machine; how about …'

At the next meeting I did get my answers. And, regarding the price per square metre, they would lower it for the areas I pointed out. That's good. Thank you very much. Yozshi and Yano seemed happy enough. *There. We didn't need a lawyer,* I thought, satisfied with my work.

'…and this is how I think the interior should look.' I face Yano and Yozshi in our loungeroom and paint them a mental picture of our coffee house. A dark-reddish, good-quality carpet. Alongside the longest wall I suggest booths with good-quality maroon-coloured vinyl; say about five, each seating four. Opposite, on the other long wall, a display cabinet, where I will display the vases, plates and porcelain figurines from Herend Porcelain. Next to it a framed board covered with red felt, large enough for pinning up a number of Hungarian doilies, perhaps even blouses and other embroidery. The wallpaper should be red and gold regency-striped. The furniture dark brown, the tables definitely round, seating a maximum of four, and covered by lacy tablecloths and, if possible, I would like bentwood chairs – they were, after all, an original Prussian design. And a true Italian coffee machine, with at least four coffee outlets. Now the kitchen. The stove, the hood, the fridge, the crockery, the cutlery, the salt and pepper shakers and the sugar bowls – the list is miles long.

More discussions.

'Don't forget about the Health Department and the City Council.' Yozshi is a builder; he knows. 'They have their own regulations: the hood should be larger than the stove, the lino has to come up to the cupboards and rounded in the corners, the benches should be …

A new day, a new problem. The coffee house would seat fifty-three. That was far too many for me and Zsuzsi to handle.

'We will need staff Yano.'

'It's not my problem; you wanted the business,' he said.

Perhaps Marlene, my neighbour across the road, would like a job.

'Marlene, would you like to work for me?'

'I would love to Jen.'

And Vera from Baker's Milk and Carol from the canteen? Yes, yes, we would love to work for you. Okay then.

'But listen girls, perhaps we will not do all that good to begin with. What if I can't pay you for the first couple of weeks?'

'It's okay Jen, we will have fun anyway.'

Thanks girls. So that was settled.

'When is it going to open?'

'I don't know yet. The opening day had been pushed back, again.'

In the meantime at home: 'Zsuzsi, pass me the Czechoslovakian cookbook that Zita sent over as a Christmas present. We will have to choose the dishes and order the ingredients. Get a sheet of paper and a biro and ask Marlene to come over to see what she thinks. We will have to finalise the deliveries.

A few days later: 'Marlene look, the delivery of Hungarian doilies, embroideries and porcelain has arrived from the agent in Sydney.'

The cardboard box was torn open impatiently by Zsuzsi.

'They are beautiful Jen,' said Marlene. 'Can I buy this blouse please?'

No way. I need it for the display. But, I suppose I can always pin a 'sold' sign on it.

The coffee arrived from Coffee Mio in Melbourne. Two twenty-kilo bags.

And the cakes?

Charlie, an Austrian pastrycook who had learned his skills in Vienna, had started a cake-baking business in Hobart and was looking for outlets for his products. Sheer luck. He walked us through his small and spotless factory and showed us the beautifully decorated tortes lined up on the shelves. What a selection! I knew them all by name; I had grown up seeing them in the cakeshops of my native city.

'Bit expensive, don't you think?' Marlene said.

'Well, customers who want to consume Viennese cakes in an upmarket coffee house will have to pay upmarket prices.'

My market research, and at that time I did not even know that this was what I was doing, was primitive, very grassroots, but effective.

'Diana, how much would you pay for a slice of cake?' I questioned the girlfriends of Stephen, George Junior and Ishtvan about their lunch spending in various restaurants and milk bars in the city.

'A-a-a-ah, perhaps eighty cents for a lamington.'

'Would you buy a slice of exclusive cake for $1.50?'

'I don't think so Mrs M.'

I did not want to sell lamingtons. But then Diana wasn't my target customer anyway. My customers were going to be middle-aged ladies and gentlemen, businesspeople who worked for a good wage and appreciated good quality. And I was going to create an environment that would support their desire for sophistication.

Music! Yozshi, we will need to install two speakers somewhere. Let's get some nice background music.

The coffee house was coming together bit by bit. Even George offered to help with fittings and turned up regularly in the evenings to assemble the booths, to screw on this and that. Yano, who was on holidays, worked from early morning to late evening and Yozshi came whenever his shift finished. There was no time for the Matra restaurant now; Latzi had to take care of that business by himself.

And the name? Why don't you call it simply Jenny's? Everyone will remember it. It sounds good too: 'Let's meet at Jenny's.'

Marlene wanted a uniform. Everyone wears uniforms. It gives you an identity with the place you work at, she thought.

'I don't really like the common uniforms, but perhaps I could make some outfits, which will be different to ordinary uniforms.'

Let all us girls go to Silk and Textiles to choose the material. We went, the girls chose and I made the skirts and tops on my Singer sewing machine. They all fitted. Great.

And the opening hours? From nine to six, with me running the business, and from six till late Yozshi will take over. We will teach him everything as soon as we find out.

We organised hundreds of things and thousands were still waiting to be taken care of.

June 1979. The European summer had begun on the other side of the globe. Yanibachi and Margaret were ready to depart for their honeymoon. Before they left Yanibachi presented me with a copy of an annual Hungarian magazine from the 1930s. In there I found pictures, photos of authentic Hungarian paintings. When framed in golden frames they made a great addition to the regency-striped walls.

'Yano, I am so proud of you and the whole family; you have done so very well. Good luck with the coffee house and see you in September.' Yanibachi and Margaret left us their contact phone numbers.

In August Zsuzsi and John's engagement party was held at John's parents' house, with many people invited who we did not know. A week before the official party, a small private family get-together was held in the dining room of our Housing Department house, where the true engagement took place with both families present.

The engagement cake, which I made for the official party, was the old favourite, the so-called 'Spoiled Cake'. Out of a large slab I cut out two big hearts, placed them next to each other on a long platter and dripped melted chocolate all over them. It was nothing even remotely similar to what an engagement cake was expected to be, but then I didn't know and no one complained.

Ring, ring. Ring, ring. It's after midnight; the phone sounds sharply through the quiet house.

'Is that you Yenni?' Yanibachi from Budapest.

He is calling to tell us that Margaret is sick and is in hospital. She has had a heart complaint for a while, but the excitement and travel has made it worse. Also, because she can't speak the language,

Yanibachi has been given a bed next to hers and now spends his days and nights there. The doctors are testing. He doesn't know how long it will take. He is phoning to let us know that most likely they won't be home until September.

It's September. Again after midnight the phone rings.

'Jenny? This is Margaret. I am calling … I … I am … Yanibachi is dead.'

'Can you speak up Margaret, the line is terrible, I can't quite make out what you are saying.'

'Yanibachi died two days ago.' I can hear her clearly now.

'My God!'

Yano comes out in his pyjamas 'Who's that?' I cover the receiver with my palm and say 'Yanibachi is dead.'

'D-e-a-d?' Yano sits down.

'What's happened Margaret? And where are you?'

'I am with your aunt in Budapest Yenni; they are looking after me. I am not sure what happened. We were going to catch the underground when Yanibachi told me to wait for him, saying, he will be only a few minutes. He placed the bag with our purchases on the floor next to me and gone round the corner where the steps led to the street level. I thought he has gone to the toilet. Shortly after he left I heard what sounded like a siren of ambulance but I did not take much notice of it.

I was left standing there and he never came back. I waited for him for four hours.' She started sobbing. 'There, in the underground, standing in one place.'

'Oh my God Margaret. Perhaps he is not dead, perhaps he got sick or …'

'He is dead Yenni. Your aunt phoned the police, all hospitals and ambulance services next morning, as soon as she could. At about 10.30 that morning I was told by her that Yanibachi collapsed, was picked up by ambulance but was already deceased. The autopsy revealed a heart attack. You see, I don't speak Hungarian and there was no one to translate.

Margaret remembered, that on that particular morning Yanibachi did not feel very well, he was tired and thought that he was coming down with something. They went to the city only because Margaret had been discharged from the hospital with good news about her heart and they wanted to come back to Australia the following week. They were souvenir shopping.

How did she get back home? She always carried the address and phone number of my aunt in her bag. After four hours waiting she walked out to the already dark street, kept walking until she managed to catch a taxi. What should she do? Should she wait a little longer or come back to Australia?

'Listen Margaret, when ever you decide to come back Zsuzsi and I will be there for you in Melbourne and then we will fly together to Hobart.'

Another early morning phone call to tell us that nine days after his death on the 26th of September a cremation service was held and attended by most of the family. Margaret was advised not to go because of her ill health. She did as they wished. She will be arriving to Melbourne on the 10th of October by Qantas flight … she told me.

'See you there Margaret.'

Two months later an article appeared by Dr Endrey published in December issue of the Adelaide Hungarian newsletter.

It said that the daughter of John Dolyak approached him and told him that the A.V.O (secret service) men took her father in Budapest and held him for two days after which he suffered a heart attack and died.

The article went on saying that: His death is a warning to people who obtain Visas to visit Russian occupied Hungary. Above all this tragic happening clearly shows that the Communists cannot be trusted.

Many thought that Yanibachi had been very outspoken, even during their stay in Budapest. He really hated the communists. Perhaps he had been watched, arrested and tortured to death.

Yanibachi's ashes arrived in Hobart after they were cleared at quarantine and were buried with his first wife. But there were unanswered questions: Why was he cremated nine days after his death? Margaret told me years after, that it was hard for her to ignore the article and what it could mean if the implications were true. Yanibachi's story is no clearer now than it was back in 1979. He was seventy-three.

❦❦❦

National Mutual informed us that part of the budget would be used for the promotion of the arcade; each shop would be separately advertised and talked about in the local media. None of the shopkeepers had any idea about just how much advertising there would be. Days before opening, radio 7HO came up with a jingle for Jenny's Coffee House and *The Mercury* called in with their photographers, all while we were hanging up pictures, unpacking and washing the crockery and in the middle of the 'How to operate the coffee machine' lesson.

The advertisement was huge. Before the opening day *The Mercury* carried a full page on the arcade: Great location and convenience … multilevel carpark … something for everyone … This is what the shoppers of Hobart have wanted for years. One step closer to shopping on the mainland.

The write-up was followed by individual advertisements for each business.

Jenny's Coffee House
and Craft Shop
Enjoy your coffee and delicious continental cakes
while you browse our range of imported arts and crafts.
Shop at your leisure.
Opening Thursday 18 October at 9 am till late.
77 Elizabeth Mall.

In *The Mercury* I read my own words about our display, the menu and my short bio, peered at the photograph of me hanging a picture on the wall, some more photos: Zsuzsi in a new Hungarian embroidered blouse, sitting in the square behind the arcade looking dreamily at a leaf on a tree; Marlene in her newly purchased blouse, showing a Hungarian vase.

Vague and exhausted, with a sense of satisfied wonder I thought of the mornings that I had stood at the bus stop opposite the entrance to the arcade wishing for my coffee house, looking at this very spot. And, as many times before, when circumstances had led me to follow my instincts, I realised that all I had to do was wish really, really hard for something, then work at it, and my dream would come true.

I had come a long way from that immigrant woman of ten years ago who could barely utter a word of English and was only good enough for washing up. Gail, a new addition to our staff, turned up with a red face, upset by a shopkeeper in the city. 'That bloody wog,' she said; then looking at me her face became redder still. 'Sorry, Yenni. But I don't think of you as a non-Australian,' and she continued her story about that bloody wog. By some miracle, with my thick accent, I became *one of them.*

As my thoughts trailed away I allowed myself a small private luxury: *I wonder if Brian reads* The Mercury. *I have lost some weight; would he recognise me in the photo? And what would his thoughts be?*

The advertisement worked like magic. The city shoppers of Hobart became caught up in the excitement of this new shopping arcade. National Mutual had done the right thing for their tenants, a great flying start.

Thursday 18 October. We have all been here since six in the morning and have no idea what to expect once the doors open. The girls look beautiful, nervously fiddling with their new outfits. Charlie arrives, carrying the cakes in large cardboard boxes. The Malakoff Torte, the Chocolate Torte, the Walnut Torte, the Coffee Torte, other tortes and the Linzer biscuits. Each is placed on a large glass platter with a lacy

paper doily and is marked with a price tag of $1.50 a slice.

'Do you know how to cut up the cakes, Yenni?' Charlie wants to know. 'Yes, with a hot knife,' I smile knowingly.

The open sandwiches, twelve of each, are made up, placed on a large tray and displayed in the glass cabinet. The sardine, hard-boiled eggs and pickled cucumbers sprinkled with caviar look spectacular, as do the diagonally laid-out pink salmon with tomatoes and parsley, and the chicken sandwiches with freshly chopped lettuce.

There is no way we could supply menus and serve our customers at their tables. They have to come up to the counter and see what is on offer. Jenny's Coffee House is the first self-service upmarket coffee house in Hobart. Every customer will choose, pay and carry their food to the table. Only the hot meals will be taken out by the staff.

By nine o'clock the arcade is filled with people, most of whom are queuing up in front of our still-closed aluminium-framed glass doors.

Hurry girls! Are you ready? A glance around the shop. It all looks just like in my dream. All is good, even though Yano and Yozshi couldn't finish the display cabinet last night and there are long planks behind the serving bench; it is okay. We all know what to do, how to operate the coffee machine and make the assortment of coffees on offer. I walk to the glass door and pull it wide open.

They come in their hundreds, straight to the food display. The queue reaches out the door. Confused orders are thrown at us, 'Perhaps that. No. Maybe the other one. It all looks so beautiful. What is it?' Within minutes all the seats are taken.

'Zsuzsi could you go to the door and tell the people that we are full but they can book in and come back in a half an hour, we will keep a table for them.'

This is new. Whoever heard of booking for a cup of coffee? But this is what is happening on that first day and, from then on, always for those who wanted to be sure to get a lunch seat at Jenny's Coffee House.

Yano calls in during his lunch hour.

'Everything is good? How are you coping?'

Good, good. Would you have half an hour to help us wash up some cups? We are running out of them. Yano rolls up his sleeves. In the course of the day the girlfriends of our boys turn up one by one. 'Can we help?' Yes please, could you help us to wash up?

Shelly comes too. Besides being a fast and efficient typist in the ANZ Bank she is very thorough in washing up. She washes everything, including the straws returned in tall glasses from the iced coffees.

'Jesus Christ, Shelly. You don't have to wash them up,' I say half loud.

'S-h-h-h-h-h!' Marlene lifts her hand to her mouth. 'The customers might hear you.'

'So?'

'It's swearing.'

'Jesus Christ is s-w-e-a-r-i-n-g? What about Oh my God then?'

'Oh my God is okay,' she says.

It became the best-known coffee house in the city, the most popular meeting place for years.

One day a customer jokingly remarked, 'Yesterday I saw you driving a new Mercedes.'

'Hah!' I said, 'That car? You should see the Jaguar I have in my garage.'

Saying that, I thought of our 1972 Kingswood and about the fact that I was catching the bus every morning. And, of course, that customer had no idea about me washing and ironing the lacy tablecloths and the uncountable number of tea-towels on the weekends, all besides my household chores.

Mami, with a sharp eye, shrewdly counted up the evidence.

'Yenni, your coffee house is a well-established business already,' she commented two weeks after our doors opened. 'Every time I walk in I see the same faces sitting there.'

She was right. From the first day the bulk of our customers were regulars.

Mami came to Jenny's twice a week, observing the people and the fashions, sometimes talking to customers, enjoying the atmosphere, the camaraderie of the staff and the food parcels I packed for her to take home. 'This is yesterday's Mami, but it's still very good.' Mami was also regularly seeing Roman after school and had English conversations with him.

One afternoon she deposited Roman at one of the booths.

'Chopi is coming to pick him up later.' She smiled and departed.

It was hard to meet Chopi for the first time in years. We faced each other a second or two before she bent towards me with her so-familiar peck on the cheek.

She had changed. There was not much left from the well-groomed, sophisticated and fashionable Chopi I used to know. My sister had become a plumpish middle-aged woman with a short haircut, no makeup, and dressed in practical browns and dark blues.

It was as if I were on one side of a ditch and Chopi on the other, just a reach away but with a fence between us. *What can I say to her?*

'Would you like a cup of coffee Chopi?'

'A-a-a-ah, no thank you; we have to go, the bus is leaving shortly.'

'It was nice to see you. Any time you are in the city, please call in.'

Roman was going on twelve. I kissed him. They left.

What made Chopi come here? I wondered. Was it one of Mami's schemes or has Chopi forgiven me for siding with Mami? Did Hans know that she had come to my coffee house and would that be a problem? How could we cross that gap, that ditch, and get rid of the fence? Where could we begin?

Roman and Chopi made Jenny's Coffee House their meeting place. It was close to their bus stop.

Chopi and I exchanged only the usual 'How are you and would you like a cup of coffee' for weeks. Bit by bit, month by month our conversations became a little more personal.

'I am going to the swimming pool Yenni; could I leave the bags here somewhere?'

Then one afternoon she came again.

'Hello Yenachka.'

Oh my God, where can I turn to hide my tears?

Even though Jenny's was extremely busy during the day, the evenings were mostly quiet.

Perhaps Hobart wasn't ready for an evening coffee place, perhaps there was a problem with the evening parking or perhaps the service wasn't good. Whatever we made during the day, a chunk of it went for the wages, electricity and other expenses to cover the evening hours. We were losing.

'Yano, I don't think we should have the business open at night. I was thinking of buying Yozshi out.'

'It's only three months since we opened. Give it time, Yena.'

'Look, every time I bring home milk or leftover bread I have a bad conscience that I am taking from Yozshi. I don't really like to discuss my plans with him either; he doesn't know the first thing about running the place. We are losing money Yano. Let's buy him out.'

When Yano told him about our desire, Yozshi thought and thought. Okay then, he will sell his half for $16,000. Sixteen thousand dollars? He put in only eight thousand three months ago! True, but look, it's a very well known and well-regarded business already; it has a huge potential. When Yano and I decide to sell, it will make us a fortune.

So, this was Yano's friend? We'd better buy him out now before he doubles the price. By Christmas 1979 we were the sole owners of Jenny's Coffee House.

It is lunchtime, Thursday. That Thursday when the pension cheques are slipped into the mail boxes in the front gardens of suburbia and the recipients, dressed in their best finery, make their fortnightly pilgrimage to the city, treating themselves to a cup of coffee and a sinfully rich slice of cake, with a guilty smile. '… I really shouldn't dear.'

Ph-ph-ph-ph, the red Gaggia coffee machine is spitting out steam. The queue in front of the display counter is growing steadily. The heat in the kitchen, just behind the beaded curtain, is rising, as the big old toaster turns out one open toasted sandwich after another.

'Tomato cheese and bacon.' 'Two banana and bacons.' 'Pineapple and …' The orders are called out alternately by the three of us through the open serving hatch and at the same time written on the order slip.

Another slip passes through the hatch. Gail grabs it. Gail is slim, young and pretty with short blond hair. Clatter, clatter, clatter. The frying pans have to be washed out.

I finish serving and walk into the kitchen. 'Boy, it's hot in here. Turn on the fan Gail, will you?' My sleeves turned up above my elbows, I dip into the soapy water.

'Hello madam. How are you today?' Marlene's cheerful voice greets the regular customer.

Marlene is always cheerful. She loves her job. We all do, and would continue to for years, side by side, day after day. We enjoy the busyness, the variety of people and the stories they tell us in the short minute that passes between cutting the cake and piping the cream on the side of the plate.

'Can you make the coffee a little stronger love?'

'Certainly.' Ph-ph-ph, the machine spits out the dark brew.

'Where's this sandwich going to, Jen?' Evelyne, the new girl, pokes her head through the serving hatch, in her hand a small basket with toasted sandwiches.

Her hair is too long and bushy, I think to myself. She should have it tied back. I did tell her the other day, but she wouldn't listen.

'One can't see your face, Evelyne,' I said. 'That's the idea, Jen,' she answered grinning. I'll have to talk to her again.

'Mr and Mrs Vienna are here,' Marlene whispers between customers.

Mr and Mrs Vienna are regulars who drink Vienna coffee and

have been patronising our coffee shop from the day it first opened. Sometimes they turn up twice a day; their business keeps them circulating in the city. Both immaculately dressed, he is a tall middle-aged gentleman and quite handsome. His wavy greying hair is a little longer than one would expect from a businessman, but well suited to a skiing outfit. Mr and Mrs Vienna hide away from the windy winters of Hobart in the fluffy, snow-covered Perisher Valley.

Standing on my tiptoes I look around to see over the heads in the queue. For a split second a vision of a cocktail shaker comes to my mind. The recipe follows: Add to the shaker two spoonfuls of chocolate scent, the essence of grilled cheese, a few drops of paté and chicken sandwich, mix it with a whiff of hairspray and perfume, and a good helping of the strong and tantalising aroma of freshly ground coffee. Shake for a minute or so, then let it go; let it waft above the lacy tablecloths and the many-coloured freshly permed heads. Let it fill the side booths with people leaning over the narrow tables in quiet conversation. Let it settle on the dark-red and golden regency-striped wallpaper, touch the golden frames of the prints on the walls and gently fall on the deep-red carpet, which swallows the bustle of many steps. Then let it rise to mingle with the soft background music and the muted clutter of the kitchen and murmur of conversation.

The vision leaves my mind.

'How are you today sir? The usual?' 'Next please. Hello madam …'

The phone rings. How can anyone be so thoughtless as to ring in the middle of lunch?

'Jenny's Coffee House.'

'This is the Country Women's Association. We are putting a booklet together and wondered if you would like to advertise with us?'

'Look I am sorry, we are in the middle of the lunch rush. Would you like to call back after three?' *People have no idea,* I think to myself.

The queue is still growing. We have to keep the double winged doors closed. Either we keep the doors closed, or we install an air curtain that will prevent the flies coming in, the Health Department informed me. I can't guarantee that the flies will not be carried in by the customers, I argue, but the Health Department stands its ground. So the doors are closed till I find $2000 to install the air curtain.

'Dear Caroline has arrived,' Zsuzsi reports, returning from one of the tables.

Dear Caroline is a man, a young man of bohemian appearance who almost daily turns up in the middle of the lunch rush, seats himself in one of the side booths, which normally accommodate four people, rolls up the lace runner and shifts the salt and pepper shakers to the wall. He walks up to the counter and asks for a weak black coffee, takes it back to his booth, produces a writing pad with faint green lines and starts writing *Dear Caroline* … and writes pages and pages.

One day I'll have to tell him to use a small table. Not today, I'll do it next week sometime. I take out an order.

'Your hair looks nice madam,' I comment, passing an elderly lady sitting very upright at the corner table. She is here every Thursday, bless her soul.

'Thank you pet. You know for the life of me I can't remember where I parked my car. Old age,' she smiles.

And then this young woman. Her cappuccino is steaming and the steam mingles with the smoke of her cigarette. Her hair piled up high, legs crossed, large eyes with eyelashes thick with mascara. Her mind seems elsewhere. But her two-year-old toddler is very much here, and on hands and knees is exploring the world of my coffee house between chairs and tables and the legs of the customers. I pick up the little boy with red cheeks. He gives me a smile, and then his lips drop. Well! I suppose the woman thinks that the lunchtimers are her free babysitters.

'Excuse me madam, it's dangerous to let the little boy go like this. Do you know how many dirty shoes walk on this carpet daily?'

The response is instant. Her eyes focus on my face. 'Sorry.' She lifts her little bundle and her handbag from the carpet beside her chair, squeezes the half smoked cigarette into the ashtray and leaves the table with the untouched cappuccino on it.

'Did you see that?' I ask Marlene on my return to the counter.

A flowery scent wafts towards the counter – Yves Saint Laurent, Paris, my favourite perfume. The scent intensifies. It is well suited to the wearer, tall and blond, her shapely legs in high-heeled courts. The V-neckline of her black jumper plunges just a little deeper than most V-cuts I know. When she reaches the counter her large eyes with a usually sad expression transform with a warm smile.

'Hi.'

'How are you Gloria?'

'You know, as usual.' The smile disappears but the warmth of her voice stays.

Gloria is also a regular, calling in twice a day for lunch and then late afternoon for a coffee. She sits in the booth, hand supporting her chin, listening to the soft French lovesongs of Sacha Distel, sipping on the short black. Then she brings the empty cup to the counter.

'Thank you,' and as she departs her scent lingers.

On one of those afternoons Gloria had confessed. Just divorced, the messy, long procedure had left her shattered; she couldn't see any meaning in her life.

'Do you still love him?' I asked directly and suddenly realised that I barely knew her.

'Not really. Oh, I don't know. But I know it will take a long time before I will care for another man, if ever.'

'We all feel the same way when betrayed. You are so young. Twenty-eight, thirty?'

'Thirty-two actually.'

'Gosh. There are plenty of men who would love to be involved with you. Just look at you. So pretty.'

'Perhaps. I have been asked out many times but I am not interested.'

'Give it time.'

That was last year and Gloria's eyes are still veiled with sadness.

And then 'Sir' turns up with his wife. He is not just 'a sir'. He is 'The Sir'. When Marlene speaks of 'The Sir', we know who she means. Sir is an Englishman in his late sixties, always in a suit and a tie, his fingernails immaculate, his broad face with smiling blue eyes. He loves our coffee and scones, comes with his wife, and after they have had their treat he carries the cups into the kitchen and places them on the sink.

'You should not worry sir, it's all included in the price.' I smile at him.

'I know,' he tells me in his London accent, and next time he does it again.

'Who is next? O-o-oh hello madam. I haven't see you for a while.' I greet the tall lady with the statuesque posture. Her face is kind, with just a touch of makeup, and is framed by snow-white, thick hair. I know her well-kept hands. She wears her rings with dignity and taste.

'My husband passed away a month ago.'

'I am so sorry madam.' A quick look at the queue. I whisper to Zsuzsi, 'Take care of the people for a second.'

'He was sick for a long time. Still, he was with me. Now I am on my own. You know dear, the evenings are the worst.'

I place my hand on her cool well-kept fingers. 'Things will change. There are lots of things you can do. It's too soon.'

'I would like to learn to paint.' Then she thinks for a while. 'Yes, that's what I would like to do. What do you think dear?'

I walk around the counter to look for an empty seat and feel the grip of cool fingers on my forearm. Her head bends a little towards my cheek as her lips touch it in a light kiss.

'Thank you dear. I feel much better now.'

The wing of the door is flung open and in its aluminium frame a tall man appears, then a second, a third and a fourth. They block out the light coming from the shopping arcade as they look around. Arms hanging, with wide steps they walk up to the counter in single file. There they stop, hands crossed in front of their groins, legs apart. The tall bodies make a living fence between us and the interior of the shop.

'Hello ma'am,' the tallest one speaks, addressing Zsuzsi. She is short, barely reaching five foot. To look up at his face she has to tilt her head back.

'… four beers please, ma'am.' He finishes his sentence and his posture relaxes, arm on the counter, the weight of his body shifts to one foot. The other three follow.

'Sorry,' Zsuzsi's confused look reaches me. 'We don't serve beer, sir.'

'What do you serve then, ma'am?' a pair of dark eyes question her.

Zsuzsi is a business-minded girl. Her brain works fast and faultlessly. These four are sailors, by their uniforms, officers from the American naval ship.

'Look at this display. We can serve you with the best cake you ever had, or some savouries from the kitchen and, I tell you what, just for you we'll make the best cappuccino in the city. How's that?' The suntanned faces stretch in smiles and the full lips uncover four sets of white teeth.

'Yes ma'am. Thank you ma'am.'

They want more than cakes. They want omelettes, grilled sandwiches and more.

'Four eggs, scrambled, ma'am,' one says. Zsuzsi thinks for a short minute. We don't sell scrambled eggs, but it's easy enough to make, and she hands the order to the kitchen.

I can hear Evelyne mumbling '… and they want scrambled eggs …'

The sailors pay one by one. I catch them from the corner of my eye as they take their seats in the fifth booth; their tall bodies bending like hinged wooden rulers as they slide into the narrow bench seats.

All the tables are taken, all the seats occupied. New customers stand in the door, look around and, when they realise that the house is full, walk out. Gloria arrives and stands in the doorway. A-a-a-ah! A customer is departing. She places her handbag on the vacant table and makes her way to the counter. In the fifth booth four heads bend in unison above the table, whispers, whispers, then four pairs of eyes follow the blond shoulder-length curls.

Gail takes out the orders.

'They want ketchup. At first I didn't understand.' She returns with blushed cheeks.

She takes out the tomato sauce and lingers around the booth, then Zsuzsi carries the tray of cakes and Marlene follows with the coffees.

I look through the hatch. Only Evelyne is in the kitchen. But not for long. She has to take out the scrambled eggs, she informs me. '… and Jen, could you just see to this sandwich please?'

No one in the kitchen and me behind the serving counter. I can hear the laughter of my girls standing in a loose formation round the fifth booth. A faint thought of disbelief at how fast a well-run coffee house can turn into a disorganised mess.

Trying to catch the eyes of any of the girls, I stand on my tiptoes once again.

There are only three men in the fifth booth. The fourth, the one I thought the best looking, has changed tables. I can see only his wide back. Gloria's sad expression has transformed, her smiling eyes deeply focused. I wonder if he smells her scent.

It's Marlene who notices me first. She understands the fast wave of my hand and hurries back to the counter. The other three are still around the sailors, as is their laughter. Zsuzsi returns.

'You think Gail will go?' she asks Marlene.

'Why not? I would if I wasn't married.'

A quick look at the large clock hanging on the wall near the kitchen door, a replica of a pocket watch, presented to me by the girls on one of my birthdays. It's a quarter to two. Evelyne and Gail are back in the kitchen, clattering, talking, laughing. Some tables are already unoccupied. The three sailors slowly lift their tall bodies and leave the booth. They go as they came, in single file with wide steps, followed by the glances of the customers. Three heads turn towards the table with Gloria and their mate sitting there, obviously in deep conversation with each other. He looks up, waves his friends on, and turns all his attention back to the young woman.

Gail is at the fifth booth, her fast hands piling the dishes onto the tray.

As the customers leave, chairs are pushed under the round tables and everything falls back into place. Only a few tables are still occupied, one of them by Gloria and the navy officer.

'Jen, look what they left under each saucer!' Gail's hand is holding four five-dollar notes fanned out as if they were playing cards. She places them on the counter under the hatch.

As things are shifted onto the shelves the kitchen is becoming organised once again. The toaster is switched off; the heat will subside now.

The see-through nylon aprons are untied from around the red short-sleeved uniforms, our latest acquisition, and are put on the hanger behind the hot-water system.

Another Thursday lunch comes to an end, leaving us with history locked in little episodes.

'Let's have a cuppa,' I call into the kitchen. Ph-ph-ph the Gaggia hisses, exhausted. We all take our seats around the first table next to the kitchen door, our staff table when the rush is over.

A serviette had been left at one of the tables, and written on it:

Well,
On behalf of
Toots and myself I'd
just like to express our
sincere gratitude and
appreciation for the fine service
and quality of cuisine.
X-mas cheer to you all.

Ho-ho-ho!!.
Thanks again.
Love
unreadable signature.

I look around our table. It reminds me of a large poppy flower with the girls in their red uniforms sitting like petals around the cream-coloured lace tablecloth, dotted with steaming coffee cups. I place the notes and serviette in the middle of the poppy flower. All the petals bend inwards, as the girls read the message.

The tall sailor helps Gloria out of her chair and opens the door, they both bow their heads towards us and they leave together.

CHAPTER FIFTEEN

Building a Mansion

A year into our operation I decided, once again copying the coffee houses in Vienna, that I would get a liquor licence. Why should the ladies who like a glass of wine or a liqueur with their coffee be cast out to those back rooms of the pubs called saloons? Why can't men and women talk business over a cup of coffee and a small glass of liqueur in an elegant coffee house?

'What do you think sir about us getting a liquor licence?' I asked one of our regulars, thinking, that all of them should have a say about the developments in the place they frequented daily. 'That would be nice,' he said, so I asked more patrons.

Most customers thought it was a good idea; why don't I do a proper survey, a petition that could be used to lobby the Licensing Board and the Hobart City Council.

People like to get involved. I have learned something new again, and set out to design a questionnaire to gauge opinions on the licence, our operation and our service, and had 300 copies printed.

A big cardboard box was placed on the display cabinet with a sign: 'Questionnaires here, please!' After closing time the girls and I read the compliments about our service and the quality of our food with pride and satisfaction.

The Health Department had dozens of objections to me getting a licence and even more conditions in case I pursued the idea.

'Here in Tasmania we have never heard of a licensed coffee house before,' they said. If I want a licence, I should lay down the rules and *then* they will look into it.

Since they asked for it, in my application I laid down the rules the way I knew best.

I approached the Licensing Board. More conditions. A woman with a coffee house wants a liquor licence? Some publicans complained after hearing about me. They had never heard of anything like that, it will threaten their business, but okay, the Licensing Board said, if I can prove that there is a demand, it would be considered. I had 300 signed questionnaires to prove my claim.

The sitting of the Licensing Board was in Burnie.

Yano couldn't take a day off his work but, 'Ishtvan, would you like to drive me up to Burnie to the sitting of the Licensing Board? I will pay for the petrol and we could take Mami for a drive.'

The board knew about me, they'd heard that I had collected pages and pages of questionnaires. Some members were eyeing the tall pile of completed forms, which I had placed strategically on the conference table at my arrival. They have no time to read them. They believe me. Because I had no police record and my bank accounts were all in order, after *careful consideration*, the board decided to issue me with the licence. Within a week or so I would receive in the mail the registration of the licence, which I would have to display in the coffee house. Handshakes, smiles of recognition. 'Well done,' someone said.

Driving back home we stopped at the beach just outside Burnie and walked in and out of the water to cool off our hot feet. *It's true, wherever you go in Tasmania you eventually meet the sea,* I thought, satisfied.

Jenny's Coffee House became the first licensed coffee house in Tasmania, perhaps in Australia. From that day on the licensed coffee shops in Hobart grew abundantly but they all had one thing in common; they all had to obey the rules I helped to lay down with the council and the Licensing Board.

Finally I proved to Yano and myself that I was capable of running a business, and from then on he never interfered.

Yanka and Honza had their second child, a little girl, and they were looking into buying a business of their own.

'Perhaps a grocery and takeaway,' Yanka said. 'Honza doesn't like it at Baker's Milk any more. We have saved up some money and I can cook for the takeaway.'

They bought a grocery shop on the road to Port Arthur, sold their Housing Department home in Hobart and rented a house close to the shop. When we visited a few months later they seemed happy enough, both working in the shop, the children, including the little one in a walker, in the back room of the shop. Untidy, disorganised as always. *That's them*. We thought nothing of it.

'Mr Milosh, would you like to take care of that money for us? It's too far to travel to the city and we can call on you any time we need it.' Honza surprised Yano and handed over a wad of hundred-dollar banknotes, maybe $5000.

'You would be better off with it in the bank,' Yano advised.

'No, no, we trust you. It's easier to have it with you,' they assured us.

Yano took the money. Some months later Honza phoned.

'Mr Milosh? You know the money? I would need it now. Could I pick it up from you say this afternoon?'

'No worries.'

He came and took the money. 'Thank you very much Mr Milosh.'

It was the last time we saw them, ever. One weekend we took a drive to Port Arthur and stopped over in their grocery shop. It was closed, the display windows stuck down with newspaper and a large sign 'For

Lease'. 'Where are they?' we enquired of the next-door neighbour.

'O-o-oh! They left months ago. One night they just locked up and went. No one knows where.'

They had seemingly disappeared from the face of the Earth. Later someone said that they were bankrupt and left for the mainland, nobody knew where. Even though Honza never recognised Yano as a friend, he was the only person Honza could trust with his money.

At the beginning of 1980 Matra restaurant was sold. A Spanish family bought it. No, they did not want any of the crockery or cutlery. Out of the whole lot I was presented with a large platter, two large dinner plates and a two-kilo bag of very dry sultanas.

'What happened to the rest of the crockery?' I asked Latzi. Matra had seated about 90 customers.

'All of them were chipped; you wouldn't have wanted any of those.'

Who cares? I thought, knowing anyway. *I will get myself a new set from the money I make.*

The freedom from the worries of the restaurant was overwhelming. A few weeks after that Yano came home smiling.

'Guess who is in town,' he said laughingly. 'I had a phone call from Elizabeth and Stephen. They are visiting Hobart, staying for a week, and they would like to meet us all.'

We organised a dinner, Rosie and Peter were invited also and we just managed to fit around our dining table.

'So, how is New Guinea?'

Very good. They have servants to do the housework for them in Port Moresby; that was one of the conditions of their work application.

'You have no idea how many Australians and Germans live there; we met some people from Hobart too.'

Stephen tells us that the country is beautiful but the people are still wild. In many parts, deep in the mountains, the tribal communities fight each other the way you see in the movies. Unbelievable. When the teachers from Port Moresby were invited by a chieftain to have a meal with the tribe, they heard that that particular tribe used to be cannibals. 'We were worried that they would have us for dinner,' Stephen laughed in the security of our loungeroom.

'Put some music on Yena.'

The first LP my hand goes to is the one from Brian. My fingers curve around it tightly. *Should I put in on? Yes.* The voice of Edward Woodward floods the room with 'The Shadow of Your Smile', and my eyes fill with tears. To disguise my emotion, also remembering Elizabeth telling me many, many years ago about this man I will meet in Australia, I say:

'Are you still reading palms, Elizabeth?'

'Sometimes I do.'

Rosie is the first one. Elizabeth thinks that by the lines in her hand Rosie is the most independent person she has ever met.

Elizabeth duly reads all the palms that are stuck under her nose and gives short and informative observations. My palm is the last one.

'In the future you are going to have a happy life and you will be quite well off.'

'A-a-a-ah! We are working on it.' I smile, looking at Yano. 'But you did not say that about Yano.'

'No, I did not,' she agrees.

'But how is it that I will be well off and Yano won't?' *Perhaps a divorce?* I think.

Her definitive voice still rings in my ears.

'Because, this is how it is.'

After that I don't dare to ask any more questions. The songs on the LP progress to that tune, 'The first time I ever saw your face'. I go out to the kitchen to wipe my eyes and then change the record.

What's that? Standing in front of the bathroom mirror, just out of the shower, I stared at the shadow on my breast. I touched it. It was hard. A lump!

I have no time to think about this now, it will go, I thought. But through the day and the next day and the next, I thought about nothing else.

After three days I visited the same specialist who had operated on Mami.

'I don't want to scare you Mrs Milosh but now it's general knowledge that breast cancer is often hereditary. Your mother had it. I am almost definite that this lump is cancerous.'

From the doctor I walked to the park, sat on the bench and was trying to put my thoughts together, trying to come to terms with the news I have just heard. So far I had not told anyone about it.

So what if I had a lump? I was not the first one. Mami had her operation three years ago and she was all right, no sign of the cancer. Perhaps she was right, perhaps she did not have a cancer only a benign lump and they cut her breast off only to be on the safe side, thinking that at her age it did not matter. In that case I wouldn't have inherited the cancer and the doctor was wrong. But even if it was a cancer I will be all right once they cut my breast off, just like Mami was. It was true that I looked after my body and was proud of it, but no one needed to know. Yano wouldn't care, I was sure of it.

As instructed, I went to St John's Hospital to admit myself as soon as possible. 'In three days' time,' the administrator said. 'You will be operated on the following day.'

Yano was the first to know. His eyes looked at me with sympathy. I burst out crying.

'Yena listen. Even if they cut your breast off nothing will change between us,' he said gently and, even though I knew it to be the truth, just to hear it from him calmed me down.

The next day I told Zsuzsi and the girls about my lump, with a smile on my face, and a facade of self-control as if to say: *Nothing to it.* Because Chopi came in I told her too, and explained that I was sure it wasn't serious. I would be okay.

'Don't say anything to Mamika. I will tell her when I find out what it is. And I don't want any visits in the hospital; I will be back in three days,' I said to the girls, Zsuzsi and Chopi.

On the morning I was going to the hospital Chopi turned up with a small parcel. Wrapped in green cellophane paper was a cake of soap and talcum powder. 'Good luck Yenachka.'

❦❦❦

A hospital is a hospital is a hospital. I am in a ward with six other women, all having breast operations the following day. The anaesthetist is going around, patting our hands saying not to worry.

A never-ending night and even longer morning. About midday the nurse is there to give me an injection.

'What is it?' I am curious. This is my first stay in hospital for any reason, since childbirth.

'It's to relax you,' she says calmingly. *I am relaxed,* I think. All I want is to get this over and done with, breast off or on, so I can return to my normal hectic life.

Onto the trolley, through the long corridor, the fast succession of fluorescent ceiling lights, then through a double rubber door. A large round light above me. Another injection, 'Count to ten,' I hear someone saying.

'One, two, three …'

The next thing I remember is that someone is tapping my cheek. 'Mrs Milosh, Mrs Milosh. Wake up. Can you hear me Mrs Milosh?'

'Ha?' I try to focus my eyes on a face close to mine. 'A-a-ah! That's my doctor.'

'Mrs Milosh, it wasn't cancerous. Just a fatty lump,' he says and taps me on my cheek again.

'Thank you doctor, thank you very much. Can I kiss you?'

'Yes, you may.'

On the final visit to the doctor I tell him, 'There is a nasty scar on my breast.'

'Yes,' he says, 'I was sure it was going to come off and wasn't very careful the way I cut the lump out.'

At least he is honest, I think, *and I still have my breast.* I skip back to work.

❦❦❦

Almost all the eighteenth and twenty-first birthday parties of our children, their friends and their girlfriends were behind us, with some exceptions. Now we had reached the stage of engagement parties and weddings.

Ishtvan, after finishing technical college was working as a draughtsman, but sitting in an office wasn't his cup of tea, he decided to travel around Australia with Pauline and George's son Stephen.

The day he left John moved into Ishtvan's bedroom and became our second son. John and I shared a mutual interest in politics and history and debated for hours, with John supporting himself on the breakfast bar while I prepared the evening meals. By him I was promoted from being Mrs M. to 'dahrlink', John mimicking my accent. The name stuck.

John was finishing his university studies in biology and was hoping for a job as a college teacher. Suddenly there was a lot of talk about marriage between him and Zsuzsi. As the talks progressed, the month was decided on. It will be in August 1981, three years to the day when they first met at *that party.*

'What do you think about selling this house to John and Zsuzsi for a cheap price and building a house on our block of land?' It sounded as if Yano had thought about it a lot.

'That would be lovely for them,' I agreed, looking around our loungeroom. It has been our home for ten years; I loved it and had no ambition to live anywhere else. Considering what Yano had suggested though, I realised that it would mean a good start for Zsuzsi and John.

'Oh Dad, thank you very much.' Zsuzsi threw her arms around Yano when he told them. Looking at those two, they made me so happy.

From that day on Zsuzsi and John saved up for a deposit on a housing loan. And they were saving hard. Every cent counted.

Yano was ready to draw up the plans of the new house. Economically it would not make sense to build a small building there; it is almost a double block, he told me. It will have to be a big house, at least two storeys.

'The process of building will go like this,' Yano put me in the picture. Yozshi will be in charge of the building and of course he will subcontract other tradesmen. Latzi had also promised to help. Yano had $36,000 saved up, plus the $20,000 and something for the Rokeby house; that should be enough, no need for a loan. By August the house would be built and then Zsuzsi and John could move in straight after the wedding.

It sounded good, I was honestly happy for Zsuzsi and John. *But, I don't want to hear from those two friends of yours, Yano,* I thought.

Yano drew up the plan and, unrolling the sheet on the dining table, pinned it down on both sides with his palms.

'Come and have a look, Yena.'

It looked a huge house.

'How many squares Yano?'

'Maybe thirty-six.'

'Why do we need such a big house just for the two of us? It will cost us a fortune to furnish it.' *Not to mention the vacuuming,* I thought, hoping that all that would change by some miracle and Yano would design something smaller. I had never liked lots of space around me. A small cosy house made me feel more secure.

'I told you, we can't build a small house there.'

'Okay, okay,' I said resignedly.

Yozshi organised for the land to be cleared ready for digging. But it turned out to be more complicated. They needed more heavy machinery as the ground was too rocky. The back-hoe, the front-end loader and the excavator arrived.

Yano was busy at work and organising the digging of the foundations, Zsuzsi and I were busy with Jenny's Coffee House and organising the wedding.

That was definitely new to both of us. How do you start organising a wedding?

'In Australia everything is done by the book. You can get a book on everything, even on how to organise a wedding,' John's father assured me. 'Whatever the book says goes.'

I bought the book. It said that the wedding should be financed by the bride's family, the whole lot, except the cars and the flowers, perhaps the drinks.

Zsuzsi and I began our expeditions to dressmakers, wedding-gown shops, photographers and possible venues for the reception. As we moved from one establishment to the other, the expenses grew accordingly.

❦❦❦

Saturday 6 June. We are just about to close the door of Jenny's for the weekend. The phone rings.

'Jenny's Coffee House, may I help you?' I say hurriedly.

'Yenni?' Yozshi's voice sounds breathless. 'Yano is in hospital.'

'What's happened?' The hollow feeling in my stomach starts rising.

'He is all right now, the ambulance took him in; we think he might have had a heart attack.'

'Thanks Yozshi, I will be at the hospital shortly.'

'What's wrong Mami?' Zsuzsi is concerned seeing my face drained of blood.

'Dad is in hospital.' I don't dare to say any more. 'We'll close now and go to see him.'

Zsuzsi and I walk into the grey, blue and white colour scheme of the emergency ward, weave our way in between the trolleys and look into cubicles with drawn curtains in the hope of seeing Yano, a nurse or a doctor. The emergency section is busy. We walk freely; nobody takes any notice of us.

Finally a nurse approaches. 'The ambulance brought in my husband a while ago, could you please tell us where is he?' I tell her his name and she goes to check it out.

'Your husband is upstairs in intensive care, take the stairs to your right.'

'Excuse me please, is Mr Milosh here?' I walk up to the nurse at the reception in intensive care.

'Just a second,' she says and disappears behind the double door. Then she comes back.

'He is on the ward. If you make it short you can go in to see him. Mr Milosh is critical, still having his heart attack, but the doctor is there to see to him.'

I am so scared. What does a person who is having a heart attack look like? What am I going to see? We walk in, me in front, Zsuzsi behind me, I am sure she has the same thoughts as I do. Yano lies in the middle of the room on the stretcher-like bed, surrounded by what I assume are doctors. He is wired to an ECG machine, his face is bloodless, almost green. I am not looking at anything or anyone in the room and go straight to Yano. I just want to touch him so I know that he is still with us and … I place my hand on his. It feels warm.

'Oh, Yanichku,' I swallow my tears.

'Dad.' Zsuzsi is at his other side.

'It's good that you came to see me. Take Zsuzsi home Yena, I will be all right, we will talk when all this is over.' His voice is tired and faint but surprisingly matter of fact.

At the reception I ask more questions. Is he going to be all right? Is it bad? How bad is it? They can't tell me; as they said, he is still having his heart attack but if I come later, perhaps after six, they might know something by then.

Yozshi comes to our place.

'Have you been to the hospital?' he asks.

I tell him what I'd been told and what I had seen. 'What happened Yozshi?'

He doesn't know. They were working on the foundations of the house, Yano in one corner, Yozshi in the other, and suddenly Yano was lying on the ground. He was conscious and said that he was in pain and Yozshi should get an ambulance. This is all he knows. Before the ambulance arrived they took him in to the next-door neighbour's place and she gave him a drink of water.

After six I am in the hospital again.

'How is he doctor? Is he going to be all right?'

The doctor can't say but he can tell me that it wasn't a massive heart attack. If Yano lives through the night without another one, he will be okay.

'Could I see him please?'

'Yes, but only for a very short time.'

It is even shorter. I walk into the ward with the doctor right behind me. Yano is lying on the bed with his eyes closed, white as a sheet.

'Oh my God,' I whisper.

The doctor touches my arm and waves me out of the room.

'He is asleep and the monitor is showing a regular heart movement.'

'Can I have a glass of water please?' I ask the nurse and while she is getting it I need to sit down.

Then I catch the bus back to Rokeby.

Yano's heart came good and he was released from the hospital a week after his heart attack. Slimmed down, he looked the healthiest I had seen him for a long time. He stopped smoking and went back to work.

The pressure was on though. The foundation of the house was more difficult than they thought. All that heavy machinery was still working there to break up the stones. This was all there was, no soil, only stones and, because of the steep slope, they needed to lay drainage before they started building. I had no idea what Yano was talking about but knew in my heart that with all the extra expenses the house would cost much more than they'd thought at the beginning. Yano shared his worries mainly with Yozshi; I was told only snippets. The house, the plan and the fact that I had no say in it left me quite disinterested. Okay, Yano and Yozshi are building a house, so what? Now that Yano was back at work, in my mind I was not worried about his health. I turned my enthusiasm back to Jenny's and to the wedding.

But Yano's health wasn't okay, he often complained about a pain in his side, under his ribs. It wasn't there before the heart attack, he said, and was ready to talk about it to his doctor when he had his check up the following week. It might be only a pulled muscle or something, Yano assured us.

It was more than a pulled muscle. He had water on his lungs; this was where the pain was coming from. And because of his history of tuberculosis of the lungs in his youth they will have to hospitalise him for six, maybe eight, weeks in the isolation unit with no visitors, at least for the first couple of weeks.

Yano went back to hospital, Yozshi was digging the foundations of the house, I was running Jenny's, Zsuzsi was organising the wedding, John was living with us, studying at the uni, chipping in with this and that, sometimes giving us a lift to the city, Ishtvan was in Perth working as a barman with his friend Stephen, Mami was regularly visiting the coffee house and Chopi and Roman kept meeting there, which gave us a chance to get a little closer to each other again.

At that time, of the whole lot of us, Chopi seemed to be the happiest.

She spent her days in her Stainforth Court flat, which she had painted white, looking after it and keeping it spotless, making German cakes, washing and ironing for Hans's household and hers. On the weekends she went to Clifton Beach, wearing long, flowing batik skirts with an apron tied around her hips, very unlike the Chopi I used to know, happily conserving the vegetables and fruit grown by Hans, taking interest in the garden and fruit trees and developing a passion for photography.

Hans in the meantime retired, bought Chopi an excellent camera and a bicycle, took her to concerts and on long walks. She also swam regularly and made sure that their diet was healthy. Chopi loved sharing Hans's house, his garden, watching and photographing the birds and butterflies, and listening to the music they both enjoyed. Roman had two homes, and the freedom of Clifton Beach incorporated Hans's discipline. Roman deeply cared about both; saw Hans as his stepfather and Hans's sons as his brothers. In return they treated him as such, took him bushwalking and, in winter, skiing. It was all good.

'Mami, Chopi is really happy with Hans, they did …' I would report since they still did not talk to each other.

'Ah!' she would wave her hand dismissively in the air.

Chopi confessed that Hans was worried about him being much older and was getting Chopi ready for the eventuality that he might die before her. As a gesture of care he kept collecting firewood from the nearby forest, stacking it in his garden for Chopi in case his prediction came true, until he filled the whole front yard from one end to the other with neatly stacked logs.

After two weeks of Yano's isolation in the hospital he was moved into his own room and we were allowed to visit. 'The days are long,' Yano complained. He had learned to play patience to fill in his long days in Vienna, while we waited to emigrate. Ironically it was the very game he ridiculed me for at the beginning of our marriage. I took the cards into the hospital. With some coloured pencils, a scrapbook and some paperbacks to read, Yano seemed to be contented. The pain in his side had gone.

'The doctor is happy with my progress,' he would say, 'and, it is quite good here.'

Zsuzsi and I had all of the wedding preparations under control. The number of guests grew to eighty. Ishtvan was planning to come home from Perth for this occasion. Zsuzsi's beautiful dress was bought and altered to fit her petite form. Zsuzsi was good at drawing, it was one of her hobbies; she designed the invitations and was busy drawing them one by one for eighty guests. The dress I chose for myself was a dusty-pink after-five creation of georgette and lace. 'Very nice; the colour suits you,' the proprietor of the bridal shop assured me.

The cars were ordered too. There will be three old-fashioned Jaguars driving Yano and Zsuzsi, the flowergirls and me into the church of St Mary's in Harrington Street. Zsuzsi and John regularly visited the priest, who gave them talks on the responsibilities and purpose of marriage. The reception was also seen to; it would be held at Newlands, an old home turned into the business of providing wedding receptions. 'I just hope Dad will be out of hospital,' Zsuzsi wished.

At my daily visits I found Yano each day looking just a little better than the day before. I felt we could look to the future with a smile.

'Yena, the Clarence Council wants us to get written permission from our neighbours because of the height of the house,' Yano surprised me one day. 'You will have to go around and talk to the two neighbours above us and those on each side to see if our house will obscure their view.'

Obviously Yozshi has been visiting Yano, I thought. 'Gosh, now? I am so busy.'

'Well Yozshi can't start building until the council's approved the plans.'

'Weren't they approved before you started digging the foundations?' *This would have been the first thing I would have done,* I thought. *And what if the council doesn't approve? Will they dig different foundations?*

'This is what you do Yena. You draw up a letter with the names and addresses of our neighbours and a short declaration that they have no objection to the height of the building. You will need four of those, one for each neighbour. The best is to visit them on the weekend and take with you the plans of the house.

Easy. I was rebelling quietly. All I had to do was start really early on Sunday, the only day I had to wash and iron the lacy tablecloths from Jenny's and to do the accounts from the week before. I would have to catch the bus to Howrah and then climb up the steepest street on the Eastern Shore and doorknock. Yano and Yozshi did not want me when they cooked up the plans of the house. Now I had to do the footwork. What kind of a builder was Yozshi that he did not know where to begin? Obviously the house was not going to be even near finished by the time of Zsuzsi and John's wedding.

I hate it, I hate it.

⁂

I catch one of the rare Sunday buses to Howrah on a very cold early afternoon. I wear my white lambswool coat with a scarf wrapped around my neck, carry a shoulder bag with four declarations and a long scroll – the plans of the house – under my arm. When I get off the bus I walk up Hill Street and knock on the door of the first neighbour.

'Good afternoon, my name is Jenny Milosh, sorry to bother you but …' and tell them what I am there for.

'No worries,' the first neighbour signs. Would I like a cup of coffee? No thank you, I still have a few visits to make.

On to the next one.

'Good afternoon, my name is …'

'Thank you very much. Bye.'

By the time I finish it is dark. The best place to catch the bus back to Rokeby is at Rosny College. I walk for three-quarters of an hour to the bus shelter, take a seat there and wait almost an hour for the bus to come. *I hate that house,* I think, sitting there freezing cold.

Saturday 15 August, Zsuzsi and John's wedding day. It is winter in Tasmania but the sun shines, reassuring us that spring is not too far away. The wattle trees are already dressed in sunny yellow pompom-like flowers.

Yano is still in hospital. Because of the special occasion they will let him out for the afternoon and early evening but he has to return to the hospital by 10 pm at the latest.

Ishtvan arrived from Perth two days ago. He fetches Yano from the hospital, then he leaves to go to John's parents' house, where John is getting ready with the rest of the boys.

My little girl looks like a princess, so pretty, so natural.

'Are you nervous sweetheart?' I ask.

'No.'

Constant footsteps up and down the corridor from the loungeroom to Zsuzsi's bedroom and back. The bridesmaids, like little fairies, are busy around her, the house is full of laughter. The flowers are delivered. A large bouquet of white tulips.

'For Mrs Palmer,' the delivery man says and for a short second I think, *Who does he mean?*

Yano is wearing the hired morning suit and he looks impressive. I do too. The door again. Barb, Clarie, John and Jean from Deloraine arrive with a movie camera. On their way to the church they want to film the last minutes before the wedding.

'Stand there. Smile. That's good. You don't have to pose, and you can talk and move – it's a film, you know.'

Three Jaguars arrive and park in front of our house, then the one decorated with white ribbons turns into our driveway. Marlene, dressed in an after-five ready to leave for the church, is in front of her gate across the road watching as Zsuzsi and Yano get into the car. Some other neighbours are also out in front of their gates. The bridesmaids take the other car. I have the whole Jaguar to myself; it smells of air freshener.

Crossing the river we drive to the west side, towards Mount Wellington. It seems dark as the sun is sinking behind it. In the foreground the Australian flag is fluttering high above the castle-like governor's house. The Queen's representative is home. The thought registers only fleetingly, then I think of my little girl; from today on she will be Mrs Palmer. *How fast the time passed.*

The church is full of friends; Zsuzsi and John look so very happy together. After the ceremony, when the last tunes of the organ die off, come the handshakes, kisses, congratulations. Mami is beaming, wearing her elegant white coat and a white hat. Chopi did not come.

She told me that she wouldn't. She will not go anywhere without Hans, and Hans did not want to put in an appearance.

The dining room at Newlands is beautifully laid out, just the way we'd planned. The speeches, music and food are exactly the way we asked. It is a great night.

Before nine thirty Yano and I go around thanking everyone. I press John, my new Australian son to my heart. 'Drive carefully and have a great weekend.' They will be driving to the Fox and Hounds at Port Arthur. One more cuddle, one more kiss and Yano and I leave to get to the hospital in time. We miss out on the bridal dance.

The new house was far from being built. They had managed to get to the ground floor, and the rest would have to come later, much later. When John and Zsuzsi returned from their short honeymoon they continued living with us. Ishtvan went back to Perth.

When the second concrete slab was laid, we ran out of money. Yano threw his principles about not borrowing money into the air and was trying every bank for a loan. No establishment would lend him money halfway through the building process. When he had exhausted all the options, he told me.

'We have run out of money; we can't finish the house.'

'What do you mean? You had over $50,000? Didn't you do a projection of the cost before you started building?' I questioned Yano but deep in my heart I hoped that the house would never be built.

They had done a projection but there was so much extra to be done. Yozshi thought that the money would cover everything, but did not count on the rainy weather, when the hired grids for the concrete lay without use for almost a month and the daily hire cost still had to be paid. And remember the digging? The amount of rock they had to dig out? And the drainage? That was all extra. And Yano had ordered a slow-combustion furnace made in Canada, only one of its type in Tasmania. Anyway, we had no more money. Could I think of something we could do?

'So how much do we need?' I couldn't care less. I considered it to be Yano's and Yozshi's project. There was not one thing I liked about it.

'Thirty six thousand dollars,' Yano told me.

I was always lucky with my requests from authorities. I went around to all the banks.

'Have they started building the house yet?' they asked.

'Yes.'

'Sorry, we cant' help you.'

My last resource, I made an appointment with the bank manager at the Commonwealth Bank, and hoped that my luck still held.

'I need a housing loan of $36,000 for our house. It is in the process of being built but we ran out of money. I know, I know,' I waved my hand in the air, dismissing the bank manager's attempt to jump into my speech. 'I know that it's not your policy to structure a new loan when the building is halfway up, but look, my husband is working for the Public Works Department, our business, Jenny's Coffee House, which is by the way frequented daily by a number of your employees, is doing very well and we bank with you. I expect the Commonwealth Bank to give me its support after I have trusted it for years with our money. Here is the name and phone number of Price Waterhouse, in case you need to know anything about our business; they are our accountants.'

I smiled, shook hands and sailed out of his office.

That particular bank manager never suspected, under the disguise of the polite and charming smile, how focused, how very determined I was, that as far as I was concerned there was no way our housing loan could be refused.

Two days later I received a phone call. The bank approved the $36,000. Good. Once again I proved to myself what I had already known for many years, that if I put my mind to something I will eventually succeed.

After telling Yano the news I caught a bus. On top of Howrah

Heights I walked through the building site and inspected the skeleton of interconnected rooms. They looked enormous, especially the entrance hall. *What are we going to fill this place with to make it cosy?* I wondered and couldn't find a speck of excitement inside me about it. The Canadian furnace was pushed into a corner on the lowest floor. A huge oblong box towering at least a metre above me, it was full of knobs, lights, doors and metres of thick cable, half of it still wrapped in a cardboard box.

To be fair to Yano, I did have the final say on colours of the rooms, floor coverings, the tiles and the design of the kitchen. Slowly the building reached the stage when it became liveable. Everybody was helping to finish it; Yozshi, Latzi, John and even Zsuzsi were all painting and varnishing. The last weekend before we moved in I decided to take part in the frantic activities. Yano gave me a paintbrush and a can of varnish.

'Go around the architrave,' he instructed. I tried. 'Zsuzsi, show me how you hold that brush, it keeps slipping out of my hand.' 'Not like that Mum; look, this is how.' She placed the brush in my hand. I tried again. It wasn't only the varnishing, I hated the sanding. My patch did not look all that good. 'You useless idiot, you.' Yano got upset and took the brush out of my hand. Lately he was even more irritable than usual.

Yano was right; I was good for fixing the bank loan but no good at painting the architrave.

CHAPTER SIXTEEN

Hand Over Hand

Even though the house wasn't completed, we moved in. The ground floor, which was to be a flat, had only a few thick concrete support pillars with some dividing concrete walls standing. It also sheltered the Canadian furnace, still wrapped in the huge cardboard box, torn in places, and the southerly winds freely swished around it in the open space. On the first level were our living quarters; the staircase leading up to the master bedroom and the ensuite was just a distant plan for one day in the future, just one empty space.

The removalists turned up in the drive of our Rokeby home and loaded most of our possessions onto the truck.

'I used to love coming home here and smelling dinner cooking,' John said. 'The first thing we will do is get rid of the smell of your cooking from the kitchen,' he added jokingly, but meaning every word. 'Only when that goes Zsuzsi and I will know that the house is ours.'

The furniture that was just right for our small house was lost in the vast expanse of the new one. The entrance hall was as big as a ballroom. And I had plenty of other complaints; the sun was at the back of the house and the only rooms that benefited from its warmth were the back entrance, the toilet and our bedroom. I hated the setting sun heating the bedroom just before we retired for the night. The view from the house was magic, though, perhaps the best in Hobart, overlooking the river, the sea, the mountain and the city. But what good was that to me? I dashed out of there before seven in the morning and returned after the sun set, to start preparing dinner. There was no time for me to enjoy the view. The windows were huge; we needed metres and metres of curtain material. There was not one corner in the house where I could curl up after work. Everything was open through the arches from one room to the other and looked twice as big with the sparse furnishing.

But things will happen when you wish strongly enough for them. Marlene's father-in-law was a fisherman from way back. Years ago he had fished out a large dining table, a sideboard and another smaller table from the Derwent River. They did not know what to do with them so they had been kept under Marlene's house for all these years. Would I like to have a look?

I crossed the road between our ex-house and hers. 'My God Marlene, it's beautiful antique furniture.'

'You can have it, Jen,' she said. What does she want for it? Nothing. Then how about Zsuzsi's old bedroom furniture for Cassy? That would be lovely.

The furniture was transported, professionally polished and placed in our dining room. It made a world of difference.

I dressed the empty corners with cut flowers, bought bottles of wine and beer, made some platters and invited the neighbours, the accountant and the bank manager for a cocktail party to thank them for their help.

'Beautiful house … magic view … I love your curtains.' Their comments flew around me and made me feel a little better about my new home.

Mr Baker paid me a surprise visit at Jenny's.

'I heard about your business,' he said with a voice travelling above the heads of my customers. He smiled and took a seat in a booth. Mr Baker had a business proposition for me. The ship was only as good as the captain, he thought, and in his eyes I seemed to know how to run a good business. Would I be interested in doing business with him? What kind of a business Mr Baker? I could name any business I would like and he, Mr Baker, would establish it for me, and all I have to do is run it for him. *Gosh, if I had known that earlier.*

'I can't now, Mr Baker. I am so busy with this shop. I am still only learning.'

'Well girl, I just came to tell you that any time you are ready, let me know.' He drank his coffee, patted me on my back and smilingly strolled out of Jenny's.

Mr Baker wasn't the only person who was interested in doing business with me. On a very warm afternoon a tall, well-dressed gentleman walked self-assuredly straight behind the counter where I was serving the customers.

'I am Sypkes.' He offered his hand.

'Are you Mr Sypkes who established the Purity chain in Hobart?'

Yes, yes. It was him. They were building a large shopping centre in Moonah and he would like me to open the very same coffee house there. He heard good reports about my business. Would I like to come with him and have a look at the new building and choose the best position for the coffee house? His car was parked outside.

In the air-conditioned black limousine with tinted windows I thought about those days of going around to the real-estate agents, when hardly any agent wanted to talk to me about my idea of the coffee house.

But there was no deal with Mr Sypkes. I did not like the position of the new shopping centre. A Viennese coffee house was good only in the city centre. I had no desire to establish just another takeaway.

'Yena, from now on don't give me any bananas for lunch,' Yano said.

'They seem to be too dense. I have problems with swallowing them.'

Hmmm! Does he have problems with swallowing anything else? No. Only with bananas. And he feels a kind of pressure in his chest. He talked to his doctor but the doctor seems to think it will settle. It was most likely a side effect of his heart attack.

The pressure in his chest did not ease though, and other food started to cause Yano problems with swallowing. He complained for months.

'How are you today Yanichku?' I would ask.

'Stop asking me all the time. The pain is always the same. I will tell you when I feel better,' he said, irritated.

The time was passing, the constant, niggling pain wasn't easing and Yano became depressed. Home from work we talked about nothing. He was not interested in the house or in the business. As soon as he had his meal he would go to bed and would read until he fell asleep. On the weekends, through the large windows I could see him shifting rocks, those that were dug out to make room for the foundation and now surrounded the house like a mountain. With a backdrop of the beautiful water views he carried the rocks from one heap to the other, trying to make a path and a place for a garden.

In the evenings alone I would spread the cards on the new Berber carpet, playing patience.

Will Yano change? Will his pain go? Will he be in a better mood? The cards never seemed to work out.

Oh dear God, help Yano and me, I can't take it much longer. Even arguing was better than this; this was no life, barely an existence. There must be something the doctors could do. It was almost a year since he had his heart attack; how long would it be before the pain went? Yano should see another doctor; perhaps it needs only a change of medication. I blamed Yano.

It was in those days that I had a dream. The details of it I will remember for the rest of my life:

The country around us is grey, the buildings are grey, we are grey. I am in my native city, Košice. Yano and I are driving in an open convertible, travelling alongside the city hospital. The convertible enters a tunnel. It is a long tunnel, feels as if we would be there forever. When the car finally emerges out of the darkness, everything around me is in full colour. Beautifully lush green trees, multicoloured houses, the streets are full of children, young women pushing prams, everyone is smiling. I am smiling too, my heart is light and happy and I am driving the car. Where is Yano?

The Christmas of 1982 was the loneliest of all the Christmases I have known.

Ishtvan was still in Perth, Zsuzsi and John were travelling on the mainland. It was only Mami, Yano and I.

We decorated the ceiling-high Christmas tree and sang the Christmas carols. The tunes echoed through the rooms and came back at us sounding hollow. After that we consumed our traditional meal. Even Yano, who in the past often criticised 'that circus', commented on the lack of Christmas atmosphere. Soon after he said goodnight. Mami and I sat around the large antique table reminiscing with tears in our eyes. The happiness was gone.

We are sitting in the loungeroom, about twelve of us, in a circle. The wall lamps are dimmed and the lacy curtains are drawn apart so as not to interfere with the glitter of the city lights through the floor-to-ceiling windows. Yano and I have invited our friends into our new home to celebrate New Year's Eve and to welcome 1983 in. We are all in high spirits, contentedly holding our glasses.

'Let's everyone say what they wish for themselves in the New Year.' Yano is in a good mood, he has felt no pain today at all, he tells me before the friends arrive.

Perhaps with the New Year that will also clear up, I quietly hope.

'I have achieved most of my wishes,' says Yano optimistically. 'I wish only for good health.'

The group of youngsters who kept their friendship through all those years progressed from engagements to weddings, with Zsuzsi and John setting the trend, followed by Pauline and George's son Stephen. He returned from Perth to help with the preparations. The wedding was on 15 January. After that Stephen and his bride were going to Hong Kong. And, because Zsuzsi and John were such good friends, they were going with them.

Yano and I were invited to the wedding. It was beautiful, as weddings are. For Yano it was a battle; he felt ill and could hardly wait to get home. On Monday he had an appointment with the doctor.

Monday 17 January 1983 at 3 pm the phone rings at Jenny's.

'Yena? I just came home from the doctor. They took an X-ray and the doctor said there is some abnormality in my oesophagus. I am down in the dumps. Could you come home as soon as you can?'

They found a shadow in the X-ray but to see what it really was they had to do a laparoscopy. 'We will do it straight away, tomorrow morning,' the doctor said.

I sat with Yano in our sitting room, holding his hand, and didn't know what to say.

That night I had a terrible dream. The dream wasn't as bad as the feeling I woke up with. A thick, hairy spider was crawling on the bedroom ceiling. I was trying to catch it but it ran away.

❦ ❦ ❦

It's morning. Yano packs his pyjamas and goes to the hospital. 'Good luck Yanichku, I will see you there in the afternoon.'

I am at St John's Hospital shortly after lunch. 'I would like to talk to the doctor who did the laparoscopy for Mr Milosh, please,' I say at reception.

The doctor comes out to talk to me. He is a short man with thinning hair that doesn't seem enough for his head. The light-blue theatre coat barely reaches around his body as he walks towards me, unsmiling.

'Mrs Milosh? Yes, there is something there but we will know what it is only after we get back the results.'

'When?' I ask.

'In three or four days' time.'

'Does it looks serious doctor? It's not cancerous is it?'

'It usually is.'

He walks away without more words, leaving me standing there in the corridor.

No! No! No! The doctor is wrong! my soul cries out silently.

Yano is still in the recovery room.

'Did you talk to the doctor?' His voice is tense.

'Yes, I did. He couldn't tell me anything; they will know when the results come back from Melbourne.'

We have to make an appointment to see the doctor in his rooms in four days' time.

It's that morning. The time drags on minute by minute. Zsuzsi is forever around me. 'He will be all right Mum, you'll see. Dad will be all right.' The girls work quietly, focusing on what they have to do, and talk as little as possible. Mami rings. 'What do you know about Yano?' 'Nothing yet Mami, I will tell you later, when I find out.' Pauline rings. 'How are you love? Do you know anything?' No, not yet.

I might not have been told, but I know. Deep inside me I know. Still, the fine line between knowing for sure and hoping lingers. One more hour. A half an hour …

On the way to meet Yano in the doctor's waiting room I walk into St David's Cathedral. *How much warmer and cosier are the sandstone churches in comparison with the big stone cathedrals of Europe,* I think, and inhale the familiar scent I associate with churches, the scent of flowers and burning candles. I stand at the door for a while and the semi-darkness kindly gives peace to my unfocused mind. I kneel on the prayer cushion in the back pew and look up to the huge suspended cross with the crucified Jesus.

Dear God. Oh, dear God, don't let Yano have cancer. Help us God.

I bow my head, close my eyes and, not able to think of anything else, I just keep repeating, *Dear God, dear God.*

The doctor's surgery is in Macquarie Street, one of those old two-storey houses with leadlight windows, a polished wooden balustrade on the staircase and thick architraves around the doors. Yano is already in the waiting room.

'Mr and Mrs Milosh,' says the doctor as he stands aside pushing the door to his surgery wide open.

'Take a seat,' he points.

The results had come back from Melbourne. There is a cancerous growth in Yano's oesophagus. They will have to operate.

I am holding Yano's hand hard and feel it trembling.

'How bad is it doctor?' Yano's voice buckles a little.

The doctor doesn't know until he operates.

'Does Yano have a chance of survival?' I ask. Everyone has a chance of survival, the doctor says. They will cut out the cancerous bit and insert a tube instead.

'How long do I have doctor?' Yano asks the question that implies that his life span is limited.

I don't want to hear the answer. In my mind I reject it as a stupid question but inside my heart it feels different.

'Can't tell you just yet,' the doctor says in a matter-of-fact voice, and advises us to register at the Royal Hobart Hospital, ready for the operation, as soon as we can.

Without a word, holding hands we walk out of the surgery. The dark Mount Wellington is behind us as we walk towards the city. Yano is going back to work. We reach the eleven-storey building, Yano stops and faces me.

'Yena, don't cry. Just don't cry please. You will be all right. Even if I die, you will be all right. You will get married and you will be happy.'

'Oh Yano, how can you talk like this? You will not die and I will not get married.'

'Yes, you will.'

He bends towards me and gives me a light kiss. 'Go back to work.'

Then he runs up the stairs and disappears in the shadow of the large entrance hall.

On my way I pass St David's Cathedral again. Should I go inside? No. I have asked for a miracle; I have nothing more to ask for.

At work, in the kitchen I tell the girls and Zsuzsi. Oh my God! They exclaim. We are all in shock. But beyond the beaded curtains, behind the counter, it is business as usual.

'How are you madam? A short black?'

'Hello sir. A lovely day.'

Pauline rings again.

'Do you know anything?'

'Yes Pauline, it's a cancer.'

'I will be there shortly,' she says and hangs up.

I sit with Pauline at the table. It's after hours, the doors are closed and the main lights are off.

'I had to come to see you love. I thought to myself, poor Jenny, I must see her. I couldn't let you be on your own now.'

'But the operation might be successful, Pauline. Nothing is definitive just yet; Yano has a fifty–fifty chance. Doesn't he?'

When I arrive home John and Zsuzsi are there. Yano is in bed already.

The three of us huddle together, arms around each other. My tears melt into theirs and we cry and cry with no relief. We can't cry out that unbelievable, that terrible, heavy feeling inside us.

Zsuzsi and John decided to go to Hong Kong; not going wouldn't help anyway. They will be back before Yano goes to hospital.

On their return Yano and I met them at the airport. Pauline and George were there too, waiting for Stephen and his wife.

Yano didn't want to talk to anyone; he walked away from our group and on his own paced up and down in a faraway corner.

'We understand, love.' Pauline placed her hand on my arm, and then I walked to Yano to keep him company.

When Ishtvan came home from Perth he was shattered.

'Don't give up Dad. You can beat it. Just don't give up.'

'Don't talk nonsense; what do you know?' Yano shut himself away from everyone.

The neighbours and friends heard about his illness; they wanted to visit, to say a kind word. Yano didn't want to talk to anyone. I stood in the entrance turning away everyone who knocked at the door. 'Sorry, he is not well,' or 'He is asleep,' or 'He doesn't want visitors. Sorry.'

'Look after yourself Yenni, take it easy,' the friends advised.

Why do I have to look after myself? It's Yano, who is sick.

We are in the hospital on the day of the operation. Yano has a room of his own. On his bedside table is the small ivory Buddha that John and Zsuzsi brought from Hong Kong. 'That's for luck,' they said, and Yano believes in it.

I am there before the operation, holding his hand.

'After I wake up I don't want to hear any bad news. All I want to know is that I will be all right.' He gives me a sad smile. Then they wheel him away.

I want to talk to the doctor after the operation and at reception I make an appointment to see him after lunch. When I return Yano is not yet back. He is still in the recovery room, they tell me. Can I talk to the doctor please? They don't know where the doctor is but could I come back in a couple of hours? But I made an appointment, I object. Sorry, come back in a couple of hours.

The anxiety weighs a ton. The sadness and worry are deep inside me. How could the doctor not keep this so very important appointment? How could a person be so careless, so unfeeling as to leave without any information about the life of my husband?

Ishtvan is in the coffee house. What's the news? Nothing yet.

'Ishtvan, come with me; we will go back to the hospital.'

The doctor has gone home. Didn't they tell him that I wanted to talk to him? Has he left a message or something? No, nothing. Nobody knows anything. Could I get his phone number please? Yes. The public phone is around the corner.

'Ishtvan, could you please ring this number and talk to the doctor?'

I am so nervous that I wouldn't be able to speak English properly. What should he ask? Ask the doctor what they found and if they got the whole cancer out.

Ishtvan rings and talks to the doctor. No. The doctor doesn't think that they got the whole cancer out but they inserted a tube and Yano should go home after the operation, forget about the whole thing and enjoy his life. Enjoy his life? E-n-j-o-y his life?

The next morning I am at Yano's bedside. He already knows the bad news but he feels all right.

As Yano is slowly recovering from the operation, I spend my afternoons with him in the hospital. His mood is also improving. While I am there he reads his book, I read mine and we hold hands.

After a week in the hospital Yano is back home and so am I; Zsuzsi and the girls are taking care of the business. I go in for a couple of hours a day over the lunchtime and Mami moves in with us to be there with Yano during those couple of hours.

Ishtvan decides to study biology at the university. He wants to be a marine biologist, he thinks. At least it will keep his mind occupied.

'It's ridiculous,' Yano says. 'At his age? He is twenty-six already.'

I change the dressing on the operation scar daily, sometimes more often, washing it with disinfectant and dressing it with heaps of gauze. Yano is slowly recovering but has a problem with swallowing. He can eat only liquid food.

'It shouldn't be like that,' the doctor says. 'You should be able to eat normally.'

Back to the hospital. After the X-ray the doctor found out that Yano was on heart tablets that were too big for his tube and blocked it. The doctor did not know anything about the heart attack and the medications Yano was taking. They need to clear the blockage. Another operation.

When Yano is wheeled out of the theatre I am there. This time the doctor comes to talk to us.

'Mr Milosh in these few days your cancer has spread to your stomach. It doesn't look good,' he says, and walks to the next bed, leaving us in a daze. The doctor doesn't care; for him Yano is only another body to cut up. Yano lowers his head on my shoulder and I lower mine on his, we embrace and both cry unendingly. What can we do? What can we do? How come the doctor did not know about Yano's medication? How come Yano had to suffer all that pain? Who can help?

Nobody can help. It is just one of those unfortunate things, we are told. Yano should go home and make the best of his time. How much time? Nobody knows.

Now Mami is living with us, just in case I need help when Ishtvan is at uni. Yano eats very little, he is losing weight, he is not on any medication, no radiation, no chemotherapy. There is nothing they can do for him; all is black and hopeless.

I go to the library and pick up heaps of books on how to beat the cancer. I read *Living with Death and Dying* by Elizabeth Kubler-Ross, other books on alternative cures, vitamins and herbal remedies, and *Life after Life* by Raymond A. Moody Jr. I know so much and yet so little. I make an appointment with a doctor who had studied Chinese alternative medicine. He is very sympathetic, holds me in his embrace and tells me that it's not enough for me to want Yano not to die; it needs to be Yano who wants to stay alive. Yano is indifferent. Someone tells me about vitamin B14. It's not available in Australia, but it's good. We would need large doses of it though. I phone a South Australian naturopath who sells a tea from the bark of a South American tree, which the locals use as a cure against cancer. Please send me the tea. Yano is not interested in reading any of these books.

'I don't mind to die, honestly Yena, I just don't want to suffer,' Yano tells me. *And he is only fifty-three,* I think in desperation. I don't want

Yano to die. I will do something. Something …

In the Yellow Pages are names of the naturopaths in Hobart. I make an appointment with one and talk Yano into coming with me. He doesn't want to, but all right, he will.

The man takes Yano's pulse, shakes his head. He has never had a serious case like Yano; all he can do is prescribe vitamins. Many, many vitamins, a boxful of vitamin bottles, about fifteen tablets to take three times a day. How is he going to do that? He has a problem with swallowing. You pound the tablets into powder and make a cocktail with some kind of juice. Yano has a sip of the cocktail and doesn't want any more. It tastes terrible.

'Leave me alone Yena. This is the last time I will let you talk me into going anywhere.'

So that's it. In the books that I read I learn that everything we do, all that surrounds us, all we eat is bad for us. The electric blanket, the dishwashing liquid, the cleansers, the soap, the chemicals in food. All that contributes to cancer. I start washing up under the running water, no more dishwashing liquid, throw out all my aluminium pots and utensils, and the plastic goes with them. Only the stainless steel and the glass stay in the cupboards. Nothing else will do and I cook everything from fresh vegetables and fruit. Real fruit juice, real homemade sauerkraut. Any naturally fermented food is good. I make my own sauerkraut and make the tea from the bark of the Argentinean tree. Yano drinks it three times a day.

'Do you feel better Yanichku?'

'I don't know. I don't think so.'

March, April, May.

Yano is losing weight and he is too weak to walk around the house; he needs support. Every time he is in pain I make an appointment at the hospital, call the ambulance, and we both wait hours there until the doctor attends to us.

We need a doctor who could visit at home, I keep saying. None of the doctors we know do that.

I think of Karl, who is a son of our friend.

I know Karl from 1976 when I suddenly developed a pain in my throat that persisted over months. My doctor sees nothing unusual. But the pain persists. The doctor sends me to have an X-ray. Nothing. All is normal. But it hurt every time I swallowed. What is it? A friend of ours suggests his son Karl, a doctor who works in a local hospital. Karl is great. He can't see anything wrong either but he has a friend, a nose and throat specialist. He makes an appointment for me. The specialist does a thorough job. After half an hour's medical examination he can't find anything. I am healthy. I go back to Karl. So what is it? Well. Have I been under pressure lately?

Have I been under pressure? My God! There has been nothing but pressure in my life for the last two years. *Breaking up with Brian, working on my marriage,* I think to myself, the rest I count out loud to Karl. Keeping two jobs, washing up late into the night in the Matra restaurant and trying to keep the house and family together. Not to mention the heartache of losing Chopi and watching Mami's unhappiness. This is it then, Jenny. Your throat complaint is a nervous reaction.

Karl is right. As soon as I find out what it is the pain slowly fades away without me noticing it. One day I wake up and there is no pain.

Perhaps Karl would like to visit Yano on a regular basis. I ring him. Of course he will.

Karl is kind and calm. He comes during the lunchtime. I see him, tall and slim, coming down the drive, stepping over the stones that Yano hasn't finished moving, and he smiles. He talks softly and long with Yano and prescribes painkillers. There is no need to call the ambulance at all hours of the day and night any more. Yano's dying becomes a little easier and more manageable.

Ishtvan comes home from uni only in the evenings and by then Yano is asleep. Ishtvan finds it hard to accept what is happening to his strong-willed father. Zsuzsi is holding the fort for me at Jenny's and comes visiting with John after work but Yano sleeps most of the time. Mami is still living with us; she finds a new meaning to her life. She is wanted. She looks after Yano while I go to Jenny's for a couple of hours.

I walk daily about twenty minutes from our place down to the bus stop. I always walk everywhere, whenever possible. This is the only private time I have.

When I get up to the end of our drive, out to the street, the whole of Hobart is spread in front of me. The sun shines with warm rays, even though it's the end of autumn. I can't stop the thoughts; they invade. I fantasise. What will I do when Yano dies? I will sell the house as soon as I can and buy myself a small villa unit. Perhaps Chopi would like to live with me; she has been very supportive lately. Perhaps I will get a dog. Yes. I would like a dog. What kind of a dog will I get? A feeling of happiness spreads inside me as a glimpse of what might happen, and then the clouds of gloom come again. Yano is dying.

Karl tells me that Yano is already on the strongest painkillers; soon they will not be strong enough and he will have to prescribe morphine.

If I don't think too much into our situation and do not allow myself to think about anything emotional I can make myself numb and just take everything as it comes.

Karl prescribes morphine. I have to administer it three-hourly, day and night. To begin with I have an alarm clock at my side but after a week my body clock adjusts and I wake up at the required time. Yano sleeps through the day and night. I have to wake him up for the medicine and he objects.

I feel drained and tired but I don't want to know. I have a sad duty to perform. Everything is on hold: Yano's dying, Ishtvan's study, Jenny's Coffee House, Zsuzsi, Chopi, all our lives.

What's that? I think, as my heart races, my head spins and I almost black out. I can't be sick now. I have responsibilities. I say nothing to anyone, walk into the bathroom, look at my sheet-white face, let the cold water run onto a face washer, wring it out, close the bathroom door, lie on the floor and put the wet cloth over my chest. After a while the unwellness goes. It's time to give Yano his morphine.

I mention my episode to Karl. 'It's nothing.' He pats my hand. But it felt like a heart attack, I object; what if I pass out? I won't pass out. It only feels like it. It's an anxiety attack. I am under pressure, this is what is causing it. Can he give me something to stop those attacks? He could but he doesn't want to because right now I need all my wits about me. It won't be too long now. I will be all right, he smiles. I am all right after that talk but the attacks come back again and again. Just hold on a little longer, Karl advises. I feel better though, because I am reassured and know what those feelings are, and I realise what our friends meant when they said to look after myself.

June. Yano spends all his time in bed sleeping and uses the bottle and a pan to go to the toilet. I am still going to Jenny's for a couple of hours. I need this change. I feel nothing, think of nothing and lock out all my emotions. When I get back from work Yano loves me massaging his calves. I do it every day.

'Yenni, you should call the priest to give Yano his last rites while he is still with it,' Mami tells me. Of course! Thank you Mami, I did not even think of it. I call the local church and talk to the priest. It's Sunday; he will come in the afternoon. When he comes, Zsuzsi and Ishtvan are there too. The priest is a kind old man, quietly spoken and comforting. Yano will be with his God shortly, he tells us, then goes to the bedroom.

'Yanichku, the priest is here to talk to you,' I tell him and he is not surprised. 'You don't mind. Do you?' Yano shakes his head. No. He doesn't mind, he believes in God.

The priest is praying and talking to Yano in a subdued voice, then he tells us that we should all say goodbye to him. I cry. This time I can't shut out my emotions.

'Don't cry Yena. I almost died the other day but someone cried me back.'

Is it possible? If this is true there must be an afterlife.

The children go one by one and talk to Yano. 'God bless you,' he tells them. *I don't want to say goodbye.* I will be still administering his morphine. Mami takes care of the priest and makes him a cup of tea. I stay with Yano, holding his hand.

The next morning Yano is in pain.

'What shall I do?' I call Karl. He tells me to call the ambulance, Yano needs to go to the hospital.

When we arrive they put Yano into a wheelchair. Yano is very tired but is still with it. As I bend towards him trying to straighten his shirt he kisses me on my cheek. This is precious. The last kiss.

They give Yano a room and I sit with him. He tells me to go home to see to the family and I gratefully abide. I need the fresh air.

Next morning I am there again. They have moved Yano into another room. He is in a coma.

The room is grey. Grey lino, grey walls, grey blind pulled three-quarters of the way down the window shutting out the light from outside. The bed is in the middle of the room, a chair next to it. *This is the room for people to die in,* I think, and sit at Yano's side for hours, stroking his still-warm hand.

'Would you like a cup of coffee Mrs Milosh?' The nurse comes in. 'It won't be long now.'

How can they talk about death so openly? I think, and I say yes to the cup of coffee.

During lunch I go to Jenny's and work there for a little while and then go back to the hospital.

The next day I do exactly the same as the day before. Yano is still in a coma.

The third day I do the same. It is Friday 17 June.

'Let go Yanichku, go with God; there is nothing here for you any more. Go with all our love.' I stroke his hand, helping him to cross over, maybe?

Zsuzsi and Ishtvan said goodbye when he still could talk to them.

I don't really want them to see their father the way he is now, a small, shrunken skeleton of what used to be a handsome man. At eight o'clock in the evening I leave to catch the bus home.

The telephone rings. It's 11.30 pm.

'Mrs Milosh, your husband passed away at 11.00 pm tonight. You are welcome to come in to see him, if you wish.'

'Thank you,' I whisper into the receiver and hang up.

'Who was it?' Mami asks.

'Yano is dead,' I say.

Ishtvan hugs me. 'It's best this way Mum,' he says in a voice full of tears.

I ring Zsuzsi to tell her that her dad had died and I would like her and John to come to the hospital with us to see him.

Mami does not want to come and I understand. Ishtvan, Zsuzsi, John and I are standing in the grey room looking at the body. It's not Yano; his spirit has left. Perhaps he is still hovering around us in the blue, faint light of the room, telling us not to cry. 'Just don't cry, please.' But we can't hear him, so we cry, quietly, deeply.

Everything what followed was important. It was important to finalise things and through it to realise that Yano was not with us any more, that he had gone, that he has died.

I rang Zita in Košice to tell her that her brother was dead. Why didn't I tell her that he was sick? Why? Because I had hoped that he would get better. What difference would it have made anyway? It would have made a huge difference, she said.

I was flooded with sympathy cards. So many friends, so many kind thoughts.

It was a sunny afternoon when our friends, a cathedral full of friends, congregated at St Mary's to pay their respect and witness Yano's shiny brown coffin topped with a large wreath of blood-red roses being wheeled through the church.

That afternoon, after the funeral, they walked me out of my own kitchen so they could take over the preparation of sandwiches, and I let them do it. Dressed in black skirt, black silk blouse and black jacket, it was only my body, numb and heavy. My heart wasn't there.

I sat on my own in the furthest room and thanked God for my decision not to leave Yano back in 1976. I thanked God that I could be with him when he needed me the most. My conscience wouldn't have let me live with the thought of him dying lonely, unloved. As if someone had cut my arm off, I felt the hurt of the wound, but the arm was no longer there.

Freedom. Independence. That euphoric, elusive state of mind, that makes nations and individuals fight and kill. Now I had it. I was living in a free country; I had financial, moral and emotional freedom and independence. I could travel, go anywhere, jump off the bridge, sleep with any man at all, no one to answer to, nobody to do things for, nobody to tell. And perhaps no one cared. A large hollow space around me, full of meaningless nothingness, and nobody could fill it; that was the state of my mind, my reality.

It felt as if I were standing on the seashore, holding in my hands the ropes to my many boats but the boats were out to sea, far, far away, with a vastness of water between us. I needed to pull them in, hand over hand, until they reached my shore and then to moor them, one by one, so they could create a structure, boundaries, handrails I could hold on to. The only anchor I had was Jenny's. It provided me with a routine that was cosy, familiar and safe.

I went back to my old working time, caught the bus at seven and spent all my days there. My anxiety attacks continued and it did not matter when, or where I was. One lunchtime I almost passed out. 'Sit down Mum,' Zsuzsi said, and rang Karl.

'Bring her into the surgery, I will take an ECG.' We went.

'Nothing is wrong Yenni; your heart is good. I will prescribe antidepressant tablets, but don't stay long on them. When you feel confident, start decreasing the dose. Okay?'

'Okay Karl, I will.'

'Mum, are you all right?' Zsuzsi hovered about me all day, every day.

'I am, I am. Truly.'

Ishtvan was just as concerned.

Yet, to look at me, there was nothing different. Every morning I made myself up with mascara and lipstick, I washed my hair and curled it up in a fashionable hairstyle, I was dressed in the latest fashion and looked good, and I pretended to be cheerful for the sake of my loved ones.

But I couldn't fool them. 'Sit down Mum, put your feet up,' said Ishtvan on my return from work. 'I will cook you dinner. Fish in beer batter. How's that?'

'Great.'

I have the most caring, the most beautiful kids in the whole world, I thought. *What's wrong with me?*

Mami moved back to her unit and kept ringing daily.

Chopi came to Jenny's almost daily, sometimes even visiting me at home.

'Would you like to spend a weekend with Hans and I?' she surprised me.

How would it work then? Well, on Saturday when I close Jenny's at midday I could get a bus to Stainforth Court, spend a night there with Chopi, and Hans would come to pick us up on Sunday morning to take us to Clifton Beach. Would I like that?

'O-o-oh Chopi, I would love it.

It was beautiful. Chopi cooked and baked for the occasion; we talked till midnight and made miles towards healing our relationship. On Sunday Hans came and was full of jokes, as in the old times.

'I got ready three pushbikes; we will all cycle around Clifton. After we return we will listen to records, then we will take you home.'

'Thank you Chopi, thank you Hans.'

Pauline rang. 'What are you doing on Tuesday night?'

Following that first one Pauline came every Tuesday after dinner, even though I knew she hated driving in the dark. She sat with me, asking questions, giving me a chance to talk about the hurts of the last six months, listening to whatever I had to say. I was looking forward to her visits.

'Do you like sewing Pauline?'

'Me-e-e? I can't even hold the needle in my hand,' she laughed.

'Would you like to make a dress for yourself?'

'You are joking Jenny.'

'Buy the material and the pattern; I will teach you.'

The confessions stopped and after a few Tuesday nights Pauline had mastered the art and completed the very first, and very last, dress she had ever made.

Pauline cares, all my family cares and the girls at Jenny's care too, I thought, and with this realisation of the love of family and friends I pulled the rope hand over hand, watching one of my boats coming to shore.

It's about closing time.

'Go home girls, it's quiet. If you hurry you might even catch the 5.40 bus home, Zsuzsi. There is not much to do here, I will finish it off.'

As soon as they leave a customer walks in. About thirty, short in stature, a fashionable haircut and outfit, a great grin on his face. He is one of our regulars. Usually he comes late in the afternoons, with one hand in the pocket of his trousers, walks up to the counter with long steps, orders a short black and sometimes, only sometimes, a Linzer biscuit. 'I used to be a priest,' he told me a while ago, 'but they kicked me out because I was naughty.' He wants to get back to his priesthood again, if he can.

'Is it too late to have a short black?' He grins.

'It's okay. Just for you. How are you?'

'And you?' He throws my question back at me.

'Fine, fine.'

'Actually I know,' he says. 'I know you are all right. I am a member of a prayer group. We are praying for you.'

'What do you mean?' His words absolutely blow me away.

He tells me that he heard about my husband passing on, so his group is praying for his soul and mine.

How could I have ever thought that nobody cared? How could I ever think that I was alone?

With everyday problems relentlessly popping up, my recovery started. I started to pull all my boats to the shore, one by one.

'Mum? What are you going to do with Dad's Kingswood?' Ishtvan asked me, looking through the window at the car sitting, still, in the driveway.

'I am not sure, Ishtvan.'

He took me down to Warwick Motors.

'We will get you a small car. Can you see anything you like?'

Gosh. Hundreds of cars, blue, red, pink, black, small and big.

'I don't know, Ishtvan.'

'How about this?' He pointed to a butter-yellow Subaru Leoni. I liked it.

The next day the Subaru Leoni was parked in front of our large entrance windows and the Kingswood was gone.

'I don't think I can drive any more, Ishtvan.'

'Well Mother, I suggest you get some driving lessons from the RACT.

The guy from the RACT turns up with his car and walks over to the passenger seat. I take my place in the driver's seat and for the life of me can't get the car up our steep drive.

'First gear!' he says sternly, and we are out on the street. We drive on the bridge, around the Domain, down Cornelian Bay and through Risdon Avenue to the zinc works. Good, good, he says. Two more lessons and you will be ready to drive. Two more lessons later I come home and tell Ishtvan that I am ready to drive. He says to get the car keys and take him for a ride. I jump into the drive's seat of the Leoni, he sits in the passenger seat and I manage to get up our drive, out onto the street. Not bad. Let's go over the bridge. Okay. Change lanes Mum. Okay Ishtvan, and I indicate.

'For Christ's sake Mother. Look over your shoulder. You can't change lanes just like that.'

'But I did Ishtvan, honestly.'

'No, you didn't, I was watching you. Let's get off the bridge and stop somewhere.'

We stop in front of Cornelian Bay beach.

'Make a three-point turn.'

'What? What's that?'

'Mum, you are not ready to drive. From today on I will take you out every afternoon until you know what you are doing.'

Since we have had Jenny's, Zsuzsi and I flew regularly to Melbourne every winter for three days to look around, do some shopping or see a show. During those three days we walked our legs off, all day circling around the main shopping block, Swanston Street, Collins Street, Bourke Street, Flinders Street and all the 'Little' streets in between, from shop to shop. In 1983 we went again.

In Melbourne Zsuzsi took over.

'C'mon Mum, you are still young; get yourself something modern. Look at those jeans. Try them on. They'd look great on you.'

'They need to be taken in at the waist,' I said. The tailors were just two shops up, the sales lady told us.

We walked into the sanctuary of many sewing machines. Yes, yes, they do alterations and will alter the jeans today, we should pick them up at five this afternoon. We did not need a ticket; they will remember us. Thank you.

We continued our pilgrimage, Swanston Street, Bourke Street,

Flinders Street.

'What was the name of the tailor, Mum?'

'I think they call themselves Six Little Tailors.'

At five o'clock we looked for Six Little Tailors. There was no Six Little Tailors anywhere.

'Excuse me, please,' I walked up to a policeman. 'Could you please tell us where is the shop of the Six Little Tailors?'

'Six Little Tailors? No idea. But wait, there is a tailor shop called Two Little Tailors.'

'Thank you very much,' I said and now Zsuzsi and I were looking for Two Little Tailors. 'But what's happened to the remaining four little tailors?'

For the first time after many sad months I laughed from deep inside me, from the bottom of my heart. Another boat comes in.

Svetya crossed my mind frequently. *I wonder how she is? Does she know about Yano?* I had not heard from Svetya for years. I could ask her to come over, now that I was driving, I could show her so much of Tasmania.

❦ ❦ ❦

It's five in the afternoon in Tasmania; minus ten hours it would be seven in the morning in Košice. I dig out her phone number and dial.

'T-o-o-o-t. T-o-o-o-t. T-o-o-o-t. Hello?'

'Svetya?'

'Who is there?'

'It's me, Yena from Australia.'

'Yena? Yena? Oh my God. Yena?'

'Hey Svetya, stop wasting time. I am calling to tell you that Yano died, I am on my own and I would like to invite you to stay with me in Tasmania for a month or two. I will pay your airfare, your insurance and your pocket money.'

'Oh my God. Yena?'

'Stop it Svetya. Get yourself to the nearest police station and ask for a passport, and then write to tell me what's going on. I am going to finish now, because it will be costing me a fortune.'

There was a problem, Svetya wrote. They could issue a passport only when she bought two hundred US dollars from the Czechoslovakian Bank. But the bank hasn't any dollars; they were getting it very irregularly and there was a waiting list for the money. What if I send her the money? I wrote back. No good. It had to be from the Czechoslovakian Bank. And if I sent it to the bank they might use it for someone who was on top of the list. But she will keep trying.

November. I felt a little bit more in control of my life. The house was on the market.

'It will be hard to sell,' the neighbour who lived above us told me. He was also my real-estate agent. 'The house is not finished and those stones don't look good around it.'

Even though I hated the house, the neighbours were great. They kept an eye on me, popping in, visiting. Bob even took out a few planks from his fence so I didn't have to walk up my drive and down his. 'C'mon, we are having a barbecue,' he would call over the fence and I would squeeze through the narrow space where the planks had been.

Christmas was nearing; I could see it on the streets and in the shops but not in my heart. I was scared of Christmas.

The proprietors of the shops in our shopping arcade were organising a staff Christmas party at Sisko's, the same restaurant where Matra used to be. I was hesitant to go out at night on my own but was looking forward to the evening in the company of familiar people.

The food is great, the proprietor remembers me and sends an extra bottle of wine to our table with the compliments of the restaurant. The wine and jokes are flowing freely, and when the desserts come a young, good-looking man wearing black tails, bow tie and red top hat walks to our table.

'Where is Jenny?' he asks.

I don't react; it must be a different Jenny.

They all are looking at me.

'Who is Jenny?' the young man repeats.

'I am Jenny,' I say, knowing in my heart that it must be a mistake. *Fancy to be dressed like he is,* I make my judgement of him.

'I have a telegram for you,' he says and starts reading it out.

Hot damn! Itz a Flim-Flam Singing Telegram stripping here tonight.
Jenny is the one to give us our Christmas fun,
she is slim and tall but that's not all …

As he sings, he takes his top hat off and places it on my head.

All her customers do love her so,
when they have a sad and sorry story to tell,
it's to her they will go …

He must be hot, because he starts untying his tie and he also takes off his coat. I can't believe it. *Who is this guy?*

To many it may just bring a tear to the eye,
but our Jenny will just sit there and cry!!!!

More of my follies are read out and, while he does it, his shirt, trousers, shoes, socks and … gosh! I can see each hair on his chest and on his stomach with the line leading down to his small jocks. And he is taking them off too. The whole restaurant, including the waiters and kitchen staff, are standing around me and him, waiting for the revelation.

And now dear Jenny the time has come to end this rhyme
and we all hope you have had really good time.
To the one and only Jenny from Jenny's Girls.

He struggles a little as he pulls his tight jocks off, down, down. *I am not going to look.* The whole restaurant erupts in laughter but I am not looking, head turned to the side, my eyes closed tight.

'Look Jenny. Look Jenny!' They are calling out. *No way,* but I risk a small glimpse in his direction. Under his jocks is the tiniest shiny black triangle.

Christmas came and went. Chopi and Roman stayed with Hans at Clifton Beach because Chopi and Mami were still not talking to each other. I invited John's parents to our Christmas Eve dinner. Mami, Ishtvan, Zsuzsi, John and I stood around the Christmas tree, singing in tearful voices. Yano's deep melodic voice was missing.

With Christmas over the city filled up, as it did every year, with a relaxed crowd of windblown suntanned faces wearing T-shirts, shorts and thin, waterproof parkas, bringing a special atmosphere to Hobart, that once-a-year atmosphere when the Sydney to Hobart International Yacht Race was on.

On Boxing Day the yachts had left Sydney, battling the elements of Bass Strait, claimed to be the most treacherous waters in the world, and after a few days of that they would arrive in Hobart before New Year's Eve.

The families of the crew were already in the city long before the yachts, clicking cameras, looking, shopping and dining.

Traditionally for the shop proprietors and restaurants the week between Christmas and New Year was one of the busiest.

The New Year's Eve party at the waterfront was always a magic night. The population turned out in thousands, walking around Constitution Dock, looking at the yachts, taking part in the festivities. There was music, drinks, dancing, singing and fireworks. This wasn't a night to miss.

'Would you like to come out with me tonight to the wharf?' Jannette wanted to know. Her husband was a pilot and was on duty that night.

Jannette came to pick me up. The great thing about it was that you didn't have to dress up; a pair of jeans and a T-shirt would do.

It's warm, no wind, only the blanket of stars above us. In Constitution

Dock the sleek yachts are lined up next to each other in the order of their arrival. With the sails tight to the mast, they are rocking gently on the dark water mirroring the lights. There are thousands of people walking, laughing, stopping. The yacht crews are calling out, offering drinks, inviting people aboard, their voices mingling with the music. Further down in the square the band is playing and some are already dancing.

The whole city is here, I think, and wonder if Brian is here too. Perhaps he is. Perhaps he is with a new wife, maybe a child? It has been eight years. Perhaps if I look carefully I might recognise him. I walk and look. We meet many people we know. They tell us jokes, wish us a happy New Year; we laugh and walk on. No Brian.

Midnight is getting close. Shortly 1983 will be history. For me a sad, painful history. The band plays and people are singing. Then for a second or two everything stops, the music, the voices. All is quiet.

Ten, nine, eight, seven, six, five, four, three, two, one, the crowd counts down in unison. *Happy New Year 1984.* They all yell, and I do too with all my heart. Happy New Year. Happy New Year 1984.

New Year's Day, late afternoon. Ishtvan goes to see a friend. I have Zsuzsi and John's favourite sauerkraut soup in the fridge. Perhaps I should take it over to them at Rokeby. I sit by my kitchen table, light a cigarette and psych myself up to drive. I am still not quite confident with my driving. Before I drive I smoke a couple of cigarettes; they calm me down. Then I go. Zsuzsi and John love the soup. When I get back home it's still daylight.

I wonder what Brian is doing. Does he live in Tasmania or perhaps on the mainland? I still have the phone number of his aunt. What if I rang? I would have to be careful about what I say in case he is married. I could say that Brian had welded up a carport for me in the past and I would like him to make me another one. I laugh to myself. That would sound quite innocent and believable. Should I ring? Am I ready to learn the truth? My address book is in my handbag. I wish my hands would stop shaking. This is ridiculous.

'Yes?' a female voice answers.

'Sorry to bother you but I am looking for Brian. He welded up a carport for me in the past and I would like to get in touch with him. Would you know his phone number?'

'Brian? He's sitting right beside me,' then 'Brayen! Phone for you.' I hear her soft Welsh accent.

My God. I think I will faint. I did not count on talking to him. Should I hang up?

'Hello?' His gentle, deep voice is familiar.

'Brian? This is Jenny.'

Epilogue

I have always believed that things in life work out the way they should. Brian and I married in 1986. We travelled to our native countries, repeatedly visited many, many other countries, and we now have friends all over the world.

After Yano's death Chopi came back into my life. She also made steps to make up with Mami, not because she believed that Mami was right but because she found it hard to live with the thought that maybe, just maybe, she, Chopi, was wrong. After a while she regularly visited Mami in her flat, but I never found out what they talked about.

The year of 1990 was another hard year for our family. In February Mami died, surrounded by every member of the family. We all witnessed her goodbye, a single teardrop rolling down her cheek just before she took her last breath, even though she had been in a coma for two days. She would have been eighty that year.

In September of the same year Chopi died after she was diagnosed with a melanoma. She was forty-eight. Before Chopi's death Ishtvan had a dream about Mami. In the dream she told Ishtvan that she was waiting for Chopi.

For weeks I felt Mami's presence in the house and in the car, sitting next to me in the passenger seat. One day I told her to let me concentrate on my driving. From then on I met her only in my dreams, together with Chopi, but sometimes I still smell Mami's scent in the house.

Hans never planned it that way. In complete disbelief he spent all his days with Chopi in the hospital while she was dying.

Hans lived many more years. We poured clean water into the glass of our relationship and made peace with each other. He loved Brian's company and Brian visited him regularly. I would send Hans cakes and he would send me flowers and vegetables from his garden or he would have a meal with us sometimes.

In his last days in hospital he told me, 'You were a very good and kind family Yenni. I am so sorry that I didn't realise it back then.' Hans died peacefully in hospital; he was eighty-four.

❦❦❦

December. The paddock and the Acton hills are vividly green after the wash of rain. I can make out almost every tree separately in the clear air as the morning sun shivers and bounces on the treetops. The northerly's gentle swish nudges the windchimes into motion, alarming the goldfinches having a dust bath on the bank under the oleander bushes. God's country, someone told me in far-back times. Back then I could not see why.

My eyes wander beyond the fence. Peace. Even though not visible past the Acton hills, I know that Mount Wellington is there behind them and I wonder what colours it is wearing today.

The roses that were moved to the front of our patio are doing well, even though they were replanted as already-established bushes. Just like me. Replanted. The roots are still covered with the old soil that became part of the new patch. The new shoots don't grow far from the bush; they are all around it. The new generation.

My accent lingers, even though the days when I used my entire English vocabulary in a single sentence have long gone.

This May it will be thirty-eight years since I stepped off the plane and touched Australian soil. Of those, twenty-two blessed years in this house.

The force of the incoming tide in Frederick Henry Bay comes and goes, its rush mingling with the sound of a faraway lawnmower. I come to know the sounds, the smells, the seasons, the music. I share years of memories with friends. I know how to compare and what to compare with.

In my memories I see years of hopes and dreams, years of trying to make the dreams come true. Then the years of initiation, hard years. Opportunities and chances and my strength to take them up. I know how success feels, the exhilarating goals with deadlines, the hard grind behind it.

I feel as if I am weaving a spell. I know the feeling of happiness. I have it now. It fills my whole life with compassion and love, because in the end nothing else matters. Love is the one that carries you through.

Yenni

Eugenia Jenny Williams is the author of *Yenni: A Life between Worlds* (Pluto Press 2002). In 2006 that book was voted one of the fifteen best loved and read books in Tasmania. Born in Košice, a city now in the Slovak Republic, Jenny and her family illegally escaped Soviet occupied Czechoslovakia in 1968. After living in Vienna they arrived in Tasmania in 1969. During 39 years in Australia Jenny has worked as a washer upper, a factory worker, a laboratory analyst , and the proprietor of three successful businesses including Jenny's Coffee House.

www.ingramcontent.com/pod-product-compliance
Lightning Source LLC
Chambersburg PA
CBHW021215090426
42740CB00006B/237